About the Author

I have worked in sales and marketing for most of my working life so have real life experiences of most business scenarios. I have created sales forces across many different business sectors.

My goal in life is to help other businesses like mine do better. There is not a great deal of help for the SME in the UK so the more I can help the better.

Would you like to get more results from your labours? Does the balance between work and reward seem to be not quite right? Are you doing all that you can and yet still not getting the profits that you desire?

There is another way to run a business!

Sales performance CAN be tweaked to win another few sales. Marketing CAN be more effective and less expensive when specific skills and 'tweaks' are applied....Profits CAN be improved when systems are refined and your business becomes more efficient.

If you want to improve your busines ... too proud to possibly learn...then there is)T keep on battling and believe it is 'j to enjoy more of this life...you never k e a call and let us chat ...it costs nothing to kick a few ideas around.

D1492754

Success isn't about achieving
something in the future,
but about doing something
right now that you love...

So forget about 'Success'
and just find
Joy, Passion and Love,
in this moment.

This is a Success you can achieve.
Just do it!

More Money, Less Stress

Growing your business does not

have to be so hard...

The Business Booster -

There *is* another way.

by Ben Kench

Published by

Filament Publishing Ltd

16, Croydon Road, Waddon,

Croydon, Surrey CR0 4PA

Telephone +44 (0)20 8688 2598

Email: info@filamentpublishing.com

Website: www.filamentpublishing.com

ISBN 978-1-908691-45-3

Printed by Berforts Information Press, Stevenage & Hastings

First published in Great Britain by Charnzak Publishing

To Charlotte, Zac and Luke,
you are my life and inspiration.

- xxx -

"... It's about being passionate, giving and committed to helping. Dedicated to learning and sharing knowledge, making life richer and better for all.

Nothing ever happens of value without a lot of effort and perspiration. If you live to give – getting will resolve itself... "

Ben Kench

Acknowledgements

Without a doubt there are many people to thank and to share the credit for this book. Throughout my life I have had the wonderful pleasure to work with some brilliant leaders who have each left their mark on how I think.

My father encouraged me to set up my first real business venture when I was just 16 and I guess from there I became hooked on the challenge that business creation represents... and learned the wonderful pleasure and joy of winning against difficult odds. Thanks then firstly to my Dad.

Indeed it was as a direct result of my father's influence that I embarked upon a selling career starting out in the replacement window industry. My early years were spent in my first sales venture, and my first real 'teacher' Dave Brazier taught me so many simple basics and put me on the right path and has remained a friend and mentor for over 20 years. Then through my years of selling double glazing, they were in a different way formative to say the least and many are remembered, but thanks particularly to my friend and boss Andy Ross... you always knew I would 'do it one day'!

Flushed with my successes from these early sales careers, I looked further at broader horizons and moved out to Tenerife. My years in Tenerife and Marbella perhaps were even more crucial to my development as I was fortunate to experience much that I wouldn't have perhaps been experiencing had I remained in the UK... and I had the good fortune to meet and watch many superb sales leaders; Paul Stewart, Peter James, Mike Evans, amongst many others, and work colleagues I revere, such as my great friend Brian Cohen who just seems to 'hit me with the truth' every time I ask for guidance. Frankly I have been incredibly fortunate and the list of those who I count as close is too long for here but you know who you are.

There have been many kind friends who were always there for me when I was most in need and there have also been hundreds of acquaintances, some brief, that too have left memories that influenced all I do. For all of you, I sincerely thank you and acknowledge publicly your influence.

Then of course I am humbled by such great teachers as Tony Robbins, Stephen Covey, Jay Abraham, Jim Rohn, Jay Conrad Levinson, James Redfield, Deepak Chopra, Wayne Dyer and of course Napoleon Hill, to name but a few. I discovered the fabulous joy in reading and learning and devoured hundreds of titles. I hope one day to meet some of you but thank you from my heart for all of your guidance.

To all I simply say 'Thank You' and I want you to know that you left behind a residue that I am eternally grateful for. To my new friends and acquaintances not yet met, I look forward with anticipation to the learning I know I shall enjoy.

No work is ever complete though without the input of professional help and I must publicly say Thank You to Filament Publishing for their help and advice in getting this finally finished and produced and delivered to you in this modern digital format.

To tie all of this together, there must be a strong thread and my family provide that cord. To my mum who must have wondered in my earlier years what she had done to deserve me! Thanks for putting up with me and loving me still. To my brothers, Dan and Reuben, who teach me still in life's ways, and my sister, Jinny, who is always loyal with her affection, and to Tom and Lucy, thanks for keeping me level! But most of all, thank you to my simply amazing and fabulous children, Charlotte, Zachary and Luke. Life is indeed rich with such blessing and words really do not do justice. Thank you for being my rock.

Finally and perhaps most importantly, I must thank the critics and the doubters! Those who say, "You're a dreamer," and forecast that 'I wouldn't amount to much' are the most inspirational motivational people on earth! Boy, did they do the most to make this happen!

Contents

Section Two - Business Booster Marketing   **143**

Section Three - Business Booster Selling - Selling the Sizzle

Introduction

Hello! Thank you for picking up this book.

I sincerely hope that as you read this today, you feel well. Don't worry that perhaps everything isn't exactly as you would like it to be in your business life, because if the reason for picking this book up is one of discontent with your current income and success level then that is good, in as much as it gives us leverage to start from. I say that primarily because my desire is to make a difference and to genuinely help you and to help improve your life. You must *know* from the outset that together we *can* address some of the challenges you currently face and you *can* change your fortunes... you *can* make your business and your life a whole heap better. It *can* be all that you want it to be.

Please allow me to explain though, that I have compiled this as a 'study aid' or a 'guide book' rather more than a book to merely read through. If you were to ask me, "How do I use this?" then I might be so bold as to say approach this book as a series of brief lessons in how to reconstruct your business in order that you might get out of it what you really, really want as opposed to that which you are actually currently getting out of it. All of the way through, I shall talk with you as though you and I are simply in conversation at your office.

My mission, as I have said, is simply to help. I passionately care about you and your business success as I know only too well what it feels like to not succeed and to endure the pain of struggle.

Why? Well partly through my own pain of running a small business without the success it needed and experiencing the demise and heartache attached, and partly because I've had the opportunity to experience first hand with hundreds of business owners their struggle and have been fortunate to share with them some guiding thoughts and seen them steer out of trouble. This book is a collection of those thoughts.

In fact this is put together, as I have said, as a guide to building your business into a superb, moneymaking, machine that gives you the lifestyle you want with the freedoms and monetary rewards you desire. It is possibly also a series of reminders about 'stuff we've already heard or known' but truthfully which we aren't doing. It is knowledge gathered through pain but shared in the hope of avoiding pain. This represents the common struggle broken down into component parts and reformatted so that you can apply bit by bit and reshape your future. Building a small business into a big success does not have to be as hard as it often feels!

As you read through this book, there are some areas you'll be more familiar with whilst others you will be less comfortable with but I urge you to simply take one section at a time and 'do it'. I often say that **it's not so much about what we don't know; it is more about what we don't do**. I do not pretend that all of my thoughts contained within are brand new groundbreaking insights but I might be so bold as to suggest that much of the material you are currently not doing fully, if at all. Thus my suggestion is that you give yourself the challenge of *thinking* it through, not just reading it through. Listen and let us learn together and then please 'go, do'. **Stop your everyday activity and actually *do* what has been discussed**. Apply each section into your business then when applied, come back and move on. Only when you have done this will you really transform your business fortunes... but when you do, you will.

And that, my friend, is all I want to say right now except, of course, to wish you well and urge you to keep in touch. God gave me an abundance of energy and a desire to help share with others... so read on and get to work, then share with me your experiences. It might at times be a slight struggle getting into some 'thinking and questioning' as I suggest in this book but please try... the more you try and stretch yourself, the greater the reward. These thoughts I share here are valuable and I promise to you, they work. Trust me please!

Go 'do' then, good luck,
Yours in success
Ben Kench

"Success Leaves Clues"

"Begin at the beginning," the King said!

The beginning? Well the whole mission here is to give you something tangible and constructive to take your business forward. The optimum way of us doing this is to follow a pattern that has proven to lead to where we want to end up. We must begin at the beginning - and that is identifying a path to travel down.

You see, what this is all about is you taking your business forward. We're going to look together at a whole load of things that you can apply but you will probably find that at first glance there are a lot of questions. You might ask, "Oh that's a good idea but how do we do it?" or, "That sounds okay, but what about my business?" So I will make sure that as we go through, we'll talk and work at a pace that gives you time for some ideas to filter down. I have included a lot of 'workbook pages' and the idea of these is that you use them and/or a separate workbook to actually break away from reading and do some thinking and working separately. As I have said, the purpose of this book isn't to fill a shelf - it is to help produce results that change and improve your life, thus I will share with you my thoughts and then there will be spaces for you to do some work before moving on and you will always be directing the pace at which you work and read.

But it really does start back at the basics. Building your business into what you dream it could give you *is* possible, but it starts with simple basic foundation thoughts. So that then is where we begin.

Don't be impatient!

Many business owners say to me they "just need to grow," that they want more customers, sales, etc. Well, in my view as a salesman, growing your business really is about sales and marketing – but this can only happen and produce really lasting benefits when the foundations are right. Your business can be enormous, if you wish; it could be small but massively profitable, if you wish. You can have your Ferrari and your villa and retire, if you wish, or you can maintain a lifestyle business and always be busy; it's your choice. It really is all possible, and the proof that it's possible is because other people are doing it now.

If the vision of 'your future' is in your head, it is there because you have seen what you want... and if you have seen it then it means someone is attaining it... and that, my friend, is great news because it means that if they can have it then there is NO reason you can't as well!

Therefore our task is to try and find patterns of success that are giving a reward you desire. We find something for us to model that when we do so, we should basically achieve the same reward – and that hopefully is what I can share with you as we go forward. I'll share some patterns of success that, when modelled and reapplied to your business, will give a similar level of return.

The ideas within this book work. They are proven, already successful.

You'll interpret them in your own way and they'll have a different application in your business, but they genuinely work. AND, even though our economic climate is constantly changing and we are surrounded at times by doomsday 'end of world/all is broken' type pessimists, there is still and always will be room for you to shine and rise above those around you.

Enterprise will always be a key to success in life. Learning to think slightly differently... learning to apply ideas when others shrink back... becoming decisive and 'action' oriented... these qualities are leadership or enterprise qualities and you will *always* win if you work on these and allow them to make you stand out.

Life is NOT all about commercial enterprise, and indeed this shall be touched upon later. Business has to have a human touch and you need a balance to enjoy the fruits of your labour, and so in this book I shall encourage you to also look at 'the bigger picture' and add to the business mix some 'life issues' that in my humble opinion then make commercial success into a real life success.

So then as we have talked about 'beginning' the journey, are you ready? Do you want to start building your new future? Let's begin, shall we?

Section One

Business Booster Foundations

Learning more is a right move, but if you don't make room for it to become applied knowledge then it will just be more accumulated unused knowledge.

One of the most common issues facing small businesses and their busy owners today is simply the apparent pressure upon you to do all of the things required to do. It feels like a manic roller coaster or treadmill, and there are many times I am sure when you just feel overwhelmed!

Thus critical to your new future is a new habit to 'Stop' that madness feeling. YOU have to take back control. Truthfully what has happened over the last few months or years is that you have slipped into the trap of feeling that circumstance dictates your action. You are spending most of your time *reacting* to the environment... choosing to do tasks because they appear and you feel that you have to do them. WRONG!! You have given away your control!

Don't beat yourself up! It's a common failing... but it is one that right now at the beginning we have to correct. You have to take back control and learn to do that which you choose and that which directly benefits you and to let go of the fear of not doing the other stuff!

As crazy as it might sound, this exercise if you do it every day becomes a mental habit... this exercise will dramatically change your future!

To make your future happen, learn this exercise well:

Stop!
(all that you are doing)

Stand Back!
(and make a little room to look at your situation)

Ask **"How Can I Make Things Better?"**

(ask empowering questions – command your brain to find better answers)

Literally make yourself stand up, shout out 'Stop!' and physically stand back so that you make yourself reflect on what is going on.

> *"There are costs and risks to a program of action.*
> *But they are far less than the long-range risks and*
> *costs of comfortable inaction"*
> John F Kennedy

When you are next at your place of work or in your work environment, please do this!

Stop that which you were doing or about to do, **give yourself 'space'** even if it isn't actually a physical space, merely a mental one, then when you have 'stopped' and in a better position to 'see' more accurately, command your brain to find an answer. **Ask out loud 'How can I make this better?'** Do this everyday as if your life depended on it and you will soon have everything you want from your business.

Pause for one moment please. Think about your last few days or weeks at work... how have you felt with reference to the time pressure and the to-do list? Have you felt constantly pulled in all directions? Have you felt that the task list just keeps getting longer even though you are chewing through it as fast as you can? Do you feel exasperated that in order to get the job done properly you end up having to do much of it yourself and thus you simply cannot get enough done?

Well that is a common complaint... but just because it is common and many people suffer from it doesn't make it what should be. It merely means that most people are also not in control and are reacting to circumstance instead of proactively changing actions NOW to make the future better.

You, my friend, have a chance now to make tomorrow better. Learn to take control back. Discipline yourself into this simple but powerful action... my suggestion is do it at least every morning and afternoon... but better still, learn to do it almost every hour so that the next hour becomes very deliberately focussed and productive.

Your first step is this simple exercise to remind yourself that you do have enough time... possibly what you lack is enough discipline and focus to make sure that you only do that, which is conducive to your forward path in-line with the goals that you have set.

Your second step is possibly a little more challenging...

If you want to 'More Money, Less Stress', then the first understanding is that **you MUST accept that it is possible** on both an outward, conscious level and importantly on an inward or subconscious level.

There can be no room for doubt.

I believe that this universe *will* help you get exactly what you want... and it hears *all* of your thoughts so if there is any room for conflict, if one part of your mind does not really believe that it is possible, then the universe will hear this conflict and interpret it as a 'stalemate'. You will not see forward movement or enjoy the giving that the universe can bestow upon you if there is a doubt as to whether you can achieve it or whether you are worthy of it.

Your job is not to know how or when right now... merely to accept that it can. I'll just say that again... your job is NOT to know exactly how your future will transform... try really hard to be less controlling and less 'if it's to be, it's up to me' in terms of specifics of how and when, but train yourself to accept that it is going to happen and that possibly a far greater intelligence than you or I is steering this path of yours. Accept that just possibly there is a force far stronger than you, and so to think for one moment that the harder we try, the more we can 'force' our future into shape... well it almost ridicules when you look at how insignificant we are in the grand scheme of things.

If you accept that there is a greater force and a greater intelligence and a rhyme and reason to the universe and its workings, then also accept that it is possible and it can happen to you!

I agree that it is difficult... I know that it seems impossible and we have a logical mind that likes to 'see' how and 'see' evidence before we can *really believe*... but, my friend, there *is* in fact evidence all around you and you have simply been playing a message in your head that it's different for them!!

You see wealth and you see business success, and then you say internally that "my world is different and I can't have that because of X, Y or Z!"

That is where you must pay mental attention, and for now, at least, please ride with this and *believe! Take control of your actions right now and* **take control of your mind** right now. Decide to make *you* the person who makes your future happen.

Thus, when I implore you to learn and repeat this simple exercise "Stop! Stand Back! How Can I Make Things Better?" It is because I *know* it will work and it will help you take control of your thoughts on both a conscious and subconscious level.

When I implore you to really work at internal quiet voices, the one that casts doubt over whether you can achieve it or not and try to work every fine detail out before it believes and sees... when I implore this, it is again because I *know* it works and I just need you to commit to the effort of developing these new habits.

The good news is simply this… once you have worked your new 'brain muscle' into a healthier habit, you will soon do it almost automatically, and when you do this you will start to see amazing things happen! The universe really will start to constantly surprise you with 'coincidences' and 'lucky encounters'! Once 'in tune' and conditioned, your mind sends out the correct 'signals' and you see the results. Indeed, almost from today onwards you will start to see things change!

Yes, from today onwards you will start to experience amazing coincidence… bumping into old contacts, meeting surprising connections at business events, having an idea that suddenly puts a new perspective on an old 'problem'… all of these things will start to occur as you start right now to take control back and to believe it is possible!

Please make a huge determined effort to practice this exercise, control your thoughts and direct the universe. Override thoughts of risk or doubt and let the magic happen!

Business Booster Foundations

Now that you have got the 'mindset' adjusted, we need to actually start some practical things to make the reality start happening differently.

To start off with then, to begin your journey forward, you need to go backwards! You cannot simply forge ahead if you haven't at first taken stock, taken a 'snapshot' of where you are and where you have come from and what actions you did or didn't do etc.

Whilst many others may advise you purely to focus on what is ahead, and indeed I will be talking with you later about focus and planning ahead, truthfully it is perhaps a little too simplistic to merely look forwards.

What if some core essential elements with your current scenario are potential weaknesses for the imagined future? If you don't learn a little analysis and examination of current process, what if one of the very keys to success in the future *is* this ability to look closely and analyse past business actions so as to plan a better course of action? What if there are frequently occurring instances or habits that you only really see when you look back a little... but that if you didn't spot them and allowed them to reoccur then they might hinder the future too? What if your aims and ideas have changes since you first set up the business and thus unless you openly and honestly write this into the new forward plan, you're likely to end up with more misery!

You *can* have all that you want and it *will* come, but for now learn to gently hold back the reigns. It is important for you to examine where exactly your business is, ask some questions and be honest with answers, and then ask clear questions about what it really is that you want to achieve.

Simple goal setting and planning basics that you know about but have slipped into not doing... simple actions that you have labelled as, "not important because I know what I am doing," have been dismissed and yet the result of this lack of attention to basics is the feeling that you are swamped, that you are not in control and that no matter how hard you try it just isn't working. The plain truth is that the lack of these simple disciplines is exactly why you haven't got it right yet!

Preparation and planning are absolutely key elements and no future path will really be successful for you unless you learn to direct that path more deliberately... and you cannot deliberately direct a path if you haven't clearly identified the path in the first place!

So right here at the beginning, I encourage you to learn some disciplines and I ask some searching questions about goals, plans; where and why?

Where are you now?

Where are you <u>now</u> in your business? What's the answer to that? Is it the very beginning of your business? A few months? A few years? Or are you further down the 'road' than that? How much money are you making? Are you feeling buoyant? Are you feeling stale? Are you full of enthusiasm? Are you knocking at the door, chasing it? Or are you sitting there thinking, "Oh my god, I really don't know how much longer I can keep this going?"

Where are you? Are you winning? Stagnant? Slipping backwards? Have you really asked yourself that question?

Do you stop to think enough about your existence and your path? The truth is that many business owners feel they are 'too busy' to stop and think; they just need to *do*! Keeping on just 'doing' is not going to help if your current 'doing' is not bringing you what you want!! Remember what they say, **"If you keep on doing what you are doing, you keep on getting what you are getting."** If you want something more than the current, then you have to *do* more than the current... or at least different than the current. Thus it is very important indeed that you examine the current. So... where are you at now?

Turnover? Income? Profits? Money facts and figures? Yes, you need to know your numbers. (Frankly it scares me how many business owners I speak with who just do not know their numbers and when asked to have an educated guess, they always guess at least 30-40% inaccurately and on the 'up' side. In other words, they think they are making more than they really are!!!)

You must know your numbers. We will talk more about that later. For now though, how many customers have you got? How many sales are you getting? How many days and hours a week are you working? Do you want to slow down a bit? Is it all a bit manic at times? What goes well in your business right now? What isn't going well in your business right now? Have you identified 'problem areas'? Have you identified 'win' areas?

These are thoughts that you need to clearly think through. If you write them down as a collection of answers, you will see clearly a picture of where you are at... and this is absolutely *so* vital because if you see clearly where you are at, it gives you a starting point to spring from and also tells you what you want to avoid and leave behind as you begin your journey.

So, keep the mind spinning... and please be totally honest with your answers. Treat this session as almost a private coaching session in which your comments and answers are always 'in confidence'. No one will know but it is important not to 'kid yourself'!

Do you think you're flying, or are you drowning? Are you treading water, but not getting anywhere and being frustrated at the effort? Where are your frustrations? Where are your 'highs'?

It's not all about money... but hey, it *is* all about the money!! Are you making enough? If not, how much are you actually making for YOU? Is that enough? If it isn't, then at least honestly write down what little you are taking. At this stage, it is deadly to lie to yourself... as maybe you do when talking with friends, family, contacts etc!! Okay, so you can have a little licence to 'exaggerate' to others but it will not help you now. Please record accurately and honestly where you are at now with your business so that you have a snapshot that we can look back upon and see how far we have come.

How do you feel about 'headaches' like staffing issues? Administration issues?

And is your business known in the market? Are you always adding new business?

Are you really gathering new customers apace, or are you very much painfully aware that customers aren't coming in very fast these days? Or are you gathering new customers but painfully aware that they're coming in at a very poor level so you're not making the money these days?

Are you finding that some of your customers are moaning a lot and therefore the enjoyment factor's gone and, "in the old days it didn't used to be like this"?

Are you finding that because of the customers you serve, maybe because they moan too much, your position in the market is wrong and you'd like to change your company's positioning?

(A good idea is to write. Use the 'Where Are You Now?' section on the page included, and honestly, simply just write down your thoughts as I ask you these questions... and please write down your answers NOW! Take action to make your future better starting NOW!! Don't put it off for later!)

Are you dealing to the middle class of your market, the bottom end, or are you very exclusive at the top end? How do you feel about your market positioning? Tell yourself about your current clients, your existing business levels and all that goes with it.

Try to involve the *feeling* inside of the answers. How do you _feel_ about where you're at? 'Where Are You Now?' is about a lot more than just facts and figures. Write down feelings that describe how you feel towards your daily grind and how optimistic or pessimistic, excited or frightened you might feel about your future.

Are you enjoying it? Are you frustrated? Which bits do you still enjoy... and which don't you like so much?

Do you think your pricing is right? How do you compare to others?

How about your energy levels? Are you tired most of the time? Has it ground you down, or do you feel it gradually doing so?

What about your mental activity? Are you awakened at night with excited thoughts and is your daytime a buzz with anticipation and vision? Or are you merely coping with everything that every day throws at you? Do you enjoy going into work, or do you feel it is now becoming a chore? If so, why? Which bits?

Do you worry? What about? Why? What do you think is the cure?

As I have already said, please write and record your thoughts honestly! What do you *really* think?

As you think, start to formulate your 'answers' *and* write them down. (It's a great habit, by the way, writing down your thought... as you talk with yourself and learn to open up, if you give yourself a creative outlet by writing the thoughts down, your mind will suddenly feel like it's being listened to and as that process starts to flow more regularly, your mind will start to produce all sorts of amazing answers! It's true! You will actually tap into a vast resource that in fact will provide you with all of the answers to all of the challenges you're ever faced with, so please encourage it by starting the process now.)

Do you think you're at the beginning of your business or approaching the latter stages? If you're in what you identify as a 'middle stage', then how did you identify that? Is that because you just think of how many years you have been doing it, or is it in terms of progress towards where you think you want to be? Are you planning an end? Do you see yourself retiring soon should finances allow? Have you an 'exit' strategy?

What about your team? Do you need to gather around you a core team, or do you have that but recognise you need extra bodies at a lower level to maintain higher volume levels? Is staffing an issue?

Tell me about your enjoyment levels... are you enjoying *all* of your roles? I mean, when you're actually 'doing what you do', I guess you enjoy 'it', but do you? As much as you always did? If not, why not? If you do but it's the other bits you hate, then write down what you like and don't like. Break your current existence down into role... tasks that consume your time perhaps, and just get knowledgeable about where you are at.

It might seem I am labouring this point. It might seem that you just want to get reading about more hot tips to build your business, but as I said previously, to attain the result you want this is such a core part of the future that right here and now you need to address the disciplines needed to see it to the end. Getting down into 'boring stuff' actually exposes the mind to real hidden motivations and without correct motivations you are not going to go very far.

And if I keep repeating something, it is because again your mind works in a pretty simple way and when it comes to learning we learn things easily when they are just repeated time and time again! Remember when we learned nursery rhymes? How did we learn? By listening over and over again! So, if this is to work it is going to work because we break the 'old mental pattern' and break away from your current business operational methods and get into a new one that can give you better results... and to learn a new one we can help ourselves by repetition.

To help you, you've got to get the brain to think on a different level. You have to encourage yourself to approach a 'new future' with a new set of disciplines, and so start helping yourself right now and address this examination of now scenario.

Please, take 15 or 20 minutes NOW and write down these thoughts as to where you are now. Write as fluently as you can. Just get used to thoughts flowing out, because it's a powerful habit.

Please don't worry about writing the correct answers either! There is no right or wrong… just start the process and then look at what you've written.

NB You'll possibly find that it's a little difficult to get the brain to start thinking and it's probably not easy to know what to write initially, but *please try*. Just let it flow, write anything in the beginning, bounce crazy ideas around in your head and give silly answers if that's how they feel, but allow the process to develop and you will find it incredibly helpful.

So go write!

After you've finished scribbling, you will have a collection of thoughts that basically show you some good points about today and some definite not so good points that we want to move away from. You're going on a journey in business development. **The future is not going to equal the past.** It can be anything you wish and if today's business lifestyle and reward system isn't giving you all that you've dreamed of (and I assume it isn't or perhaps you wouldn't be reading this now), then you have to know exactly what is not right about today's business lifestyle. You need to understand what you do not like and for what reason… and then you can recreate your business lifestyle to one that suits. As has been said, this is a journey… and every journey needs a start point. Find yours.

(Scribble time! Take your chance now to answer these questions using the thought prompts you've just read. Go back and reread the questions, and write *fully* a 'snapshot' of everything describing your current 'status quo' and then do the same *fully* for each section.)

WARNING! WARNING! WARNING!

Have you done the writing??! Were you just about to carry on reading??!! Remember, please, before you just read on... if you want to simply read on, then probably you are only thinking about this at the same surface level as you've become accustomed to and that will probably imply a level of application much as you've previously become accustomed to. If you do that then the 'same as before' in application will produce the same as before in result. Please, stop now and take a few minutes to review these questions, ask yourself more and examine where you are at with your life, your business life especially and write a clear account of what you like and dislike, and give yourself an accurate start.

Business Basics

Where are you now?

_____

_____

_____

_____

_____

_____

_____

_____

_____

_____

Where do you want to be?

_____

_____

_____

_____

_____

_____

_____

_____

_____

_____

What are my goals? (Simple, overview aims)

_____

_____

_____

_____

_____

_____

_____

_____

_____

_____

Why am I doing this? What do I really want to achieve?

_____

_____

_____

_____

_____

_____

_____

_____

_____

_____

Where do you want to be?

Every journey has a destination, an end to aim for, so the next area for you to look at is, 'Where do you want to be?' You've got a 'start', so now see if you can put an 'end' together.

Where do you want to be? *Do* you have a clear and specific 'end goal', or a just loose thought of what you'd like if it all 'goes according to plan'? Genuinely one of the major challenges in attaining anything is the 'define it' challenge. Most of us are almost programmed not to aim for much because then we avoid disappointment... and thus we have only vague notions of what we would like to achieve in life and indeed we only set very moderate aims usually again because of an inbred belief that we aren't really ever going to make it, so why dream and be disappointed?

However, please believe me; to make your life a success IS possible. To achieve much greater things than that which you currently have IS possible – but it is much less likely if you do not know exactly that which you are aiming for. Thus, a very clear and precise written goal is a key ingredient of your forward journey. Lots of people have a very loose end goal but that's why they never attain it. In order for you to attain your goal, you must have it specific and clear.

As before then, please write down some thoughts on where you want to be and I'll 'prompt' you with some thought provoking questions...

Do you see yourself on a beach retired?

Do you see yourself owning a huge company, but having a less active daily role?

Do you see yourself having sold out and not owning anything and starting another one?

Do you see yourself quitting this daily grind and actually then just doing what you really want to do, which is have fun, play golf, fly aeroplanes, do whatever?

Do you have a hobby that you'd like to do, and work is a necessary evil at the moment?

Do you see your business expanding nationally, internationally? How about locally by adding outlets or branches, but keeping it fairly small and manageable?

Do you have a *personal* 'fame' or 'recognition' goal? Or do you see it as *business* branding that you want to achieve? Or is it nothing about that, that it is merely a lifestyle/income that you want to achieve?

(It perhaps isn't easy to get your brain 'muscle' thinking beyond your usual daily thought level. You see, generally you will find that most day-to-day activity isn't thought out. Most day-to-day activity is where you get sucked along with what's happening around you. And that's given your brain a lazy get-through-the-day attitude. Your brain isn't *driving* you; it's just coping with what you're doing. So when it comes to driving forward, we are now having to think and it doesn't come naturally! You have an awesome computer between the ears, but it isn't working at much of its capacity so let's try hard here to stimulate it into overdrive. Train that mind muscle and it will soon become strong, as does any other physical muscle like your bicep.)

As a tip, try looking at all of the 'Where you are at' items, such as money, hours worked, number of staff, premises etc. and then look at them and ask 'Where do I want to be?' It will give you an answer... write that down and let's aim for that!

And what does it mean, all this writing down where you're at and where you want to be?

It means taking control and putting your brain into *active* gear, and then saying, "No I don't want that, I want this". It means you **stop drifting and start steering.**

It means that as you develop these skills and retrain your 'mind muscle', you gain more and more control of your life and thus increase hugely the chances of getting what you want out of it. Don't be lazy! Do not get swept along in an aimless drift!

It simply means that pushing, when it doesn't come easy now, will directly impact what you get out of your life. It means it is worth it!

What are your goals?

Next then is Goals. Goal setting!! Not new... something I am sure you have done before, but let me quickly ask you... have you set goals before? Have you achieved all or even most of them? Honestly?

Why do you think you haven't?

Well, my guess is that actually when you set them you didn't actually write them down specifically clearly enough and then the actions plan to achieve them wasn't closely linked enough.

No problem... but let's change that and make certain that this time you are equipped and capable to actually achieve that which you have set as a goal.

So, what are goals?

Perhaps one goal might be to sell the business and get the Ferrari. One goal might be to get the Ferrari, the private plane, the beach house in four destinations around the world! How big do you want your goals to be? Where are they? What are they? Do you have goals? Some people have limited goals, some people have great big goals; what are yours?

Think for a moment about what you would like to achieve... in your personal life, or in respect to your health or your contribution to your community? Do you have ideas in these areas? If you felt that you could achieve it, would you want to include activities in these areas?

Tell me, how do you feel when thinking of goals? Do you feel silly sometimes? Many people, if they're honest, feel awkward. If you do, then please recognise that feeling and let's consciously smash that restrictive thought. All that is happening is that you are hearing someone else's conditioning that you absorbed as you grew up... someone who had little faith or aspiration trained you to think in a limited fashion. "You aren't ever going to get that so why bother... it's for others, not for the likes of us" etc.

Well, that has to stop! You have to believe that tomorrow can be a lot different to today if we change our thoughts and actions. Indeed, you telling yourself that you "don't really believe I can have it"... that awkward feeling... that is telling your subconscious mind that you don't want it! But you do! So stop the negative internal language!!! Stat really trying to have belief!

A great way to do that is to set goals that you feel are achievable and then work up in smaller steps. It is possibly true that the universe can make you a millionaire literally overnight... but if you have been struggling for 20 years and haven't achieved more than £30,000 a year salary, then you might struggle to believe that within a year you can become a millionaire!

Now, in another section we will look at 'Mindset of Millionaires', but for now whilst it may be possible if you don't believe it to be then you will have a negative subconscious input and that will mean non-attainment. So, choose for example an increase from £30,000 to £50,000.

Remember also the point we made earlier that "Ours is not to reason why, ours is just to do or die". In other words, you and I, we are not all powerful! We don't know everything! We don't know what magical powerful connections might happen in the next month or year... we don't know who can be steered our way, or what incredible idea we might have, or what opening might suddenly be created to exploit that idea you already have! You do not know... you sometimes just have to have a little faith and belief in the universe and its ability to provide!

So, going back to the issue of goal setting. Try to stretch yourself into a goal that you can almost see achievable but not one that you really cannot believe.

And as before, whilst I'm not saying how much you should write, I just want you to flow. Please try and get it to flow. Don't just write a word or two but try *describing in full* your lifestyle with colour and clarity. It isn't merely "live in Spain, own a Ferrari"; it is a full description of the villa, its location, its gardens, your full lifestyle and the other toys you have alongside the Ferrari. You'll find actually that when you do start to get it to flow, then you'll find that you can't stop it. But just initially, let's get used to thinking a lot deeper.

Again, let me share a thought with you as we're talking. All the people that 'make it', all of the 'success stories' and the entrepreneurs or stars of film and music... one absolutely 100% common thread is that **they all knew what they wanted and were 100% focussed on getting it.** There wasn't any half-hearted approach of, "Well, if I get it, it would be nice". There isn't any talk of possible other careers, just in case. The ones that 'make it' are the ones that *accept nothing else as an option* and are so totally committed and focussed on their goal or outcome that the universe accepts that's what they're going to get and gives it to them.

Their success measured exactly their expectations because their expectations were precise. They were specific. They were crystal clear and non-negotiable.

Clarity of focus and absolute driving energy towards a solid visualised goal are number one prerequisites to your success so if you aren't really sure about what you want, if you only have vague ideas and "it doesn't really matter as long as I'm okay", then you must do some work in this area now. DO NOT read on and DO NOT try to trick yourself that as you go along all will become clear like some 'road to Damascus' type experience. It won't, so stop now and examine where you want to be, what goals you're aiming for and then once they are clear, you can work precisely on how to get them.

One final but very, very important point you need to be aware of when considering goals and goal setting etc. is the S.M.A.R.T. goal setting - Specific, Measurable, Achievable, Realistic, Time framed approach.

This is excellent advice and you would be well advised to always break goals into this *type* of set up. However, I have an issue with this... Allow me to explain:

How do you evaluate what is achievable or realistic?

The only way you can is based upon what you 'know' to be true. You will, for example, believe something to be 'achievable' when you can 'see' a path to achieving it. When a path is completely unknown to you, you will assume that it cannot be achieved. Indeed, you will assess 'realistic' as 'possible based upon what you know is achievable...' and what you know is achievable is at best a) past knowledge and b) your limited experience of the world and all of its mechanics!!

How arrogant we become when we as mortals assume we know all of the realms of physics and future possibilities!!! How crazy that when we cannot even predict the weather accurately, we presume to know enough to judge whether something is possible or realistic or achievable or not!!!

The point is you will make a judgement based upon very limited knowledge!

Again, here's an example... assume you want to increase your income from £30,000 to £250,000. Now that is a quantum leap! Do you even know anyone who makes £250,000 a year? How on earth can you 'see' that much money as possible when your only 'knowledge' is of a world of £30,000 to £50,000???

However, if you knew people who earned £250,000 a year, then it might change your opinion. If you knew several people who earned a million a year... or even a million a month... then again your knowledge of that world might change your belief that it is possible. (You might still argue for your limitations. You might still say, "Yes, but I am not them and I can't earn a million a month!" but we'll work on that!)

So, the bottom line is... goals are critical to have because they are the driving energy that keeps you working when you feel tired and want to stop. Dreams and goals are the motivation behind effort... without something to drive you, something that makes it all feel worthwhile, without dreams and goals you will not even get on the next rung of the ladder. BUT with the right focus and belief, then suddenly your dreams become much bigger and much more powerful and then magic happens!! Please then, dream! AND write clearly those dreams and goals! Be inspired to push! Dream with clarity, faith and certainty.

WARNING!!!

As before, PLEASE DO NOT READ ON UNTIL YOU HAVE DONE THIS WORK WITH YOURSELF!!

To help you, I have included a worksheet for you to work on. Use the questions asked in this section along with the ones on the sheet. Please do not read on and skip the work... that's what you've always done, remember??!!

Your future is in your success habits. One of them is Stop, Stand back and ask 'How Can I Make It Better?' Another is doing the work!

You make it better by breaking the old habit of skipping exercises! Do the work and allow yourself to create a future you want instead of remaining in the present you don't much like!!

And if you can identify some goals, then the natural question to follow is:

Why?

Okay, so we've looked at where you're at, we've looked at where you want to be. We have identified some goals. Now let's look at perhaps the most crucial point – why are you doing it?

The question that lays the cornerstone of our foundations is "**Why am I doing this?** What do I really want to achieve this?" You MUST have a focus on the underlying driver for your end goal.

And because of all the interruptions and hassles of everyday business life, you need to be focussed on a daily basis. All the other hassles that go on around you knock you off course, and if you're not constantly pulling yourself back on course and refocussing on why you're doing it then you end up in a totally wrong place. It's no good getting to the end of your working life and saying, "Oh pants, we're in the wrong place", because it's too late. But you <u>do</u> have the control, and what this is all about is taking control of what you've got. You <u>do</u> have the choice. You <u>can</u> be in the destination that you want. Focus on your why? What's driving you, what's it all for?

(You need to be able to write down some whys, and some answers to, "What do I really want to achieve?" And it's well worth taking time out periodically to ask yourself these questions and keep going back to them.)

And it might help you if you remember that if other people can get to the destination that you've identified, if other people can show visible evidence of attaining what you are after, then <u>you</u> can attain it.

The only thing or person that stops you… is you.

You get knocked off course one day, which is entirely understandable and possible… but you have to pull yourself back on. Sadly what often happens is that people just carry on. You, on the other hand, must recognise that you are temporarily 'off course', pull yourself back and remove the 'fluffy' state of mind. If you don't pull yourself straight back, you'll drift, and that easily then sets into big drifts and then after several years, well, you're miles off.

So please start **pulling yourself back into line on a daily basis**. (Hence the Stop, Stand Back, and 'How Can I Make It Better?' Mantra)

Take notes now – use the spaces provided. Learn to write your thoughts frequently and just keep pulling yourself back, every day, every week, and every month. Where are you at? What do I want? Why? Why? Why? What am I <u>really</u> after?

Do you *really* want this wealth and fame and fortune and retirement because you'd just love to drive a Ferrari 24/7, because that'll soon get stale? You can only drive it so many hours a day! You really would get fed up! If that's the end focus, you may have a problem! So what else are you going to do with your time? You don't want to fall into the trap of some people that when they retire they then just literally die because they've got nothing to live for.

When you have all of this wealth, what will you do with it? Would you possibly not work so much? If that is the case then... is it wealth that you want or free time???

When you have all of this wealth and time, *who* do you want to share it with? If that is the case, why don't you just set out to spend more time with them now???

If you keep pushing to learn and grow, what are you planning to do with all of the knowledge when attained? Share it? Help others? If that is the case, what could you do right now that helps others in a similar way???

Here is a thought: scientists have proven that brain activity is directly correlated to age and lifespan. Learning a language or a musical instrument, for example, is often recommended for retirement because they're two things that really stir the learning patterns in the brain, and brain stimulation or activity is essential to life. And as I say there's research that shows it <u>physically</u> extended lifespan. So, think a little deeper about your future. Learning and sharing and remaining outwardly focussed are great habits for survival!

"I'll tell you what I want, what I really, really want", to paraphrase the Spice Girls. Because it's what you <u>really, really</u> want that matters, and sometimes the first time you write this down, the goals that you write, the end is very glib. It's commonly 'millions of pounds, retirement and

Ferrari'. That's rubbish; it's not what we *really* want. What are you going to do when you've got that? Who with? Where? Why? In fact, it's probably not even your own goal! It's one that you've heard, thought is pretty good and adopted; but is it really your own choice?

Do you want to give all your family lots of money to ease the suffering, perhaps? Do you have grand ambitions to provide employment for loads of people in your area? Or to create a shelter for the homeless, a care home for the elderly, an education programme for underprivileged kids, a sports academy for tomorrow's hopefuls?

I'm going to let <u>you</u> think about that for a while and let <u>you</u> write and let you talk to yourself at your leisure. I want you to come back and revisit these pages.

But as we move on, allow me to share another thought: the group known as 'mankind' share several core 'needs', two of them being the need for connection and the need for spirituality... that is a basic need for 'connection'. Connection is a word to describe that feeling of belonging and being liked... that feeling of being an important part of a group, even if only a small part. In a similar fashion, the need for a spiritual awareness or recognition of a higher power is pretty much within every human. That feeling that you're not completely alone and that you do matter to someone, somewhere, that there is a reason why you are here and a broader plain perhaps. It is about reflecting on our creator and looking to the universe for answers or a God for support.

This is actually built in us all, because like it or not, try to ignore it, bury it or kill it, these feelings are in us, and sooner or later come to the surface.

The point is thousands upon thousands of 'successful people' report that the fame or money that they strived for, once attained, still left them feeling empty or still unsuccessful. We don't need to relive old clichés, such as money cant buy happiness, but actually they are true and as you start to think a little now about your 'why', I promise you that merely having a material 'why' will leave you empty even when you get it... and I'll wager that the odds of you 'getting it' are lower too.

Try to think then of a 'why' that is bigger, a 'why' that involves sharing and giving. Try to think of a 'why' that is 'other people focussed', not 'you focussed'. Think perhaps of being a servant to your clients to save them from all of the other cowboys out there! Try to think of your job as a mission to prevent your potential clients ever suffering the pain of dealing with lesser providers. Think of your 'why' as not what you get out of your business but what you can *give* with your business. Think of a 'why' that involves 'connection' and 'contribution' and 'humanity'.

I believe that when you find this, not only will success be far easier to attain, but massively more rewarding when attained... as I said, just a thought...

Okay, so we've been stirring the grey cells a little bit. But a word of warning, a common habit is not listening to yourself and not asking properly, and not really trying to find an answer. There is a part of our human psyche that says we are afraid. It's very, very simple. Most people do not set goals or examine daily activity – where they're at or why they bother – because if they *really* looked, they wouldn't like what they heard or saw. If they really looked at their lot in comparison to their ideal, if they really looked at goals and said, "Oh, I'd love to have this", a voice inside their head at the same time says, "But you can't". And so to avoid the pain of disappointment, they stop going for it and they come out with this silly line, "Well I'm happy anyway". That's pants! Have the courage to stand up for what you want and then have the real strength to ask for help getting it! Don't ever give up and stop trying!

For most it's a 'bury the head in the sand' approach, *existing* not really living. I want <u>you</u> to know right now, I am here to help you *really live*. Remember, **you *can* do it… there's no such word as *can't*. Ask instead, "How can I?"**

Building a better business to make your future better is only going to be achieved if you improve your habits! It's not what you 'know'; it's what you 'do'. If you've read on to this point without stopping to do some 'exercises', then I appreciate that you have heard all we've said before… I know that you know… but do you *do*?

Spend a few moments writing. Let words and thoughts merge and play games as to how big a picture of your future you can paint. Test yourself. Be 'crazy like a child'. Allow your true desire to surface and instead of feeling silly to want it, have faith that you can have it and have courage to ask for it. Then when it is out into the open, the process of attainment can actually start… and I promise you that attainment is supremely possible, so do not feel silly to be bold. Be proud, adventurous and honest with yourself… and then we can move on and aim for something that fires us up.

This is your 'blank canvas'. Be bold, crazy and childlike! Write ALL of the 'things you want'… paint the picture of your ideal future.

Remember always that the vision you hold inside of your head as an ideal 'perfect' you… this image is only possible inside of your head because you've seen images *outside* of your head… which means you've seen it already, which means it exists already… thus there is no rule whatsoever in the universe that says you cannot also have it!! The most fantastic news is that if it already exists, then you can have it also, so don't be afraid to dream! Paint your picture now!

My Perfect Vision

(What do I look like? Healthy? Shining? Bright-eyed and bushy-tailed? Relaxed? Etc.)

_____

_____

_____

_____

_____

_____

_____

_____

_____

_____

_____

_____

_____

_____

_____

_____

_____

_____

_____

_____

_____

The Importance of Planning – Do you plan to fail?

Right, now that you've done some basics – understanding where, why, etc. – the question is, *how* do we go forward to our identified goals? This work you are doing is about an end result. Okay, you appreciate the process and will learn from it, be blunt, it's all about getting what we want which is more than you've got now!!

Here's a question; do you plan to fail?

No?

So <u>why</u> do you <u>fail</u> to plan? If I asked you, do you have a current written business plan, have you?

Again, I'll say it, this isn't about knowing stuff, it's about *doing* stuff. That's the difference.

You know that you should have a plan. What you may not know though is how to make one that works as an ongoing document and maybe you don't see the value of making one.

Firstly then I'm going to suggest right now that you go and write a plan. It doesn't have to be *War and Peace*, it can be brief. It just needs to tell <u>you</u> a suggested route to the previously identified goals with time frames attached so that you can see milestones along the route. As you know, this isn't rocket science but it's amazing how often it is not done.

I shall share some ideas with you now to help you break it down into simple steps and then actually create a useful, workable and helpful plan that will get you what you want. Sound fair?

"If I don't plan to fail, why do I fail to plan?"

You can write on the pages included, or better still, get a pad and write, **"I must make a plan because I do not plan to fail".**

To help you, start with the broad outline questions; "Where are we now?", "Where do we want to be?", "Why?" Fill in your answers to those and the next question is, "How do I get there?"

At this point you must reflect upon the identified goal… and in truth a plan suggests actions that you can take in order to inch forward towards the goal. Plans are all about actions. To make it a working document and one that actually helps instead of merely being an exercise for a bank manager… to make this a reality… the plan needs to be specific and precise with action steps identified and suggested results noted.

How do I get from point A to B? What sort of activities will I need to include? Who will I need to work with? What will be my anticipated costs? What extra resources of people, money, and time will I need? You'll just flow, and some silly answers will flow but these might be great ideas!

Again you probably know that when you first start a business, especially when you are asking for someone like a bank to lend you money to start your business, you understand that writing a plan is a good idea. You recognise the need to write a good thorough plan to go and raise money against.

Today, however, many weeks, months or years later, you go to work every day… why? What do you go to work for, if not to raise money? And so what we have here is a situation that even you can see is crazy… on the one hand, to raise money you absolutely appreciate that you need a good and thorough plan (or else the lender will not entertain the idea of lending)… and then on the other hand, when you're raising money by just working for it, you don't see the need for a plan. Why? What's the difference???

Well of course the difference is no one sees the fact that you haven't got a plan so you assume it doesn't matter but I'd like you to just remind yourself of the reasons why a bank manager wants a plan.

Firstly, it shows that you have thought it through, that hopefully you've covered all eventualities and nothing unseen is going to suddenly come into view and ruin the business and result in him losing his money. Secondly, it gives you a path to follow so it eases the mental struggle so common in new businesses and new business owners. Thirdly, it should also have highlighted many areas that must be worked upon, outsourced, competitors to be aware of, costs to watch in case they spiral etc. etc. and these are watched on a weekly basis to stay 'on plan'. Thus making a plan is a very helpful exercise... and that doesn't change just because the bank manager isn't going to see it!

"Proper Planning Prevents Piss Poor Performance!"

Here's a suggestion. If you like, you could probably write some of these little sentences on yellow Post-it notes as mental reminders on a daily basis around your office, around where you work.

To sidetrack a moment, I'll tell you a little story about Ben Kench, just so you know that I'm only the same as you. (We're all only the same in as much as we all have 'challenges' to deal with and often very similar ones too.)

A few years ago, I did pretty well here in the UK selling double glazing and made lots of money and went out to Tenerife and bought a nightclub. I had a gorgeously beautiful girlfriend and a nine-month-old baby, bought a nightclub, rented out my three houses; I was well on my way.

We'd been in Tenerife probably less than four months when my little girl caught meningitis. It was several years ago now in Tenerife, and really people didn't know about it. It chokes me up just to think about it, but she was dying. We took her to four doctors and in the end she was rushed to Santa Cruz Hospital. They wouldn't let me in because we weren't married (it was a very Catholic country back then). They let the mother in and they read my daughter the last rites, and got the priest in and shaved my daughter's head and put pipes in etc. because she'd had this condition now for about six days and she was only 19-months-old. She was dying and the doctors were preparing me for the end.

And in the ensuing hassle, my daughter did survive. She's fine, but the entire world I'd built around me tumbled in. I'd gone to Tenerife as I thought myself to be a high flyer on my way to being a millionaire at 30 and quite literally within six months I was on my arse! Our relationship disintegrated, my baby was dying, the stress of it all; a new nightclub, a new country, new homes, everything just was too much for us; we were both so young... my head was so messed up!

My girlfriend decided to clear off with another man and they took the nightclub off me and I lost my three homes back in the UK. My head was messed up big time! My dreams, my relationship, my houses and my business had gone. I ended up with no money, completely on my own.

I didn't have the money to get home; I didn't have the money to *ring* home. And somebody came along to me and he said, "Here you are, mate", and gave me a book and he helped me on a path of learning. It was *How to Win Friends and Influence People* by Dale Carnegie (Sean Smith, I thank you eternally), and I read it and set about applying the principles to rebuild my life.

One of the things I did was to take positive messages from that wonderful book and create notices all around my home that constantly branded my troubled mind with uplifting thoughts. I literally brainwashed my mind into a better thinking process. I trained my mind to dwell on good things, not all of the bad that I could so easily drown myself in. I <u>literally pushed in helpful messages and pushed out destructive ones</u>.

I love every day now and I'm passionate about sharing some things that have worked. So whilst we go through these ideas, one of the things that worked was **little Post-it notes all around my environment**. I had sentences all around my flat - on the shaving mirror, by the kettle, by the cereal bowls - little sentences to just reprogramme the brain.

And so that's what I'd encourage you to do, just reprogramme the brain on some of these habits. Get some Post-it notes, or make something bigger, and place all around you these helpful daily reminders like, "Do I plan to fail... then why do I fail to plan?" The 6 P's is a good sentence to put up. 'Do I plan to fail?' is a great question to put up.

And it's a great book by the way, *How to Win Friends and Influence People*. Read it if you haven't already and if you have read it, read it again. And I only share that story with you because I know from painful personal experience that **the way out of any hole is just to share knowledge and to learn... and that simple things work**. So try putting messages all around you.

"Plan your work and work your plan"

Just have these gentle daily reminders right in front of you and every time you get up or go into your office, you'll see and you'll think, "Yes, okay, I've got to plan this out a bit better". It's so simple, but it's so powerful. Plan your work and work your plan.

The Financier's View

As you set about writing yourself a plan, consider this thought. Try thinking like a financier. The financier's view, as I call it. What do I mean by that? Well, have you ever tried to raise money, or know someone who has?

Financiers are a breed unto themselves, because they absolutely do see it just in their terms. So you have to be able to speak their language. But what a financier always asks you is 'What if?'

You will put down the best plans in the world of how many widgets you're going to sell and how much you'll make on a widget and how many people are going to buy widgets twice and third times and it all looks great, and you do all these spreadsheets and what your costs are going to be, and your wages, and how many people will you need, and it's all great. And then they say, "Well, what if you don't?"

What if...?

And you say, "Yes, well of course I'm going to, I know I can."

"Yes, but what if you don't?"

So I want you to ask yourself as you're planning and improving, "What if?"

If your plan says I'm going to, for example, gather another 30 customers this year, and those customers are going to give me £100,000 this year.

Ask: what if that £100,000 of work creates a need for another member of staff?

Or, what if you don't get £100,000 out of 30 customers but you <u>still</u> have to add admin to cope with 30 extra customers? How are your costs going to look?

What if you get 30 customers and your average sale value is lower, or what if you get your £100,000, but it's taken 50 customers?

How does that affect your admin and your costs?

Get very, very good at asking yourself 'What if'?

So, a little Post-it note somewhere on your wall, as a reminder, and your brain says, "What if this doesn't go according to plan?" and keeps you looking and thinking. Because it means when you get up on a Monday morning and you've got your plan, "I'm going to do this at 10 a.m., this at 12 p.m., this at 2 p.m., and this at 4 p.m., then I'm going to do this on Thursday and that next week." And then something completely goes off course, like your IT system screws up, or two of your key members of staff are off sick. What are you going to do?

So get used to asking, "What if?" Because the best laid plans of mice and men, as we know, don't always come off. We have to have a fail safe. Because you <u>can't</u> turn around to yourself and say, "Well I didn't get it, but it's not my fault because I didn't plan for that". It doesn't take away any pain and sure doesn't help pay the bills! You MUST think it through and be properly prepared for some unexpected happenings.

The Devil is in the detail

It's very boring sometimes to go through lots and lots and lots of writing and facts and figures, but it needs to be done occasionally. I'm not into 'paralysis by analysis'. I don't want you to get bogged down, but I <u>do</u> want you to understand the clear variations.

Simple steps. I'm not going to say to you, "Get all technical about this." I just want you to pause for 15 minutes every day. Just pause every morning and say, "Right, what am I going to do?" And don't let the world that swallows you up every morning take that away because if you don't pause, you'll end up in a very reactive environment every day and you'll never strategically push your business where you want it to be. Every morning, take a moment – Stop, Stand Back, and ask 'How Can I Make This Better?'

And when you've decided what you want to do, which might take five minutes of planning, just ask yourself that question, "What if that doesn't happen?" It might be that you're going on sales calls, and you're going out to see a sales potential and you're going to try to get an order, and that's really as lose as you've made it. Well what if he doesn't go for that? What are you going to come away with? Have you got two or three options before you go on that sales call in your mind?

Have you got the materials with you to show those options? Are you properly prepared? It might be that your objective is to get the order, but if you don't get the order, you're going to get a smaller order, and if you don't get any order you're going to come away with some referrals. Or, you know that it's a two stage process so you're going to have to go back a second time, so your objective the first time is to get another name and another meeting set up because it's a larger organisation and you can't do it just with one. What if they are not in or it isn't convenient; are you prepared to call somewhere else to make full use of your precious time?

It's about pausing to plan properly, including your "What if?" Proper planning would ensure that, if you can, you find out before you go in whom the other people are that might be the decision-makers. Proper planning might ensure that before you go, you look at the website to find out some information about the company, instead of just what you've already gleaned from your meeting.

Proper planning might be that you look at that company you're going to see and look at what they're currently doing. So you're going to sell them a website or some transport services or some IT infrastructure or whatever. <u>You go in there armed</u>, you know what they currently have as a set up and you've found out who they've dealt with in the past or who they are dealing with still.

You go in there with objectives and you're prepared because you've done some research. Don't be like the amateurs, the 'also-rans' who just put it in the diary and turn up. Arrive mentally armed for any eventuality and stand out as a winner. A winner who appears to have all of the luck!

"Luck is the meeting of preparation with opportunity"
Anthony Robbins

And isn't it <u>amazing</u> how <u>lucky</u> some of these successful people are? Because when they get there, they come out with more feedback, better appointments or bigger orders. But that's because when they were in there, they handled it better because they were operating from a knowledge base. Because they took those 15 minutes of preparation time and they didn't just turn up on the call. And remember the definition of luck... "The meeting of preparation with opportunity".

So make yourself a note; preparation, planning, time to stand back, ask yourself the 'what if's. It's simple stuff but it's the difference between world leaders and also-rans, because everybody else is too busy getting up and running around and doing what they've got to do. From now on you're going to get up earlier, <u>stop</u>, and in the <u>calm</u>, go forward. And as we talk together, if this isn't your current daily habit, then exercise some disciplines and I promise you <u>can</u> be very lucky.

And before we move on, before we leave this foundation place, here's a thought; look again at your goals and plan. Here's what usually happens: your goal is vague, it's general. It's good because it's better than nothing, but it's very fuzzy. Remember we've said this 'muscle', this mental muscle of writing and flowing and getting what we want; it's very out of use, it's not good. So when you first write what you want, it would be fairly vague.

For example, 'recoup investment'. Okay. Yes. You need to work and make a good living. That's generic, isn't it? It's vague and broad. Here's what you need to do...

The Butler

I'd like to introduce you to my friend and your servant – The Butler.

Let me use my illustration of a Butler or manservant who is employed by you to get what you want, to be your servant acting upon your instructions... a bit of a 'gofer' (go for what I want) type of person. (Many years ago, higher society homes would indeed have a Butler or manservant to attend to the needs of the master, and so visualise it in these terms.) Anyway, we have a situation where I believe there is a butler or servant for each of us at our command who will willingly go and get anything we want from the universe... if we ask him to.

Now, imagine calling in your Butler and asking him to "Go and get me rich!" Or telling him, "I want more money and to be successful'. How would he react? What would he say to you in return? Is there enough information in that request for your loyal and willing servant to do as you request? Imagine if you were issuing instructions or requests to an employee or family member, if you were vague and non-specific for example. A request to a sales team member to "Go and get more sales" might lead to more sales of the wrong sort or of too low a value or a request to a family member to "Meet me later" could lead to massive communication and frustration if details aren't also included to make it specific and actionable.

With vague 'requests' such as 'more money and more successful', could a Butler go and get your request? Probably not! Chances are he is going to want more information! Like, for example, when you say you want to be rich, maybe he would want to know what 'rich' means to you? Like how much money do you want? *Exactly* how much? And by when? Or you ask for success and he says, "What does success mean to you, Sir?" The point actually then is very clear, isn't it? The point is that if issuing instructions to ask for assistance in getting what you want, then your **instructions must be clear, precise and specific**. You need to tell him exactly what you want by when and what it looks like; otherwise he isn't likely to get it for you!

Have you read Napoleon Hill's *Think and Grow Rich*? (Buy and read it, if you haven't. It's a classic, another 'must-read').

Let me tell you briefly my story. I read it first time many years ago, as recommended, and I read through it and thought, "Yes, that's a good book, but hey, so it's a good book"; the 'secret' didn't stand out and hit me. And then about 15 years later, I was having a conversation in my office with another hard-working long-term friend of mine, and we were sitting there reflecting upon the recent success of someone we knew saying to ourselves, "We are the ones that have been working hard for years, being honest, so why aren't we the rich ones?" (Ever had that conversation?!) "It frustrates me. We work bloody hard and all those other people are getting rich... ", because at the time somebody we knew had just landed a great big deal and made a load of money and they weren't "smart people working hard", like us! You know how conversations like that go!

By chance, on my bookcase to hand was *Think and Grow Rich* and I just thought I'd pick up this book and start reading it again and do, you know, something? Seriously, I read the first chapter and it just went 'bang'! It hit me for the first time all those years later. The 'secret' to untold wealth! It is about *how we think* and *how focussed we are* and how we need to know *exactly* what we want. *We need to issue specific instructions* to the universe before it can conspire to give us what we ask for. That's the secret!

So having learned the lesson, I pass it on and tell you, my friend; you must learn to give very specific instructions to the universal messenger.

If there is a messenger or butler out there to help us (which there is) and our current instructions are vague like "Increase turnover. More sales! Be rich!" What's the Butler going to do? What's he going to say to you first of all?

"When?" "How?" "How much?" Amongst other things.

You see, you put it in a real simple situation like that and we can all appreciate that our goals are instructions and that for them to work they must be more specific. Your instruction or goal is too vague and the Butler needs more information before he can go to work.

So go back and look at your goals that you have written down, and pretend I am your Butler. Now tell me what you've written and see if I've got enough information in what you've written to do it. Play with me – tell me as your servant, the goals that you wrote down earlier and see if they are *specific* enough for me, a humble servant, to get for you... and if they are not, then simply go back and revisit them to make sure you are absolutely clear as to exactly what you are asking for.

"The universe will conspire to give you all that you ask for"

Better still, to ensure you do this and help yourself to the future you want, go back and write your desires or review the goals sheet that you filled in and then ask a family member to play the role of 'Butler'. Ask them to enter the room then issue your request. Play the game and imagine they are your manservant and ask them out loud to get you what you have written... and then ask them if they genuinely were 100% sure they were clear as to your instruction and felt as though they could in fact have got what you want. By playing this role play scenario, you'll see where you're being vague and be able to correct it.

And then, I suggest you 'Ask the Butler' – every morning and every night. "Ask and you shall receive"!! Trust the universe and attract your future!

Goals revisited

With that Butler and 'specific' thought in mind then, it might be a good idea right now for you to review your goals again. Write them down again. Because what you've got to be is very specific... it's about just training this 'muscle in your mind' so that you become 'fit thinkers' and succeeding in business isn't hard at all then!

On the 'Goals revisited' sheet, write down your goals. Start at the top 'Five year goals' and then work down the page.

Where are you going to be in five years' time? Multinational? National? Several outlets? Three, four, five shops around the area? Do you want to win awards? National awards? Do you want to be on the TV?

Do you want to be famous as an individual, or do you just want to have the company badge up in lights?

Is your goal 'income' derivative, or 'fame' derivative?

It might well be that you have a personal mission so you want to be able to stand up and be known as the man/lady that solves these problems (in your field), you want to be the name, like Saatchi and Saatchi have become in the advertising field.

You might want to be, for example, absolutely synonymous with your industry in your area, like the brand. The 'Hoover' for vacuum cleaners' principle.

But if you don't have that issue and it's just about money, what do you want? £500k? £2 million? Cash savings or assets? Do you want to go on and own several businesses?

Write something that you think you can achieve in five years... and remember with today's instant communications five years is long enough to rise out of nowhere, be a global phenomenon and die into obscurity again... ask some of the pop stars we've seen!! Gareth Gates, anybody?!!

How about your different streams of income? Are you thinking there are several channels you'd like to grow - for example, Business to Business and also Business to Consumer? What about the Internet? How do you see that as part of your business future? Are you keen to develop a hobby and let this also become an income feed? Perhaps through gaining referrals or actually by making a business of your hobby? Think deeper.

Five years is a long time but it can also flash by as we know when we look back! You must be careful that it doesn't flash past unproductively for you.

And then quickly address your three year goal. Again, where can you be in three years from now, just ask yourself that question. Where could I be in three years from now?

Do you want to have a second shop/premises open? Do you just want turnover in your one place of business to be increased, and you're not bothered about other stores or outlets?

Do you want personally to be on a three-day week because you don't need to put any more in because you've got great people there?

Ask the questions but be specific so that instructions to the universe can be successfully handled by your Butler.

What about the size of your team? Are there specific people you have already identified that you'd like to be onboard? Do you want to focus on creative thoughts you have, like writing a book yourself, and if so where is this going to get done? What can you plan in to make it happen?

Write something that you know you can achieve in three years.

And then underneath it, again just off the top of your head, what can you do a year from now?

To help you, think of this as a challenge. If you've suddenly got to stand in front of people a year from now and say, "This is how I've got on", you're going to be mighty embarrassed if you haven't got anywhere, aren't you? So a good exercise is always to think and create leverage by planning to do something. So you might tell me publicly you're going to do a certain thing, and then I'm going to make the arrangement to meet with you again and you're going to have to come back and prove that you've done it.

I guess the key here, my friend, is that **we must be specific, mean it and commit to it**. It will help massively to write it down and as you travel along your journey, it is absolutely likely that you will adjust your focus and want different things. That doesn't make this a waste of time. On the contrary, it makes it even more valuable as you will be able to see your development in a series of old passages like diaries of your growth. It will be fantastic, enjoyable and rewarding as you plan to achieve, and then achieve and see yourself growing.

(Hopefully you will look again at this and this will become one of your habits, success habits as I call them, on an almost daily basis, but if you look again at this at another stage you'll probably see something different and that's why you need to keep looking at it. For now, just write something that first comes into your head.)

Goals revisited

What are my five year goals? (Financial goals, company status etc.)

_____

_____

_____

_____

_____

_____

_____

What are my three year goals?

_____

_____

_____

_____

_____

_____

_____

What can I do in one year?

_____

_____

_____

_____

_____

_____

_____

Revisit the goals and make them correlate

Okay, finally then, look at what you've written on the five year, the three year and the one year. Have a look at the gaps between one and three, and three and five. Look to see how they might go together, or indeed be too separate. Can you see a relationship between them? Is the jump between each sensible? Because some people put a five year goal, e.g. £3 million turnover and a three year goal of £1 million, but then in their first year only aim to get themselves to a level of £100 000... well that leaves a massive jump in just two years. Now that is entirely possible but what have you put into your plan, or what do you need to put into your plan, to make that happen? Or do you want to revisit the goals and make them correlate?

So have a look and see if you've left the correct hurdles between one and three, three and five, one and five. Can you safely say, "Yes, I can do that"?

Creating massive leverage to ensure action follow through

To take your goals and your life to another level you have to make certain that they don't stay as mere wishes. You have to push something inside of you to make certain they are attained - simply put, you need leverage. Better still, you need massive leverage and if the dream and pleasure of being the success you've written about isn't enough to pull you towards the success no matter what, then you need a pain or punishment threat to push you towards it. So, here's my challenge!

I'm going to say to you, "**Make a commitment. Write to me now telling me your goals and what you *will* do in one full year, then in one year from now, I'm going to have one of our team call you to see how you have got along**". Do you fancy that challenge? Can you handle that? I dare you!!

If you can, write to me NOW and I will promise you, you will hear from us in one year's time and we can see how you've got o"! (Or, for help along the way, check out www.thebusinessboosteracademy.com and www.thebusinessbooster.co.uk)

Now that's leverage! Now you have got a leverage of pain... potential embarrassment... you've said you're going to do it and when we come back to you and you haven't done it, what will you feel like? So, if you want to really make this happen, then give yourself leverage but bear in mind also that what we're really driving at here is to make the goals something that you can achieve based upon what you know of your resources and abilities... and give yourself a stretching task but one where you're in with a sporting chance of achieving it!

Please, please, please sit down and give yourself a specific target, a thought through plan and best of all, log onto our website www.thebusinessbooster.co.uk and give yourself massive leverage!

Activity is the key

So, we've made our goals a little more specific... what about our plan? Our activity to make the goal happen?

On the sheet provided, **write down an activity plan to achieve your one year goal**.

You've said, "This is what I can do in a year", so now write down *activities* that will get you to where you want to be in one year from now... and think a little before doing this because actually a lot of folk get really lost here. The day ahead is not usually planned! For many the day's activities are driven by what is going on around them which we will look at in a moment, but for now please think about your immediate one year goal and define actions that specifically will help to get you nearer.

<u>What</u> will you do? <u>Who</u> will you visit? <u>How</u> often? How many of activity X? How much of exposure Y? Ask yourself some questions, give yourself an activity plan. Let's assume that you and I are having a virtual meeting together on Monday morning. I'm going to be virtually in front of you saying, "Right, where are you going today? What are you doing this week?" What would you show me?

The focus is always on what's in front of you.

If that's your daily habit, it'll only get better. Make it a daily habit, <u>the activity you need to focus on is something very specific</u> which would be, for example, four phone calls or two visits. Make your activity something accurate and precise. In the past when you have turned up at work, you've said to yourself, "I've got to grow the turnover, I've got to get more business in", but it didn't tell you <u>what</u> to do and very often the day's got lost in a blur! So get used to taking the goal down to an activity.

For example, a financial goal of hitting £Xs - which equates to so many sales - which equates to so much activity per man - which is so much activity per man per week - which is so much activity per man per day - which equates to a number of physical visits - so the bottom is X amount of telephone calls to achieve the required number of visits.

I know I'm labouring it a little bit but that's only because it's important and I care. If it's not a muscle that's already well trained, train it; it will help. If you get into the habit of breaking everything down, you will achieve more. **Break it down and write it down.**

Peter Thompson refers to it as "chunking it down", because people start with great big bits and they make it into little chunks, so your goal needs to become something that's 'one small step for man'.

For example, "Four phone calls to existing clients, two phone calls to potential clients, one hour preparing for tomorrow's visits, doing one hour's research about what my clients are using so that when I go in tomorrow, I'm better armed." Specific activity will give you much better guide.

It's about managing yourself towards success.

As a manager you ask good questions of your team, so as a self manager, ask good questions of yourself. A timely reminder to think of Rudyard Kipling's six wise and serving men, Who, What, Where, How, Why and When, but in essence ask great questions and lots more of them. (Now that is perhaps a Post-it note type of reminder?)

For example, four questions I always work with; where are you going? Why are you going there? What do you hope to get? How will you know when you get it? Because if you keep asking yourself those questions, you don't go and do the same set of mistakes the third or fourth week. If you didn't get what you'd hoped for, you'd change your actions. (Tip: write these questions on Post-it notes as constant reminders until you and your team have them branded in the mind.)

So give yourself the power of questions and ask yourself where you're going, why you're going there, what you hope to get, and what's it going to cost you to get it. **Get specific about your activity**... how many phone calls, how many face-to-face visits, what literature do you need to create, letters to write, what specific marketing activity are you going to engage in? To get how many enquiries? At what cost? How many will you close?

There is simply loads you can stir your mind towards thinking and as it becomes clearer your self belief will raise... and then your chances of success rise and you will feel fantastic! It is an upward circle that keeps lifting you higher so you will start to live an incredible life!! I promise! Just start with simple specifics as to what **exact activity** you are going to do.

And then retrospectively analyse your activity and see how it can be refined for the week or month ahead. Manage yourself.

So quickly write now some specific activity plans for you to action tomorrow morning because what I want you to be able to do is start your success journey and creation of success habits tomorrow morning. **Tomorrow morning is a new slate**. You're going to sit down early, you're going to take some space to plan, you're going to think your plan through and say "What if?" You're going to make yourself some goals and plan an activity... and you are going to start getting what you have always wanted! No more dreams or wishy-washy vague thoughts. No more half-hearted faint commitment that means nothing. Instead solid, focussed, specific endeavour towards genuinely identified clear and precise goals. **Tomorrow your new life starts... go make it what you want!** (Please, please do this, because simple things like space and planning will give you much firmer control and direction!)

AND before we close I can perhaps hear you saying that "it's alright for others but in my business I cannot just do what I have planned because the phone rings or a customer walks in and I don't get any time."

Beware 'Reactive' chaos!

Well, in some circumstances, there is an awful lot of activity that's very 'reactive' because of the nature of the business, especially in retail with customers walking through the door, etc. And sometimes you end up with a day where you think, "What the hell have I done?" I appreciate the comments.

For you, avoiding the 'reactive, unplanned customer-led' environment might be an issue. But it's an issue in print, and it's an issue in retail, and it's an issue in computer support, and it's an issue in business services, because <u>every business</u> has the same constraints. And I totally understand how you see it in your world, and you're right. In every business one could argue that you've got to jump when the phone rings or drop everything when a customer walks in, because "You need to keep the customer happy or you'll lose customers".

I fully appreciate that, but remember **"There's no such word as can't. Ask instead, 'How can I?'"** Ask yourself, what can I try doing to buy me some space? *Who* else could I delegate to that would give me an hour or two to work on planned activity? *What training* can I pass on to my team so that they do things my way? How could I *educate my clients* so that they plan ahead more and make both their business and my business less stressful? There <u>is</u> always a solution if you ask better empowering questions.

The fact is that carrying on in a reactive state doesn't help. You have to learn to take control so that you can focus on YOUR specific objectives. You have to drive your business forwards towards your identified goal and your business isn't going to get there if you let other situations constantly drag you back. Stop being a 'reactive victim' and start being the director that you call yourself!! Direct, don't do!!

Analyse what exactly keeps pulling you back. Is it poor service creating ongoing demands? Is it poor products that actually you possibly shouldn't sell? Is it poorly trained staff because you never truthfully really bothered to train them? When they said they could do it, you assumed that they could do it your way!? Is it poor clients? Those who always moan and never want to pay or appreciate good service? Whatever the drain cause, YOU are in control (if you choose to be) and YOU have the power TODAY to make things change.

For now, try simply listing specific activities that you do on a daily basis that could be classed as a 'drain' – and then proactively address them over the next few weeks with your team to reduce your reactive time consumption.

Secondly, more positively, make a simple list of all of the growth and positive activities that you could do that when consistently achieved will bring you to your goals.

It is an incredibly helpful discipline and one that in turn can be very rewarding because you can get a real feeling of self approval and satisfaction. Make yourself a commitment to plan activity precisely and give yourself daily clear task lists. Make a commitment to be in control of your time and not in a reactive trap. Make a commitment to make your future happen and not accept any more pretty pathetic excuses!!

Try being imaginative and creative! Remember you set your own limits... if someone out there is already experiencing the life and wealth that you desire, then it means it can be achieved!!

Okay, enough about goals and planning... go to it. Do the thinking and then start *doing*!

Time Drain Activity Sheet

Things that currently consume my time:

_____

_____

_____

_____

_____

_____

_____

_____

_____

_____

_____

_____

_____

_____

_____

_____

_____

_____

_____

_____

_____

_____

_____

Activity sheet

Specific things I can do to take me nearer to my goal

Monthly Activity Plan

(What will I do? Who will I visit? How often? Etc.)

_____

_____

_____

_____

_____

_____

_____

_____

_____

Weekly Activity Plan

(Who will I call? How many visits? What should I write? Etc.)

_____

_____

_____

_____

_____

_____

_____

_____

_____

Systems and Process

Well, to make sure that 'The Butler' can fetch all that we *specifically* ask for, and to make sure we process the 'how' into the end result goal, we need to focus on systems and processes.

Systems are critical

... systems are absolutely critical.

You may not think you've got systems, apart from perhaps IT. It's common for businesses to start out with the originator and that person does everything... and then gradually adds people who take over roles and activities that are passed on from person to person without much specific thought, other than obviously making sure the new person does the required task effectively.

Well, what I would like you to do is think for a moment about the different areas of your business and let's see if we can identify systems and processes that are critical to your business... and once identified let's see if we can improve them.

The prime question I guess is very simple... do you ever feel that you are very busy with loads of things that you need to do, and yet despite all of the hard work and hours, you come to the end of the month and you are not making loads of spare cash??

It's not a blanket rule but usually the fact is that if that is the case then the work that you are currently doing is taking too long to process and demands too much of 'you'... and in both cases it means that you can make huge strides if you re-engineer the systems and internal processes a little.

So, what are the areas of your business that you currently 'do'?

As an example, you are involved in sales at least some of the time, because every business has to achieve sales, so what is your sales process? Where does it start? Who touches it? Where does it end? What measurements are in the process?

Do clients ring you, or do you ring them? Do you visit them, or is it all phone and mail? Is your sales process all about you, or is there a team? Who else is involved?

To help you make any improvements at all to any system, it will help you if you first draw the existing system as a diagram. For now then, as you are looking as an example at the selling process, write down that process in a simple flow chart style then add a name next to each identified stage. See who touches it and where it ends up.

The next question then when you've identified the process, is who does what in that chain? How much of that chain do *you* do?

(Warning! If you do a lot of that chain, you've got a job, not a business because you're trapped by it. To make it a real business, you need to create a recognised role and then fill that role so that business happens and income is earned without you being there.)

You have to look at that chain and say, "Where can I put other people in?" "Where can I involve automated processes with technology?" "What about adding another person at a junior level perhaps? When you've got a process that goes from A to B, B to C and C to D, and it comes out the other end and you're not really involved, then you've got a systemised business. And that's a) valuable to you, and b) valuable to somebody else.

Ask yourself a few more questions in order to help complete this exercise. As I've said, do clients ring you? Do you ring them? What happens after they have touched you? Is it a letter? Is it an appointment? Is it two appointments? After you've had the appointment, is there some paperwork and the agreement to purchase? Who does that?

What happens to the paperwork? Do you process it, or does someone else process it? How much is paper, and how much is IT? And then the job is done, or the product is delivered. Is the product delivered? Who does the job if it's a service element?

At what stage do you get money? Do you get deposits, or is it all balance payable at the end? At the end of your payment, do you give them receipts, or is it automatically generating a bill off your computer?

Is there a follow-up call at the end to make sure the job was done correctly? If there is, who does it? Is it a physical call, or a telephone call?

Then you've got a payment process. A deposit collection and balance collection. Who does what? How much is/can be automated? Where are there drawbacks?

For example, a kitchen sales company I worked with collected most of the money prior to fitting but allowed retention of a small amount by the client payable upon completion. They asked me to help because they found a lot of clients were holding back final payments on grounds of some very dubious complaints. It amounted to a lot of money and most of it was their profit as the costs had been paid out of the previously paid monies. Thus I helped them 'tweak' the process. We looked at the workmen fitting the kitchen and their attitude to work *and* involved *their* payment linking it to client final payments. We also involved a tweak with paperwork and client 'sign-off' at fitting completion to be done whilst the fitters were there. The end result was payment collection on every job, even higher standards of workmanship because the workmen were literally working for *their* money and they felt more involved and important to the overall business, not just relevant to a part of it.

Another possibly more common example was a web development company that had a challenge with a sales process. They had a lot of clients who would agree to working with them and the usual payment process was upon satisfactory completion, but as is often the way, a company requiring a new website hadn't got together all of the content and generally made completing the projects very difficult. This meant that the company had a serious cash flow issue as employees need paying for their work but clients weren't paying as completion hadn't been achieved. The tweak was to create a staged payment process and 30% deposits. It wasn't the 'normal' way and the business owner at first doubted that clients would accept it... but he soon realised that if he didn't try it, then his survival chances were poor! In the end, serious clients agreed and it spurred them on to being more diligent with content provision and those who didn't agree walked away with their poor business proposition to drain another competitor!

So these are just examples, but think through all of your process.

Is money collection and cash flow an issue? If it is then we need to look at the sales process and ask empowering questions like, "How can I improve this?"

Again, another example on this subject. Because a lot of businesses assume they can't ask for the money until the client has received the goods or service, I worked with a supplier of promotional goods who was having massive cash flow challenges. Again the usual 'payment on receipt' process meant he was always paying out sometimes weeks before he got delivery and then it was often 60 or more likely 90 days before he got paid!

We tweaked the process and simply asked for monies up front. Now that sounds simple but actually my client had a mental block because that 'wasn't what they did it', it wasn't the way they worked and the industry didn't normally do that. Well I got him to start asking for monies right up front when he had a commitment on the order and guess what? His clients didn't mind! They realised that to get anything these days you have to pay and to get great service, there needs to be a cash flow to allow survival - thus we framed the cash request as *a benefit* to them (the client) *because it allowed enhanced service*. If they were genuinely wanting the goods then they have to pay sooner or later, so why not sooner... and in the end we resolved a massive cash flow issue from having slow payments, often 90 days late, to enjoying a majority of monies in advance! He's now using other people's money to run his business, not his! Much better! And all because he opened his mind to another way other than what 'he did in his industry'.

It really does help. Please, have a look now at all of the areas of your business and identify processes and the system it flows through.

How about an after sale follow-up procedure? If you haven't got one, then it's an area you've got to include. Does anybody call and ask "Are you happy with the job?" Things like that, consolidation, must be included but look at your process for getting it done, assign a role responsibility and a task expectation and then as you develop, look to take yourself out of the roles that you are filling and replace with others or software.

Which leads us to "Who does what and where?" You don't need to examine it now, but ask yourself, (write on that same sheet), who does what in that chain? Are you doing it all? And the next powerful question is who else *could* do it? What have I got to do so that other people can do it? How can I get other people to effect this process so that I'm taken out of it?

I always remember a quote from Sir John Harvey Jones essentially saying that management was not about you doing what you can but about doing what *only you* can – "Only do what only you can do". Identify the process from beginning to end as a flow diagram (see illustration) and then once all of the individual steps are noted, put a name or a machine next to each step. You then question why you are doing each area if you indeed are.

Again it hinges upon our use of excellent questioning and I shall prompt you to help your mind flow because the more you ask questions, the more you find a solution.

It might be, "Who do I have to talk to for help in outsourcing? Is there a service provider that can help me with this particular area, thus freeing me to do a more valuable role?" Again I shall offer an example. When a design consultant client first started in business, they quickly found that their time was being consumed with phone calls and struggling to complete proposals, often working well into the night which was almost a good thing that they were busy but which meant that they were getting less actual sales time. I helped them realise that they had to delegate the phone answering receptionist type work but they felt challenged with costs of employment. The business was too small really to carry another wage, yet growth was being held back due to not having another person.

The solution? They found a very efficient phone answering service that became a virtual secretary and for the cost of probably three days' wages, they got a month's service. The clients ringing in assumed they had hired a secretary and she told them that the client was out or busy, thus creating a very positive impression and they got all messages relayed in time to make important return calls. It also filtered out the unwanted incoming sales calls and they were free to apply themselves to selling and growing the business. It illustrated the simple need to let go of some tasks of lower value and even swallow hard and commit to spending money which isn't yet earned but in order to make room to earn it! This can then be extended to virtual admin that takes even more of the load off.

Have a long hard look at your business in ALL areas and just clearly write down the steps and highlight the people involved and then ask questions that guide you to possibly 'tweaking' the process and creating improvements.

"What business can I look at to give me a model? Who can I turn to or ask that might have 'been there, done that' and I can learn from them?"

Consider McDonald's — they systemise properly!! If you were to become a franchised outlet, they tell you how much fat to use in the fryer, what temperature the fat is to be, what type of fat, they tell you what type of meat, what type of bun, they tell you exactly what weight, exactly what sort of potato, what size of potato to chip in. It's just amazing.

Now imagine if your business was like that. Imagine if everyone in your business knew exactly what to say, exactly where every piece was, and in the eventuality of something not going right, where to go and who to see. Imagine if every interaction of your business had somebody who said, "I know what goes now. Ooh, that's happened. I'll go and do this". Imagine how smooth your business could become?!

Another example in the selling process is quote or proposal writing. How much time does that consume? Well can it be improved? Can it possibly be done by anyone else? Is there a way to minimise your time if indeed it still needs your input? Is there a piece of software that you can install that makes it a machine task, not a human task? What about the use of template proposal forms where you alter particular details to suit the new client but basically the body of the proposal remains the same? Or is there specific software that creates quotes? (Have you ever asked these questions, or merely complained about you having too much to do???!!)

There is always an answer that represents an improvement... and by going for these perhaps 'new to you' improvements, you will go towards your goal. If, on the other hand, you make silly excuses that it isn't right for you or you just can't do it now, well then you will remain in your current level and you hold yourself back so try this, please.

There will be systems and processes in lots of areas of your business that actually you haven't really looked at in a detached perspective before, and when you do you will see a workflow. So doing this now, creating a workflow similar to the example illustrated on sales, really helps. Please Stop! Stand Back, and do this now for each area of your business.

Allow me to share yet another example. I was working with a client who developed and sold software for the financial services industry. Their sale process involved enquirers being sent an information pack (whether they had specifically requested one or not) and then a telephone call a week or so later to confirm that they had received it... and then they were promptly sent another package containing a trial disc of the software.

I asked why this was the process and the reply was merely that "We've always done it this way". No one had questioned it! I asked the Managing Director what cost his packages were that were being sent out and he discovered they were £11 each! (He'd never really questioned either; it was just 'assumed' that it was the way to do things and that this cost was a necessary evil). We pretty quickly tweaked the process and asked many more smart questions during the first incoming enquiry call to prevent wastage of materials being sent out.

The critical point here is that there is often no qualification process early on in the workflow. Too often, incoming telephone enquiries are taken and immediately messages are passed on or action is taken without asking about the enquirer's need or time frames. My simple but powerful suggestion is *always* to make for yourself a pretty comprehensive 'Enquiry Sheet' that asks all of the relevant questions of the enquirer so that the enquiry itself can be properly evaluated before action is taken and cost occurred or your time consumed.

Ask lots and lots of questions because questions give you the answers, and the answers mean that you'll end up with a <u>system</u> that handles your sales, not a <u>person</u> that handles your sales, and <u>then</u> you've got a business.

There is huge power in this process. The insights and the release that will come to your business when you have drilled down through the 'way you do things' in each area of your business...and whilst sales have been used as the example, your task now is to ask all of these questions and do the drawing for all areas.

What other areas of your business are there?

Administration, for example. Do you ever get clogged with admin, paperwork? It's alright doing the business but it's sweeping up this messy office stuff that's a drag! It might be wages, it might be bookkeeping, deliveries, stock control, ordering of supplies, checking goods in or customer orders out. Lots of areas where there is currently a system but you're not really aware of it in an analytical sense.

What about when you've got more staff? What's your staff management process? Do staff get managed and trained or do they just turn up and get shifted around jobs?

Allowing a process that says 'just turn up for work and be shown' in a pretty disorganised fashion might be all very well when there's only a few of you, but when you start to create a business model, you've got to address the issue of training. Even if <u>right now</u> you don't need to have a training facility because it's only you, recognise that to grow a good business you'll need a training facility or training time allowance, so it's got to be there in your overall process.

If you don't plan it in, then what happens? What if you suddenly grow and add a person, and then you suddenly grow again and add a person, and again you suddenly grow and add a person, and none of those people get trained and they all just 'learn as they go along'? They might all be doing bad habits.

And when you've got five people all doing bad habits, you've got a lot of bad habits in your business, and then it's hard to change. But if it's in your process at the beginning, as you add people they'll say to themselves, "Oh, got to go through this" and they all learn correctly and the job is done properly throughout. I promise you, thinking now about your business process, taking time out now to do this work, will seriously help.

So have a think about sales, have a think about admin, have a think about production, have a think about purchasing and supply chain process, have a think about your delivery, have a think about the maintenance of your vehicles, have a think about your training, have a think about all the various areas, and then try and think through a system or a process of where it impacts your business and who is involved in it. Use the flow diagram I have included and draw one similarly for each identified area of your business.

This not only helps you become massively clear of all areas but sometimes you'll examine an area for the purposes of this exercise and immediately see something that you know can be improved to make you more money. It was always there but you weren't looking!

Ask questions all of the way through this exercise. Ask if the outcome could be achieved with a different route. Ask if the route could be including other stages. Ask who does each section and then ask why.

It's a good exercise to add names, especially if currently you are doing most of the work in your business. As was mentioned a few moments ago, whilst you might be doing most of the work now it is critical that you identify exactly *what* you are doing so that you can evolve and replace you... remember that if you don't replace you, you don't have a business, you have a job... and that is even worse than being employed as there isn't even any sick pay or holiday pay! Who touches what? Write a name next to each stage.

AND here's a thought. It is often the way with our delicate human psyche to feel a need to be important. A core human psychological need is for value or significance. Thus it is common for people mistakenly to cling to their precious knowledge so that only *they* know it and *they* have to be consulted. By holding back from sharing, *they* need to be kept around. Very often indeed, especially in larger more corporate entities, this 'management by clinging on to tasks' is the management style and yet this is sooo not the way to grow an organisation! Importance isn't achieved by holding onto knowledge. Significance is not recognised by secretly guarding... it is by sharing and helping the team. Real management is about getting the job done with the least effort and the greatest return. In your business you must identify areas *you* are involved in and then **only do what only you can do**... the rest you offload! And the next step is to show others the bit that 'only you can do' so that too can be released and you can move upward. The goal is to be doing nothing other than that which you choose to do and still be earning all you want to earn.

Sales Process - illustration of workflow

Firstly, list all areas where there is a 'system' already e.g. sales, admin etc.

_____

_____

_____

_____

_____

Enquiry in

(from a marketing process)

↓

Sales telephone call made to qualify the enquiry

(or enquiry is incoming call so qualify at same time)

↓   ↓

Sales visit arranged   Sale not immediate

(literature sent, future action

forward planned)

↘   ↙

Sales call

↓

Proposal/quotation prepared

↓

Sales call to deliver proposal and seal order

↓

Order taken - process paperwork to sales support/admin

I sincerely hope you are able to pass on all of your knowledge as often as possible because until you do, you are actually trapped! DO NOT fall into the trap of many 'important' managers.

Tell them when you see them, **they are not important, they are imprisoned!** That might help them to see their life more clearly!!

The Importance of Gearing

We have so far looked at where you are now and created a clear 'snapshot' to help you with clarity. We have examined where you want to be and 'specifically' written some goals. Next, we talked about how you are going to get there and you have written a step-by-step plan, or set of actions, to take you to the identified goal. Importantly, you have also examined why we want to be there so that you can maintain momentum and always be driven to achieve... AND you have now examined and pulled apart and started to re-engineer the actual processing of the work so that you can get more done and make goal attainment more certain.

But what do we do when we want to ramp it up? When we want to go faster, what happens now?

Well let's look at gearing.

You want to grow your business. You're thinking now about being bigger and that is going to mean work increases and generally everything speeds up. The new growth will be driven by you and you will be revving yourself up. Now if that means revving up to go faster, that's good, but if you rev up an engine and just keep revving it up to go faster, then what's going to happen to the engine?

It blows up, doesn't it? And that's what happens in business. People just rev up because they think that's the only way to go faster until one day their engine bursts and they fail terribly. What we've got to do here is look at gearing.

As an analogy, very simply using a car as an illustration, when driving and reaching a certain speed but wanting to go faster, what do you do? To go faster without blowing the engine, you slot another gear in.

So if we talk in business terms, a gear might be a person. Now it is accepted that as you grow you are going to add a person, but what is most important is *how* that person slots in.

If you've got a process for the gear (or the new person) to mesh entirely into, it will give you more speed and less revs, but if you've *not* got a process then actually adding a person could be more headaches. If that person isn't involved in 'synchromesh'-type training, then the new cog might in fact not engage and seriously damage the engine!

We've all seen, or experienced I'm sure, training that goes a bit like this:

New person comes in called John. "Hi John, welcome to the company. This is Freda; she's going to be helping you. Sit here, watch what Freda does. I'll be back later. Have a good morning."

Thus, John is 'onboard'.

Later on, John gets told, "Right, come over here and spend an afternoon with David, because you'll have to cover a bit of his job as well." At the end of the first day, John is asked, "How did you get on, John?", and he says, "It was good. Yes, I've seen a bit of what's going on." And John is then told to go on and continue, comments such as, "Listen, it's a bit 'in at the deep end' around here because that's how we do things, but you'll get the hang of it."

And then, John goes on to work with the company but regularly makes mistakes. He's forgiven though because everybody makes a few mistakes... "That's the way things are around here!"

Possibly you can relate to the illustration. Maybe you have experienced it first-hand, but honestly is that the best way to run a company? Is it giving John or the company the optimum future? Is this the way to add staff, or is there a better way to 'gear up'?

So, recognising that you can't just build your business by revving it but that you've got to 'gear it' and add people, your systems must be ready for gear addition *before* the attempt at adding. Are yours?

Have you got a recruitment process clearly written and understood so that when you need to gear up, you can start the process correctly? Do you have a specific written procedures manual? (You wouldn't expect to mend an engine without a book of instructions, would you?)

How about your training programme? Is there an organised step-by-step approach where a new person's knowledge is tested and new specific knowledge imparted so that you absolutely know they are doing what you need the correct way?

The question to ask: Are you geared for success?

For example, do you ever have an issue on recruitment? We mentioned McDonald's earlier, but as an example of a possible high staff turnover environment, do McDonald's have a problem with it? NO! They just have a system; they bring them in, they train them, they ship them out. They know they're going to last two or three months, in some cases two or three days, but it doesn't matter... they've got a system. 'Recruitment in, training, do this, do this, you're bored, okay, off you go, recruitment in, training, do this, do this... ' Just a system.

You might think it's bad when you've got to find staff now and again. Imagine having a recruitment rate of 260% staff turnover! Imagine having to find everybody two and a half times a year! They manage it though because it is just a machine... they just roll a system and keep feeding one end.

Your business MUST develop these types of systems. Your business needs a manual for each process so that knowledge about how to make each process happen correctly **is available when required, not limited to inside a person's head**.

Very often in a business, specific key knowledge is contained not within a folder, but within a department manager's head. What would happen if that person's head suddenly got lost and access was denied? Your business would suffer! Think about it please... is there a person in your business that you have to ask in order to ascertain key information regarding an order or a client status? If that sort of critical information isn't in a system somewhere, then you might be heading for trouble one day!!

To be safe and to prepare for going faster, make sure you start today at compiling a set of documents that describe each system and task expectation so that another gear can readily slot in. **Take information out of heads and into systems. Make your *business* intelligent not reliant upon intelligent people!**

To create your future how you've dreamed it is entirely possible but it requires a little work now; preparing, planning and thinking.

Remember, there's no such word as can't. Ask instead, "How can I?"

The Bible says, "Ask and you will receive" - because He knows about the Butler!

If you ask the Butler clearly, he'll go and get it. Do you want proof?

The proof is out there with other people that are living the lifestyle you think of. The fact that other people have built their businesses into large success stories where people are added and profits are made and the business owner is released from daily stress, is proof. The fact that you can see examples is proof that it is possible. The universe *can* provide, it's just not coming to you *yet*, but tweak a few of these ideas into your business and ask correctly for support and help from your 'Butler' and you can have all that you want.

So, let's double your business tomorrow; you can do it. Just adjust or improve one or two things.

You <u>can't</u> do it if you don't change your gear. You <u>can't</u> do it with some of your processes because you'd all clog up. You <u>can't</u> perhaps do it with the audience you're serving, or the prices you charge, or the type of product you're actually delivering, or the way you put the products together... but all of those *can* be changed if you want to do more.

There is no such word as can't, ask instead "How can I?" Your brain will conspire with the universe to give you empowering answers. Fact.

"How can I gear my business?"

Thinking of the areas where there are identified 'process and systems' (the list you made earlier)... at each stage, think of what is required to 'gear' your business.

Start with the identified stages where *you* are currently doing the work. Then go down into each area and ask "What would be a better way to 'gear up' this area?" Ask yourself honestly, "Could anybody slot straight in and do it instead of me tomorrow?"

If the answer is "No", then ask "Why not?"

Is it because the knowledge they need is all in your head? Then you need to get it out and document as much as possible.

Is it because they need training? So what training process is there? Is there a training manual that documents clearly each required operation?

And do this for each area and each person. Make time for this because it is vital. 'Stop! Stand Back... look at the business and ask "How Can I Make This Better?" Remember, you have a very precarious business if it depends on you being fit and able to drive it, and secondly you certainly have no value in it as a business to a perspective investor... they know that without you it doesn't operate!

Brainstorm

What could help me grow? Who could I slot in? Where could I duplicate roles? What knowledge is in my head and needs to come out? Could I eliminate a stage of the process to improve?

How to do it? Who is possible to slot in? How? What is involved? Etc.

_____

_____

_____

_____

_____

_____

_____

_____

_____

_____

_____

_____

_____

_____

_____

_____

_____

_____

_____

_____

Testing and Measuring

Getting systems right is an excellent idea, but how do you know when they are 'right'? It's no good just doing all of this, and then not knowing if it's really working. So what now?

Whilst you consider making these suggestions evident in your business and indeed whilst you are operating your business as you currently are, a good habit, a 'success habit', is that of testing and measuring everything you do. Is it working?

You could be asking "Does that work?" and you're saying to yourself "I *think* it does."

How do you know? Don't guess or assume that because you're getting the business in, it's working the best way. That isn't a safe way to operate. You need to <u>know</u>, you need to be sure, so test what you do and measure results.

But if you were testing and measuring everything, you'd soon know. It's worth pointing out here though, no matter what we do, sometimes we'll screw up. But if you're testing and measuring, then you don't screw up twice.

Test everything, measure your return. And if you haven't got a system that tells you that you can test it, then guess what you create? A system! Because if you're going to spend any money, you've got to see it return.

If you're going to go out on sales calls, what do you get from them?

If you're making adverts or creating flyers, or doing any sort of promotion, what are you getting from it? How are you tracking it?

If you've designed and distributed loads of flyers, have you got a little reference number on the back? Have you got your staff trained to say,

"Where did you hear about us?", or, "Can I just ask, what's the reference code on the bottom of the flyer?"

You've done the hard work to create the flyer, you've maybe even thought about putting a reference code on, but your system isn't complete because when they ring in no one asks them, or they get asked but it doesn't always get recorded.

So just think it through. Everything from recruitment to sales to advertising to time spent on jobs to adequately perform tasks... test it and measure it. Put a system in your business to test and measure. Make a form that all incoming enquiries are recorded upon and ensure that upon the form is the question, "Where did you hear about us" This tells you then the effectiveness of your promotional activity.

Allow me to give you an example. A client of mine who was selling websites thought advertising in the Yellow Pages was a good idea. I questioned this and he thought me to be crazy, after all he clung to the idea that, "Yellow Pages advertising is a must and everybody looks in there." My question wasn't based upon Yellow Pages working, more was Yellow Pages working for *him*. So, we made a definite effort to track all incoming new enquiries and then we could clearly establish the lead source... and guess what? He did get some enquiries from Yellow Pages but nearly all of them were pretty poor quality where the enquirer was ringing round and shopping on price and actually didn't want to pay my client's prices. Yellow Pages worked on the surface as it created a lot of enquiries but in fact Yellow Pages ads *didn't work* for my client because they didn't convert as it attracted the wrong type of shopper. However, had I not insisted that every enquiry was tracked into a system and measured against a source and a cost, he would not have known and continued to waste effectively several thousand pounds each year. Don't let that happen to you.

For _all_ activity where spending is involved, make sure there is a question asking, "Where does it come back? How do I know?"

Again, I shall illustrate. I worked with a very successful retail outlet that had been established 24 years. They were well known around the town and turnover was £20,000 - £30,000 per month. The owner was spending approximately £50,000 each year on various printed media to keep the name out there. I questioned why he was doing it. The reply was firstly along the lines of "Why do you think? To make our name known." I asked, "Is it possible that you are making your name known, but not actually getting any return from it?" I asked more questions - was it making the name known to the right people, or was it in fact a waste because spending in the local news media was 'general' and his client was perhaps a little more top-end? Was the advertising money being spent to reach the wrong people? I simply asked what he was getting back from the adverts. How much sales could he directly attribute to the spending? He couldn't do so.

Next question I asked him, and one you should ask yourself too; if you hired a member of staff and you couldn't _really_ tell if he was working or actually doing anything for you, how long would you allow it to continue? Would you keep paying someone to work for you, if you couldn't see if they were working or not? Would you tolerate paying somebody to work for you if in fact they didn't work? Absolutely not!!

So why spend on advertising unless you can absolutely prove it is working for you? And DO NOT believe the advertising speak that says, "It must work or they wouldn't keep doing it!!" That's just telling you the others don't know it isn't working either!! My client in fact then cut his budget from £51,000 per year to £11,500 and we in fact doubled his turnover in the next year through other activity!!

The moral then is simple... test and measure everything especially what you spend!

Measuring your business

You have to know what you spend and where it goes and particularly what your business gets back.

What do I spend? (Advertising/promotion, sales staff, admin, production, etc.)

_____

_____

_____

_____

_____

_____

What do I know I get in return?

_____

_____

_____

_____

_____

How could I possibly improve this? What question or measurement can I introduce to make sure I track what I spend?

_____

_____

_____

_____

_____

Strategy and Tactics

We have looked already at a few critical areas of your business that when tweaked will radically improve your life and your business success, but an area we next need to examine is, how do you actually spend your time? What consumes your hours? Is that the optimum use of those hours?

It's often said, "There just isn't enough time in the day", but it's also true that many of those hours are ill-spent. Time management is always an issue and it can be difficult to see the wood for the trees when you are in too close to the business so let us look now at how you can make time work for you. You only have 24 hours in a day... and some of those you will need to sleep and rest, so how can you squeeze more out of the hours you have left?

I'd like to suggest this:

"It's not the hours that you put in that count; it's what you put into the hours."

So, please reflect for a moment on your actions, your daily activity that consumes your day, and ask, "Is that activity a reactive one or a proactive one?" How much of your time, expressed as a percentage, is directly consumed by what goes on around you? How much of 'what you have to do' is as a reaction to what is happening?

For many, it is almost 100% of their day that is being controlled by 'what they have to do because of things that are happening'. Certainly it is common to be above 75-80% and the often quoted saying is, "I can't do anything about it!"

You now know though that "There is no such word as can't... ask instead 'How can I?'"... Thus, "How can I get more results from the same or less hours?" or "How can I use my time differently so that I get a different result without letting everything slip because jobs aren't getting done?

What is your strategy?

Understanding and appreciating that most of our time is spent in a reactive manner helps a little, but are you consuming your hours with strategic activity or tactical activity? What is the difference and why does it matter?

Well, for example, during a sports game when one side is winning it might tactically substitute an attacking player for a defence player and close ranks to protect a lead and secure a victory. This is a tactical decision as a reaction to the prevailing conditions.

Or again in sport, a manager might rest senior players and play junior players in a league game when all of the season is ahead of them and there's little at stake but might call upon the more senior players in a cup game to ensure progress into the next round... this would be a strategic approach thinking and acting proactively to determine the outcome of future events.

Can you see the difference in the two approaches? Can you see how a tactical or reactive approach deals with 'the now' and a strategic or proactive approach plans and creates a 'desired future'.

Now imagine this for a moment... wouldn't it be better if you spent most of your working day *creating* _what is to be_ around you, rather than *reacting to* _what is_ around you?!

If your goal is to double your business in a year, but your activity plan is to talk to inactive existing customers tomorrow morning, which may not be the right activity for that strategic goal. So let's assume that to double your business needs a lot more client flow and probably pre-qualified clients.

Now a strategic move; Monday morning might be to go and meet with leaders of identified organisations or feeder groups. So, for example, a good source of feed for an outdoor activity store selling camping or walking gear might be a Ramblers Association or a Camping Club, or if you're selling bicycles you might identify that a good source of feeder would be Cyclists Association.

On your activity plan that you created whilst considering goals and planning, you might have written, for example, to 'make five phone calls and send out five letters to people who have recently bought bikes'. Whilst this is not a bad idea, this is dealing in ones. Possibly a better *strategic* plan would be to go and make arrangements to meet with leaders of Cyclists Associations, because they might have 2,000 members that might feed in.

A strategic plan for something like IT/PC sales might be to go and identify, perhaps, schools and talk to leaders of local education authorities and make sure that you're au fait with all the educational authority heads that lead to budgeting, so that you might get in the back door of bigger orders. Sell bundles of PCs, not one here and there.

It'll take you a long time to make the relationships, and you'll have to go to several places, but *strategically* then when they come in, they say, "Yes, we need to kit out the whole room" and you pull off an order worth 20 to 100 times greater! Much, much better!

If you are selling a bulk mailing service, for example, your activity plan might be to send out some letters to potential customers, i.e. the data agencies in the middle, but a strategic move might be to go to talk to the list suppliers and find out who they sell data to in large chunks so that you can then go straight to a large chunk data buyer and try to get work that way. Strategically you're going right the way around, and your activity is not going to give you instant results, but long-term it is much better because three or four months of schmoozing gives you double or treble the business effect.

So, this is the important factor. We've written an activity plan and it's good, but is it strategic? Is it strategically aligned to your goal? To achieve your goal, you'll probably have to do some bigger actions, so a strategic action would be something that is probably not immediately returning. Have a look again and reflect on some strategic action.

It's always difficult. But if you never start doing the strategic and just concentrate on doing what you've always been doing, then you only ever get what you've got, which isn't your goal.

So, have a think and write for yourself. Understand the difference between strategy and tactics and ask the question, "What is my strategy?"

Strategy is massively different from tactics. Beware though! You have got to have balance! You can't do the pendulum swing because then you won't have the income coming in next week. But by the same token, if your activity isn't strategically set up then you will not get your goals either; you'll just keep surviving at this level.

When you take a few moments to do this, when you try thinking perhaps on a 'bigger picture' level, you will feel fantastic! You will have a lot more clear thought every morning, you'll know where you're going, you'll know why, you'll know how you're going to get there because of your plan, and you'll know that because it's strategic you're going to get your big goal. So you'll feel inspired, motivated.

Part of the battle is that every morning when you wake up, there are so many other things chipping away at you. From the second you wake up, the environment you're in, you might have a great day... until you get out of bed! And then it could just go downhill! Anything could trigger a 'bad day'... the kids scream, the wife's in a mood (or husband!), you haven't time to have your breakfast, whatever. You've got to iron your shirt or the clothes you wanted to wear aren't there. Then you go out of the door, you get in the car, the car's not starting or the weather's rubbish or the traffic's a nightmare and you get to work, and there are so many things that can erode your day. So it is all about how you *think*. Most of these success habits revolve around your mindset... but keeping it strong and still focussing on a 'bigger picture, strategic goal' and action plan will be the difference between you achieving it or forever dreaming of it.

Look at your business then and clearly identify the sort of work you *prefer* to do. Again, let me share an example. A building firm client of mine expressed concern over the state of the market. They were fairly large, successful construction clients engaged in public contract work, such as schools and hospitals. Prestigious contracts, some might say. The complaint was that there was just so much hassle and all of the jobs were being screwed down in price by the purchaser. There were constant health and safety issues and generally he just couldn't see a future. He felt like the future prospect was to continue making hardly any money but keeping a load of others in work.

Was it building as an industry, or an economic climate then that was at fault, or was there something we could do?

I asked my client to focus on what he was in business for... his answer to make a healthy income. I asked what he wanted to do to make the income... build hospitals and schools, or did he much care what he built? The answer; he didn't care much what he built. He was a builder with a good team of lads but hadn't thought of doing other than that which they had always done which was schools and hospitals and large contracts.

What did we do? We repositioned his excellent firm into an 'exclusive home' building company, building swimming pools and gymnasium extensions for the wealthy clientele. He saw a strategic path towards much higher margins by deliberately looking for and digging out lower value but more lucrative private clients. His tactical reaction had always been to cope and to cut costs... the new business approach gave him a *strategic* development plan and a fresh optimism. He soon found his way to massive profits, less hassles and a far better business from far less business!! Strategy, not tactics.

Could you do the same? Is there some work which you get better margins on? Is there some work where you get great referrals on? Is there a feed channel that you could link with that once activated could feed you literally loads of work? Ask these questions and then when you have identified the targets, the feeder groups, the referral channels, then you deliberately nurture these channels.

It will mean time out from 'doing'. It will mean time out from chasing that which is on your desk to do, but it will also mean a much better tomorrow. You see, the truth is if you carry on coping with today and using the excuse that you don't have time because you're too busy, then the fact is you will always be too busy because nothing will ever change unless you change it. All that you ever do is repeat today! Thus, it might be a 'swallow hard and grin and bear it' process... it might mean that you'll need to juggle hours and tasks and things like that... but the end result is you'll get what you want instead of what you're getting.

Your task now is to sit and clearly identify your better work. Look at what you want in terms of contracts and types of client... then look to see where they might come from and what you can do to gather more. Take time out to ask for assistance if it doesn't come easily. (A great resource might be www.thebusinessbooster.co.uk or www.thebusinessboosteracademy.co.uk which provides you with coaching support and documents too!)

Remember, "There's no such word as can't, ask instead 'How can I?'" and remember the Butler... he is on your side, you know, and he's pretty loyal!! Go ask him!

Your business strategy

In an ideal situation, what work (contract type or size) would I <u>like</u> to win? Where does it usually come from?

_____

_____

_____

_____

_____

_____

_____

_____

_____

What could I do NOW to take me a step nearer to winning that work? What activities could I diarise to strategically take me to more ideal clients?

_____

_____

_____

_____

_____

_____

_____

_____

_____

Who do I know/could I know that can lead me to more of the work I want? Where might they be? Where could I strategically go?

_____

_____

_____

_____

_____

_____

_____

What skill or knowledge level will be required? What do I need to do NOW so that I am prepared for the work I aim to win?

_____

_____

_____

_____

_____

_____

_____

What about other team members? Is there strategic activity for them that I need to include NOW?

_____

_____

_____

_____

_____

_____

_____

The Importance of Data

One of the areas to pay special attention to, an area that'll help you fly to unprecedented levels when you master it, is the capture and management of data. So we're going to look and focus our attention for a few moments on the data that you have, the data that you can get, and why you want data.

And again, to help you, I've come up with a very unique and scientific approach to gathering data.

Shall I share it with you?

Here's a scientific and foolproof approach to gathering data – **Ask!** Ask everybody, all the time!! And store and record their answers!

(Obviously you're asking lots of questions already in your head about what to ask, how to ask, when to ask of whom and why? I appreciate that, and I shall share with you some thoughts now but please commit to making this a primary function.)

So what do you know about your clients? What do you need to know about your clients? Why should you know more about your clients? Who do you ask? How do you ask it?

Data is very, very important because if you're going to grow your business and you're going to start to rev the engine and go faster, you'll need to know more to make the higher speed safe. If you want to increase your turnover and more importantly increase your profits, you've got goals which need more money than you've currently got, and you have ambitions on a totally higher plain which all mean you can only do that if you're much smarter. If you just work harder, it's like blowing your engine. So how do we work smarter? We have to have more knowledge, especially about our clients... although we will also need more knowledge about our role and business operations and, as we talked about earlier, some of your time must be planned in for learning, reading, training etc. You are not going to be able to compete with higher flyers if you're not intelligently on their level but for the moment specifically we're going to focus on client intelligence.

Have you noticed anything about the larger supermarkets in the last few years? Along the lines of intelligence?

Supermarkets are clever now. They gather loads of data at point of sale from their customers by using loyalty cards that are swiped at purchase recording against each member what they bought! They swipe loyalty cards and it tells them everything about your shopping habits with them. They're smart because they gather the data, they know what you've bought every time you swipe, and so they bring and create a pattern to buying habits. So when they send you the vouchers as they do in promotional mailings, those vouchers are strategically aligned to things that you regularly buy. So they're talking your language and you go back for more.

The question is, what do you know about your customers? Do you know what your clients regularly buy? Do you know who your client is so that you can go back to them? Do you know enough to entice them into extra add-on sales and keep them coming back? Well that's where we're going. We're going to look at capturing, recording and managing that sort of intelligence to massively increase your business effectiveness.

Our ideal aim is to build up what I call a 'profile' of your customer and, by the way, we're going to refer to them as clients because it denotes a far greater relationship, as we shall cover later.

Okay then, let us assume that you know some or most of your clients, certainly the regular ones, but how well? Do you merely recognise their faces as they walk in? Do you remember all of their names? How about remembering what they told you last time you chatted?

Imagine how they might feel if you did? How do you feel when you go back to a place, perhaps after only one visit, and they remember you… how do you feel? Pretty good, don't you? Even better when they remember your name and especially when they recall what you talked about. You're left feeling 'wowed'… you just don't expect it and it makes an impact on you to the extent that you will try to repay that courtesy and respect by returning and giving that store your patronage. Your internal representation is that you'd rather give it to them than someone who doesn't know you, as they deserve it… and that, my friend, is a hugely powerful feeling to invoke. Imagine if you invoked that sort of buying bias in all of your clients!

So, looking then at your client base, let us assume that you do not know all of them or indeed many of them at all… there's some work to do. How do we do it?

Simple. You're going to ask loads and loads and loads of *good* questions.

From today onwards, you are going to be a 'guerrilla'. You're going to be thinking like you've never thought before. You're going to be gathering intelligence and storing it, watching for signs and reading situations like a guerrilla might when planning a military campaign. You see, let's very quickly understand this. Warfare used to be fought with two great big armies having a bloody fight in a field and basically the one with the biggest army won. That's what fighting was all about - size. Strength was a function of numbers.

Then, in the Vietnam struggle the huge might of America was, for the first time, totally unable to command victory purely because of its size. The new style warfare was launched… the 'guerrilla' soldier was born. These were frighteningly effective and yet micro in comparison. They had no real army, no real size and weight, but yet with seemingly deadly accuracy they took out enemy strongholds and fought off the weight that immense money bought. Guerrillas challenged and effectively won, causing an embarrassing withdrawal by the USA.

Now we know that there are often many comparisons drawn between a military struggle and a business one. We appreciate the similarities in the fight... so let's learn from the guerrilla analogy. What made a guerrilla so deadly? How was it possible for a guerrilla force with so much less in all resource utilisation to beat off a giant opponent? David and Goliath again, in fact, wasn't it. So what was the edge they had? Intelligence?

They learned to listen, watch, study the movements of the enemy and then, by watching carefully, they would see what is always there – a weak link. They used patience and intelligence to find an 'Achilles Heel' and with one shot, took out the enemy. One small pebble correctly aimed with a sling, one neat arrow that slain a legend. These are timeless principles, stories we know well, but ones we should remind ourselves of now to drive our battle forward.

Truthfully, my friend, in your business battle you do not have the luxury of huge armies... probably manpower itself is limited and the tasks outnumber at times the soldiers. Then of course the enemy we fight might appear to have bigger armies... they have huge budgets to fight their battles with and we can't compete on displays of strength through media to brainwash the masses... so we absolutely have to have the intelligence. We have to know where we can aim the small pebble and we have to totally see where our arrow strikes. Intelligence, my friend, will always win. Brains over brawn.

One quick thought though as we proceed with gathering, storing and using data to make our fight 'intelligence driven'. We need to comply with all current legislation regarding data and so I suggest you register for the Data Protection Act and make your process correct. It is true that most of the data you will use is in the public domain i.e. phone books, but for the sake of getting it right, just register.

Secondly, again because it is one of those housekeeping points that so reflect the world we live in today, check all data against Telephone Preference. Some are TPS (Telephone Preference Service) registered, people who don't want to be called, so please check all lists before ringing to make sure you don't break a law by ringing someone who has requested they be left alone. The same with faxing... check the FPS lists and keep your process from upsetting anybody.

Ok, housekeeping done; let's get smart.

Question: in your business at the moment, do you have accurate records? Do you have a database? Do you have a CRM system?

If you don't, you must. It's as simple as that. You must get your business a **contact management system** to store, manage and use data with. There are several on the market... some are 'cloud-based' being Internet sited solutions, such as SugarCRM, and some are server-based for your office, or computer installation such as Sage ACT or GoldMine by FrontRange. I personally highly recommend using www.fusemetrix.com It's both customisable and flexible enough for almost any business and I have seen it transform many of my clients' businesses as it has with my own. However... whatever system you get, get one! Get it, use it as I shall guide you, and you will soon look back and wonder how you ever got along without it!

What is a CRM, or CONTACT MANAGEMENT SYSTEM? Well it is simply a modern day 'little black book' with all of the names and numbers in but added to that is a record of all of your notes relevant to each client, a diary to plan your work in which is linked to clients' information. It incorporates reminders so you won't forget tasks and it even links with accounts packages so that you can analyse client spend or sales performances easily through one application. I promise it is superb for any small business and as I have said, when you get used to it you'll wonder why you never bothered before.

So here's an action plan, specific action. You <u>MUST</u> buy/<u>get yourself a data management system</u>. (You could just use a database, something similar to Microsoft Access, or Microsoft Outlook which will be on nearly everybody's computer, but my recommendation is that you use something a little bit more specifically geared towards marketing, such as a designed CRM programme.)

You will want to know which campaigns have worked, which staff members earned you the most, which call ratios are working for which person at which time. You'll want to know ratios and costs for people and places and events and mailings and you'll want to be able to pull reports on that to confirm and discuss. You'll also want to be looking at the whole history of each client, at the same time as knowing that all of the letters or emails or invoices that you've sent them... they're all attached to the client record, everything. Open the folder and there is everything.

Having established and installed a proper system, you need then to populate it. You need data on clients and prospects. In simple terms, it becomes THE storage place for ALL data – clients, prospects, suppliers, staff etc.

It might be a member of staff; you'll still want their phone number somewhere, won't you? You still want their address somewhere. And you may, in this legislative society we live in, at some stage even with members of staff have to record certain things like meetings, disciplinary procedures, warnings, sickness records etc., and so why not keep it all in one place? So even with members of staff, put it all in, because it would just have a source code, 'staff'.

Suppliers? As business owners, we all buy stationery, we pay landlords even if it's only taxes, we buy print work, and we'll probably have vehicles which need maintaining. We'll have all sorts of suppliers, IT, Internet providers... why not keep details on them all in one place? And let's have a record of everything we've purchased, everything they've said that we're going to get when we've paid our money. Keep a record of the meetings we've had.

Existing clients are obvious, but what about prospects? Contacts that we have made that might one day become clients. Or contacts with which we have not yet had contact, perhaps data we have purchased ready for use... it still can be stored. What about our peers who might one day not be clients or staff but might be introducers, or joint venture partners. In fact, everybody you know. Because it's so much easier to keep it in one place.

And if *you* know, your business *staff* know and that can be massively powerful. For example, when a client rings in and it's Mrs Jones, your team member can quickly ask who is calling and as the client is saying who they are, the team member brings up on screen the clients details... confirming with the caller specific details... which makes the client calling in very impressed. You know who they are and that feels like they are important enough to be remembered, and that as we said earlier is a fabulous start. And it can get even better... imagine if the client records had been correctly updated with details of a conversation you had with them yesterday... maybe when you offered to give them a special extra bonus gift or delivery date or price reduction or something... imagine if you had recorded that information and then when the caller rings in, your team member says, "Oh, I can see Mrs Jones that actually you are very lucky... you've been granted an X!" Now the caller feels wowed that you are so efficient and impressed that your word is not only going to be kept but that the others know about it. Believe me, that is so rare that you will win clients forever with these simple touches... and you cannot ever do this if you haven't got the right system.

Now would you like your clients and your customers to think like that? Every time they ring in, if the person answering the phone went, "Just a moment, oh yes, Mrs Jones, Anywhere Street", and identified them straight away, the client ringing in would feel "Ooh, they're on the ball." And subtle things make massive differences. If your impression given out is that you're very organised and very professional, people comment and talk. It's about positioning. You suddenly start to get much more respect and that equates to higher revenues.

When enquirers are ringing in, you can ask them a couple of questions that identifies who they are. You can teach your system, or teach the people in your team to ask key questions, and if you keep the system open on the PC, correct client record details can be brought up onto the screen as the caller is on the phone.

Or how about somebody who might have rung in last week, and spoke to another staff member who isn't currently in the office. The client rings in and asks, "What's happening? I spoke to Ben last week." The original staff member (Ben) hasn't relayed to you the details because they haven't seen you - you've both been like ships in the night so you don't know what the caller was talking to your colleague about, but you open the system and say "Just a minute, David... oh yes, I can see. Ah right, yes, I know Ben's dealt with that. In fact, it's noted, dealt with, delivery expected here Thursday morning and he's got an appointment in his diary for Friday at 9 a.m. to bring it to you." The client calling is suitably dealt with and happily comments, "Oh great, lovely, thanks."

Now, if you haven't got that information, when somebody rings in, you'd say, "Look, I'm really sorry. I haven't been able to speak to Ben. I don't know when I'll see Ben. I'll find out and I'll get back to you."

Now what have you just done? Firstly, you probably haven't impressed a client and possibly added to his frustrations, but also you have instantly created two jobs. One to speak with Ben and remember the client's issue, and secondly to get Ben to call the client back (and hope he gets them first time). Instantly two more jobs in your already busy schedule! It just piles up more pressure, doesn't it? So I'm talking practical things here, my friend. If you've got access to information, it saves tasks, and in an already overcrowded world where you're trying to grow, you've got to save tasks because that equates to time and stress.

So, apart from the proactive advantages, the tools that we're going to grow with, it's very, very useful just internally. Like anything, you'll have to have the disciplines to make sure it's used, because input is the key and you will have to commit to a learning process before it's a comfortable addition but the longer term benefits are well worth it.

So get a CRM programme and use thoroughly from today onwards!

And just one thought to bring home the value of this type of programme in a monetary scenario. Let me ask you a question. In your last two years, did you do any networking at all, any big meetings or business gatherings? How many people do you think you've bumped into? In all of your business interactions, how many would you say you've touched shoulders with?

Can you imagine all of the people that have walked into your shop, all the people you've had conversations with, you've had coffee with, all the people you've bumped into, and you just going, "Oh alright, how are you? Busy, yes, see you again sometime, okay."

I would say it's probably a couple of hundred, at least.

Okay. So, out of all of the potential customers, not all of them that you meet have a need, so what do you think is that ratio of more serious potentials? Would you say probably half the people you meet have potentially got a need, and half haven't?

So let's say half of the people you meet are interested. Do you know what your ratio of sales 'pitches' to conversion into paid work is?

For an example, let us say that your closing rate is one out of six. Out of every six that are interested, you get one sale.

Out of the two hundred people you've 'bumped into', there's approximately **sixteen** sales!

Your average deal might be worth five thousand pounds, **so there's nearly a hundred thousand pounds worth of business you've just missed and kissed goodbye to!!**

Now if I was to say to you in the next two years I could show you one simple way that would get you an extra hundred thousands pounds worth of business, but you might have to spend one thousand pounds getting some IT together, what would you do?

Exactly!! Spend a little, learn a little and reap back a heck of a lot! It's not difficult, it's just different.

So what I'm saying to you is that *possibly you are not looking at what you're losing.* A hundred grand, possibly, is lost because you're just not recording who you're meeting. And then you're not going back to them and keeping that relationship going. It's *massive* value! From today onwards, *please* make it one of your action plans.

To help you remember, please allow me to share with you the following acronym... courtesy of a friend and an absolute networking master Mr Will Kintish: F   U   K   I   T

Follow   Up,   Keep   In   Touch!

The cost of NOT keeping in touch!

In the last couple of years or recent history, how many people have I met? (List the places you have been and possibly how many contacts you've touched)

_____

_____

_____

_____

_____

_____

What is my average conversion rate - sales opportunity to sale?

_____

_____

_____

How many sales could I have missed? (Number of contacts divided by conversion rate)

_____

_____

_____

What is my average sale worth to me? (Either profit or total value)

_____

_____

_____

How much have I lost?! (Number of sales X the average value)

_____

_____

_____

If I continue at this rate and style of sloppy business, how much will it cost me over the next two years?

_____

_____

_____

How do I feel about this? (Recognising this is within my control)

_____

_____

_____

_____

_____

What action am I going to take NOW to make this huge loss become huge gain in pocketed income? (E.g. install and manage correctly a CRM programme, follow-up leads etc.)

_____

_____

_____

_____

_____

_____

_____

Profiling

Following on then from the Contact Management and data capture thoughts, you need to start to think along the lines of intelligence winning the day not merely strength... again our battle analogy, and thus using the data and intelligence systems we need to look more closely at the ideal client scenario. We need to 'profile' clients and targets.

Do you know who your customer is?

Do you know who your ideal customer is?

Do you know where to find more of your ideal customers?

Do you know what language your ideal customer speaks and do you know therefore what to say to your ideal customer to get him to come to you?

Now if the answer to any of those is 'No', let's do some work on it. And that work is called profiling. So, let's look at who buys from you.

Write down, for yourself, who buys from you... and just try to identify them. Now again, whilst you're doing this, think of me as your Butler and I am outside now awaiting instructions from you to get you more clients; I am your servant. You've just got to tell me who you want me to get. So I'm out here and you're saying, "I want more customers", and I'm saying, "That's fine, I'm ready. I'll go and get them. Just tell me who."

So tell me, your servant, who to go and get. Describe for yourself now the ideal client profile. Write that question down, **"Who is my ideal customer?"** Describe for yourself who they are... and remember, being vague is not any good! Be specific.

Allow me once again to briefly share a thought...

All around us is light... we are so used to it we barely notice it. It doesn't really attract our attention as it is always there pretty much, and we just don't notice it particularly. Now, take that light and focus it through a magnifying glass. What happens then? Well you soon start to notice it because when it's focussed, it burns. Now, take it one stage further... take that light and make it so focussed it actually becomes a laser. What you have now is something that will cut through almost anything! It is still just light but when focussed it is no longer 'missed'.

Your marketing message is 'light'... when it is aimed at everybody it is so vague, so spread around it is like light everywhere and it is unnoticed and missed. Take your message, however, and focus it and it becomes noticed... focus it accurately and it cuts through almost anything.

Make your message laser-like... focus it exactly where you want it to work.

Thus, with that thought in mind, let us address the issue of our instructions to the Butler and exactly what sort of client we would like to have more of. (Remember, don't ever say, "Oh, anybody", because that isn't going to help you!)

How old are they? You'll always get variables but as a broad base? You might, for example, have people that buy when they're kids and people that buy when they're 90, but the bulk of your customers or clients may well be 45 to 60. So who buys? How old are they?

And if it's a B2B environment, how old is the company? How big is the company? If it's a B2B environment, is there a pattern amongst them? That most of them have three years' history, most of them have got four to six employees, most of them are turning over between half a million and two million pounds?

Is there a pattern? Are you dealing with bigger companies, medium or one-man bands?

If you're dealing B2C, are you dealing with youngsters? Are you dealing with males or females? Are you dealing with old and retired couples? You MUST know.

If dealing with corporate clients, for example, do the bosses play a lot of golf, because that's how they do their business? Or are they in buying groups? Or are they also in local societies or Chambers of Commerce? Or are they in a Trade Association?

Think about your best client and then say, what does he look like? How big is the company? How often do they buy? What does the person in the company look like? The people that I deal with, what sort of characters are they? What would they read?

What about their social habits... do they have a sport or hobby in common? Do they all drive perhaps certain top-end motor cars? Do your clients predominantly all enjoy living in certain demographic areas... perhaps certain suburbs of towns or possibly they frequent a type of nightly entertainment venue?

Look for clues and patterns by asking each buying client some broader questions and storing the answers to create a picture of their habits.

There will be clues. Ask lots of questions because you will find a profile... and then the next bit is easy. If we know what to look for, we understand some of their habits and we will know by default where to start looking to find more of them! It's actually pretty easy!!

By asking things like what do they do with their spare time when they're not at work, you build up a profile of your ideal client... and the strength of this is that by nature we humans like to mix with people like ourselves. As the saying goes, 'Birds of a feather stick together', and so where your client enjoys a particular sport you will find by virtue of his tastes being similar to his peer group that many of his sporting colleagues will probably also like what you sell. Thus following the trail laid by your client, he leads you to many more just like him you can sell to.

Think about it. When we're out socially, do we mix with people that we totally dislike, or do we mix with people similar to ourselves? What do we do?

We mix with people similar to ourselves. So, if I am your ideal client, and I spend two days a week playing golf, or I'm into motorbikes, or I'm really into football, or I'm really into computers, or I'll buy a lot of clothes, or I eat at a lot of great restaurants, or drive a certain car - if I'm your ideal client and I mix with other people like me, follow me around and you'll find lots more potential ideal clients!

You've just got to record what I do. So this is why I talk about data capture, because if you start to build up a profile, the potential end result is immense.

You might start with very little data like where I live, but that should be postcode driven.

Postcodes indicate demographic areas; good quality areas, bad quality areas. If you see a pattern of your customers all in good areas, well then you can hit the rest of those areas. You want your computer to tell you in a second your postcode areas. Start asking for them, get your staff to ask for them, and put them in the system that we talked about.

Better still, put a piece of paper into the system that dictates what they ask. Postcodes are so simple, so you might start off with just name, address, postcodes and phone numbers, but then you've also recorded obviously what they've bought, you've recorded how they paid for it, and probably in general chit chat you may have asked about the car, the home, the career roles etc. Now though, instead of merely using that information as conversation to be pleasant, you are recording it and gradually building up profiles on all of your clients. It's gathered in a harmless even enjoyable fashion and yet leaves so many clues.

Now if you suddenly went back to your data of 200 people a year later and asked it to give you the names of all of the people that are business owners, and it spat out another 120 that own their own business, would that be valuable? It would if you were focussing on selling a new service or product aimed directly at business owners.

So, get the system set up and then get a process that includes asking the questions, and then put the question answers in, and start to drive marketing from intelligence.

From this intelligence approach you then look at who you'd like to deal with, strategically, and say "Right, I want more of those. How do I get them?"

In business, most people merely accept what comes to them but that is NOT what you have to do. You have to say, Stop! If it comes to me, I'll accept it, but I'm going to go out and get what I really, really want. And I know what I really want because I've written it down, I've identified it, and we're now going to go and get it.

So please pay attention NOW to this idea of profiling your clients and begin to deliberately ask for and store added information. Be focussed on smarter business in the future and pretty soon you will find it so easy to make more money!!

Data – Predicting Trends

One final point on data and intelligence gathering. It could be very, very useful in a number of ways. I'll relay a story, again another one of my clients. In a former life, he was marketing director for a large leisure company who owned a lot of the nightclubs in the UK. More specifically, he was the marketing director for a company using marketing data and concentrating on the value it really shows and he was talking with a club manager in one of their venues who couldn't see the value.

Here's the scenario: club being open, people coming in, intelligence driven marketing saying we want to capture this data, so they issue these membership swipe cards. And every client gets a swipe card and as they come in they're encouraged to just swipe it because they get bonus points. Now guess what this card does? It tells you who is coming in. The question is, if you were a nightclub owner would that matter, or would it just matter that you'd got people coming in?

Well, you see the nightclub manager in question and a lot of people like him, they don't *think*, they don't go through business with intelligence, they're just there to do the job. "It's busy; we're taking the money, what more do you want?" Intelligence, above, asks who's coming in, who's coming in, who's coming in? It matters. Of course, the manager didn't see the need to bother with this bit of plastic. He just wasn't into the system, couldn't see the value of it and it wasn't really pushed enough.

Of the people that were swiping, they started to see a pattern. Postcodes, demographics, poor areas. And the warning from above was very clear; you're getting the wrong sort of people in. The manager said, "Oh, it's only a few people. I know them, I can handle them."

Long story short, the nightclub closed nine months later. It became overrun with the wrong sort and consequently fights and drugs became a major issue. Now how many millions of pounds does a company lose when it closes a nightclub? Several millions.

So, millions of pounds lost because they didn't predict a trend because they weren't thinking smart. The trend from intelligence indicated poor demographics, wrong people, inviting trouble, drugs and crime. And guess what happened? It didn't become apparent straight away because the wrong people were the minority. But gradually the right people who were in there started to say to themselves, "Oh, I don't like the sort that's coming in here now. I won't come back again." And gradually the nice people left, which left space for the non-desirables and the whole nightclub started to get fights, started to have a drug issue and was closed by the police.

The manager had constantly stated he didn't have a problem because he was measuring the attendance level and spend level only... surface measurement. Sub-surface data showed the problem.

So data doesn't *just* drive forward to grow, data starts spotting trends that could be dangerous and protect. You cannot afford not to know.

Another example. Do you know where your average sale is? Do you know what your average sale margin is? What if you were still selling what felt like loads of sales and actually because you are only looking at total figures, not margins, you are constantly striving to maintain a level when actually to maintain that level is straining and overloading the people. The result is you are working flat out but not making enough money. So often, it happens... business owners are so focussed on maintaining turnover levels and yet they don't look below at average sales values... and in order to maintain the turnover when average prices drop, the staff work 20-40% harder merely to stay afloat! In the end you get mistakes and disruption and it implodes!

Merely measuring totals isn't enough. You need to watch average sale values and average margins to make sure they don't slip.

Or are you just going to find out one day you've got no money left?

Do you know who is buying and how often they come back? Because if you knew that usually people buy three or four times a year, and now they're buying just once, you might want to do something to correct that before it becomes that they don't buy at all!

A printer, for example, is very good at design, and they get a lot of people in for design. But unfortunately, once they've got all the design work done, there is a danger the client can then just farm the print work out to somebody for a reprint at a lower cost. Now if you were aware of all the people that bought once for design, and then weren't buying again, you'd think, "I've got a problem here." But guess what? Most people are not aware. They do all the design and they don't think about them coming back. They do the hard part, the expensive part, the labour input part, they gather and they sell and the reproduction, the run offs. Where the profits are, they're not getting.

You see, brain wins over brawn every time, doesn't it?

Some of the great, great business leaders of today, they aren't big employers. Intelligence wins, muscle doesn't. So think how much of your business is driven by muscle, and think how much is driven by intelligence. Just ask yourself that question. Because if a lot of your business success is driven by 'effort in', it's going to come to a halt one day.

We gather the data because it directs our future marketing and it also predicts current trends.

Your action plan therefore is to absolutely make sure from today onwards your business fully uses a contact management system and all of your people and processes are gathering and storing information so that you have an intelligent business that survives and flourishes.

What does my 'Ideal Client' look like?

List the characteristics of your best clients? (How many staff, how many locations, turnover/size, payment period, ease of dealing with, etc.)

_____

_____

_____

_____

_____

_____

What else might be a common characteristic? Think of their habits/ lifestyle/leisure interests (cars, holidays, gym clubs, schools, sports links, etc.)

_____

_____

_____

_____

_____

_____

Where might be a great place to meet more of these type clients?

_____

_____

_____

_____

_____

Your 'Ideal Client' Circle of Influence

This is a critical exercise in learning how best to drive your business forward. When you can truly understand your ideal client's circle of influence, then you can strategically take dedicated actions to meet with their influencers and thus 'bump into' more of your ideal client sort (or get lucky as some might prefer!). What else might they buy? Where else might they go?

Add an 'arm' for each supplier type that they might spend with. On each 'arm', list a type of product or service they might purchase and then list at least three specific examples of this type of provider. Then you have a very specific targeted list of people to approach! Easy!

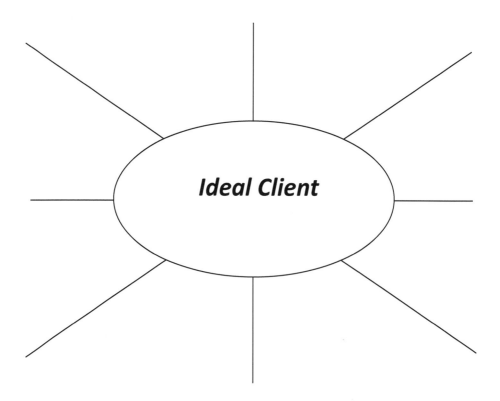

Business Booster Foundations – a quick recap

We're in business and we want more. You want to grow your business and be wealthier than you are now and I guess probably you want more free time and less stress. To get that, you want to grow... and to grow your business to more than it's currently at, you've got to *do* something different, because what you've currently been doing has only got you to where you currently are.

There is absolutely no such word as can't... we ask instead "How can I?"

Well how you can is by following these simple steps:

To grow a business you've got to go backwards. So, let's briefly recap on all that we've covered so far... repetition to help us brand it into our minds.

Absolutely the first thing you have to do is **STOP!** You need to **STAND BACK** from your business and look at it in a different light and **ASK HOW CAN IT BE MADE BETTER?** Stop doing the same old reactive stressful way! Make a pact with yourself now to stop the old because it isn't getting you what you want. Stop the old and add the new...

You've got to look at yourself and say first of all, **where are you at now?** Write and clearly talk with yourself being totally honest. Do not just keep saying the same old tired lines. You're not completely happy so be brutally honest, uncover some truths and then you can go forward.

Then find out **where you want to be**, write your lists of clearly identified goals, not forgetting, of course, that the Butler is your servant but he cannot get you anything that is not **specific** or he won't know what to get! Make your goals clear, specific and issue your instruction as if to a real person that you need obedience from.

... and then ask yourself **why**?

Remember your why is the most important. Your why is more important than anything else. Because, if your goal is purely finance, a million pounds and a Ferrari for example, that's easy when you're hungry and you're driven... when you're on £20,000 or £30,000 a year, a million pounds and a Ferrari answers all your problems, but when you're on two hundred thousand pounds a year, you haven't got the same problems. In fact you're probably pretty damn comfortable and, "Hey, well if I don't get my million, I'm alright." And the problem, the issue with finance-only goals, is you will not reach them because on the route you'll get comfortable. And once you get comfortable, the impetus has gone out of your goals. **Comfort Kills** when it comes to finance goals. So a word of warning, if your goals are financial, just be prepared to think of something stronger than that.

So, you know where you're at, you know where you're going to, you know why.

Now that you've got a really big strong why, you're determined to do it so you've got to decide on your **how?** You're going to look at **planning**.

You need to make goals and then break the goals down, and then **write a plan as to how to get there**, and we're going to take that plan down to a level where we can shout to the Butler *exactly* what he wants to get you. Okay.

You have a mission servant in the universe. The Butler is outside your room now, but he can't go and get what you don't know he's got to get. So, you've got to give him *specific* directions for your goals, and you've got to give you *specific* directions for your **activities**.

You've got to know for, example, on a Monday morning that you're making four phone calls, two visits, etc.

Then of course, you absolutely MUST remember that some of that has got to be **strategic activity to get the bigger picture**. Strategic activity might be schmoozing an influential industry figure or a large potential account over several meetings with no immediate payoff... just remember you need to have a strategy.

Having thought enough then to have a planned strategic approach, you are now realising that intelligence wins the day. **You invest in, and use, a CRM contact management system**.

Put all this together and you start to get smart and **gather data on your clients**... because data provides intelligence, and as you now know, brawn doesn't win. Brains do.

So instead of fighting every day to try and get around to a hundred calls to find the five that want you, sit down for two or three hours, maybe over two or three days, and find what identifies the five and then we just go and talk to five.

You gather data on what makes the people that buy from you in a category, and then approach them. Simple really!!

Okay, so I think you have learned a lot, thought a lot and like I said when we started out, I hope you have taken each step slowly and stopped reading to actually write and think for yourself. This isn't a race... and perhaps we should remind ourselves of the story of a race between the Tortoise and the Hare... who won? Yes, the Tortoise... he didn't go speeding off, he slowly took one step at a time... so please don't race on ahead with 'reading just another book'. Stop and make sure you have worked on all we have talked about.

Mindset Of A Millionaire

One final thought you will do well to ponder on for a moment or two as you read this today... How Do You Think About Success?

How do you feel about really achieving? What goes through your mind when you are talking or dreaming of a brighter future?

When it comes to investing possibly in new systems or engaging a designer for a more corporate makeover... or spending on a new Internet site that actually uses back office process, not merely a brochure???

How do you feel? What are your thoughts about money?

Well often there is a scarcity mentality at play.

That is, a person thinks that actually there is not enough to go around and therefore their monies have to be divided and something has to give. Have you ever heard that? Said that?

Well, my friend, ponder on the thought of a more abundant earth!

Millionaires have many common success habits, some of which we have already looked at, but truthfully one of the most prominent is that of 'an abundance mentality'. Truly rich people share a belief that there is always more and so focus on the bigger picture, not the smaller 'fear based' thought. Making millions means believing that there are millions to be had and that having them does NOT mean wrestling them from somebody else!!

A Millionaire Mindset then is where you strive to make yourself be. Yes it can be difficult... maybe your childhood or early conditioning taught you to believe that there is no money and the rich have it all and the rich aren't nice people etc. etc. Early environments possibly endorsed by recent experiences have left a belief that there is not enough.

Everybody is complaining about having less than they need... but in fact globally there is a massive supply. It might need some redistribution... and some of it your way, but in truth there is no shortage. Your mindset, however, determines what comes your way.

Thus your task is to think like a millionaire. When it comes to spending, especially when it is for something in your business, call it investing. Make sure that it is of course an investment into something that makes a difference in the future, not merely a flight of fancy now! But if it means investing in an education programme so that with your higher level of knowledge you can speed up your journey, then that should be done. If it is possibly, as already mentioned, a new image, a new website, a new CRM system, all of these are vital to the success that you ache for... and a millionaire says, "if I need it then I have it and I work harder at making it pay back."

Your new future is as certain as your belief about it.

If you have a doubt and hold it back in anyway, then you effectively hold back any success that you desire. Only YOU can make it happen... and only YOU hold it back!

Yes! Your current mindset and attitude towards learning, growing, changing and investing are all the reasons why you are where you are at. Make determined mindset shifts today to think like a millionaire and you will see massive and rapid improvements.

For example, where do millionaires socialise? Is it down at the local bar where all of the occupants spend the little money they have and moan all night about the world letting them down? I think not!!

Where do millionaires spend leisure time? Is it in front of the TV watching mindless soap operas and talk shows? I think not!!

Where do millionaires eat? Is it the fast food/junk food takeaway that almost demands being overweight? I think not!!

Your future reflects your thinking. Your habits reflect your thinking. Your habits impact your lifestyle and your colleagues and your influences.

Make changes in all of these areas and you will see amazing things happen as 'coincidences'. They are NOT coincidences, by the way... they are the universe's way of rewarding you for making that step up. When you change a habit of going to a local bar and mix instead at a leisure centre that is serving a higher demographic, then it might just be 'purely coincidentally' you start talking with a really nice and quite connected person!

It might just be that when you stop eating at a fast food diner and push yourself into a better restaurant where healthy vegetarian food is served that you meet a local business leader on the next table.

It might just be that when you think like a millionaire and move your leisure time from TV to the business networking events in your area that you bump into a terrific potential client and almost land a large new contract!

The universe will conspire to give you what you ask for... and what you show that you believe that you can get by your actions.

A Millionaire Mindset shows. It's visible. It is reflected in your clothing, your stance, your language, your walk, your friends, your habits... it is evident in everything... and when it *is* evident in everything, then you will see the millions. You have to become that which you want to become.

Your habits attract people to you... make them millionaire habits and millionaires will come into your view. Your attitudes are reflected in language and energy. When these reflect your belief in success, into your field of view will walk successful people to carry you on your journey.

I promise from my heart that this is tested and proven. This is not about the outside world; this is about YOU.

Your future, your business success, can and will be directly proportionate to how you think and believe.

The ideas in this book work, but they have to be applied and committed to... and that is down to you.

Having a millionaire mindset means that you WILL commit. It means that you WILL do each step systematically and thoroughly. It means that you WILL push yourself to manage your thoughts and your actions and reflect the millionaire you want to be.

So, my friend, I urge you from my heart... believe in you. Believe in the universe... and demonstrate your millionaire mindset right now, tonight, in everything you say and do.

Then you will reap the rewards and the future will be all that you want and deserve!

Section Two

Business Boosters Marketing

"Remember there is a natural season for planting, there is a time to grow and then there is a time for harvest. Do not try to short circuit nature... better to work with her and make your harvest bountiful."

"I have more respect for the fellow with a single idea who gets there than for the fellow with a thousand ideas who does nothing"
Thomas Edison

What you need to do now is build on the foundations that you have learned about. You're going to get up every day and start with a different practice. You are going to Stop! the old and in its place start to implement a new approach.

When you do this your business day should already be better... truthfully you should be clear-headed and be feeling less stressed because, whilst possibly you aren't seeing massive extra income yet, you should feel much better about *why* you're doing it and where it is leading you. Indeed you should feel less stressed because you can clearly see systems and intelligence and a little 'planning before action' taking effect. Yes, you now will be living with better foundations and that in turn means the time is correct for 'growing' upon those foundations.

The task of growth then, implies that you must examine your marketing activity and essentially generate better enquiries. In fact, 'enquiry overload' as I like to call it.

Marketing is not, as some people assume, an expensive advertising and brochure exercise. I call marketing **"the art of making people beat a path to your door"** and by people I mean targeted, suitable, potential clients. Marketing, I believe, is an art. It is a science and it has its rules. Marketing is an all encompassing word – but let us break it down and understand a little more about what is involved.

Firstly, it is understood that there is a process of relationship development that you need to develop with your clients.

Some of them at the bottom end will be 'suspects' that then will become 'prospects' that then filter all the way through until they become 'raving fans' at the top end and start giving you so many referrals you can't handle them.

If you were asked, "Who is your client or who would you serve?" prior to giving it a deeper thought as has just been covered - what might you have said? Sadly many business owners would say, "Well anybody really with a pulse!" because they think that anybody's money will do.

Now I'm not saying that if someone comes up to you waving a fistful of dollars, you won't accept it. In that sense, it is true that anybody's money will do. What I am really saying is that being more selective about who you actively 'chase' is a far more productive approach and thus in essence it isn't just anybody. You don't go out and stand on the street corner and say, "Does anybody want to buy my goods?" because that isn't going to help you. So now we know about the profiling, it's going to be a lot easier.

What we're going to do is drive lots and lots of people of the right sort through your ladder (see diagram – marketing ladder).

As you can see, the way marketing is defined from my perspective, is, 'The art of making clients beat a path to your door'. It may be using different mediums, such as advertising, telemarketing or direct mail, but marketing itself is the art of making people come up to you and say, "Please can you talk to me about your 'stuff'?"

So, we've got to start out by finding suspects, and then filtering those people into prospects, and then filtering them all the way up the ladder.

It might be interesting to note here, that the dictionary definitions of 'customers' and 'clients' are very different... and the use of even a different word can have a profound effect, as we will talk more about later, however for now the definition of a customer is "somebody who purchases goods or services", in other words a person who just spends once. A client is defined as somebody "who is under the protection of another", or perhaps in buying/selling language, someone who is a frequent purchaser and is 'looked after' by the person/company they purchase from. It implies a *totally* different relationship and responsibility.

My thought here is that if you view them all as clients, the way you handle them from the first time you interact with them because of you seeing them as perhaps more valuable would be more conducive to them buying again.

The Marketing Ladder

"Marketing - The art of making clients beat a path to your door"

Ben Kench

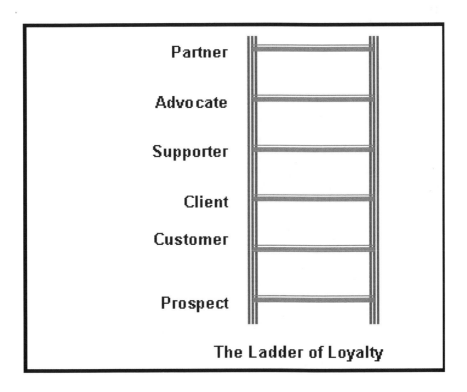

Just a thought but I believe an important one... view every person who approaches you as a 'client' and treat them accordingly and you will more likely be rewarded with the relationship and loyalty that a client relationship usually engenders. For now though, in the name of 'marketing' let us focus on attracting enquirers...

Who do we want? From where? How do we attract them?

We talked about profiling, and you should now know who your ideal customer is.

At this juncture I am suggesting that you have access to all of your client records... all records of those who both purchased and enquired from your company in the last year or two. I possibly will concede that you don't have this at the time of reading but as we have covered this critical issue in our building foundations section, I am going to presume that you have run out and installed a CRM system and loaded various bits of data that you have and also learned a little about how best to drive the system. If you haven't then it makes this marketing 'Enquiry Overload' section very difficult. If you have, you will now see the power of what you have done!

Okay then, as I say presuming that you do have your data to hand, your task is to produce a full list or report of all of your client (your system should have a 'reports' facility and you will be able to pull 'lists' based upon search criteria and data recorded) especially those purchasing over the last two years. Then collect a list of clients that have bought frequently or bought more than once at least. And then look at just those customers and see what you can see hidden in amongst the obvious. For example, what are they like? Do they have common threads, such as types of industry purchasing a type of product? Do you have threads that link volumes with geographical areas? Is there a type of client that seems to buy more frequently?

(You will see all sorts of links when you look closely, as we discussed when we looked at profiling, and that is where we need to pick it up again.)

Once you've spent a bit of time just asking yourself those questions, you'll have a good idea of the profile of who they are, where they are etc. Can I ask you though; have you ever asked your clients <u>why</u> they bought from you? I mean, really asked them for a genuine reason why they chose you, not another competitor?

If you haven't, I really recommend you do. Make time in your planning process, to go back and talk to your clients, even when they've bought from you. If you've got a relatively one-off purchase, for example, financial services on a mortgage, it may be deemed that once the mortgage is done and dusted, they're happy, it's gone through, you don't need to talk to them again. This may be the case with a mortgage... but is that all they are going to ever buy? Is the mortgage in fact a one-off purchase these days? Again the assumption is very often that, "When they've got another need, they'll come back", but I assure you this is a fools assumption and it merely leaves valuable cash lying on the side for competitors to steal.

Whatever your scenario - fitting out an office IT infrastructure or building a website, selling them garden furniture or selling them a business service - whatever the instance, find an excuse to speak with your client again. Plan time into your process to talk to them again and ask, "Out of interest, what was it that helped make your decision to buy from us?"

And don't ask them straight questions without giving them alternative answers, because people are reluctant. Initially they'll be resistant; they won't think.

Give them alternatives like, "Was it the positioning of our offer, or was it the price, or was it the way we approached you?" Give them alternatives. And they'll probably say, "Oh yeah, I like that." And try and widen each question. For example, "Was it the friendliness of our staff?", "Was it their helpfulness?", and "Were they knowledgeable?"

Personally *I* believe that if you do a survey of your ideal clients and why they buy from you, you will find a key factor will be because you're friendly and you give them help. I believe service on a *truly human relationship level* is paramount. Whilst I will suggest to you many a time that service in itself is not good enough alone to make a client choose you, they probably won't know about your service until after they have bought and thus it doesn't help gather sales in the first instance, but truly human, sincere feelings of concern and well-being that are portrayed and projected to the client during the service or selling to them causing a bonding with your 'personal touch' *will* directly increase sale likelihood. They will state this as a reason they bought... and remember it afterwards.

I also believe that in your relationship you must impart knowledge freely because it engenders loyalty. When asking them, "Why did you buy?" try also asking them to give their opinion on how knowledgeable you or your staff are. My guess is that you'll find a correlation... the loyal clients who responded to the personal touch will probably also identify the level of knowledge imparted as a key reason as to why they chose to buy in the first instance. The more you're perceived to be the expert, helping them with lots of knowledge, the more they'll respond and deal with you. They won't even know why they feel like they have to respond. It's a human 'condition'. We have a programme in our mind, inbuilt into us, that likes to reciprocate. It's called the Law of Reciprocity. We feel obliged. If someone gives us something, we will look for a way to give something back; we'll feel the need or obligation to repay. (Think for a moment of your Christmas card list... what happens when someone gives you a card or a gift that you weren't expecting? You absolutely feel obliged to give one back!)

Strangely enough, if your clients perceive you as being knowledgeable, and you've given them knowledge to help them in their buying decision, they have probably felt more loyalty and feel bound to deal with you when it comes to buying. Thus if you use this to your advantage, if you become the <u>giver of knowledge</u>, you will <u>bind</u> clients to you, but do a survey first, find out why they bought, and then we'll go and find ways to bring them to you in their droves.

Another question: Ask yourself this; "What makes me memorable?"

Is your offering an infrequent purchase? Is it a once in a while, possibly a year or several between purchases? If that is the case, then usually it will also relate to a higher ticket item and thus quite probably a fair sized profit from the sale.

You see, the question as to whether your clients remember you or not is critical if you sell a less frequently purchased item. NEVER allow yourself to believe that it is a one-off purchase and that they will not be in the market again. These days even purchases such as houses, vehicles, home improvements or investment products that on the surface are a larger seldom bought item are repurchased with surprising frequency as people move home, get divorced, win the lottery or enjoy the realisation of greater wealth that is very possible today. (The challenge is that they should come back to you and you should be getting a nice large profit second time around if you did your job correctly *after* the purchase.) You need to learn a factor that makes you memorable.

By examining these two points, you will retain huge percentages of your clients. If you can truly find out what it was that made them buy from you in the first instance, and then if you apply action and communication frequently after the purchase to continue conveying this same message, you will see huge dividends. However, more importantly right now, after having studied a list of *clients* and learned reasons *why they bought* from you, <u>you now have a huge weight of argument behind you that simply knocks the prospects you're talking to into your net. Now we are *really* ready to begin gathering volumes of enquiries!</u>

Armed then with this intelligence and mindful of some useful human factors such as reciprocity, let's look at generating more enquiries for your 'new' business than you can shake a stick at!

Enquiry Overload

I believe we can get your business to have literally hundreds of people saying, "I want to buy." And more importantly, once we start to really turn the tap on, we then filter it so that the quality of those people enquiring is even better.

We're going to look at the sales process later, (even with loads of enquirers, you've still got to convert them into <u>buying</u> customers) but the truth is, if everybody coming to you is of the right <u>calibre</u>, more of them will convert. To generate real Enquiry Overload you add onto the intelligence we have gleaned thus far some techniques that create massive impact.

There are of course hundreds of ways to market your business but let us look at a few of the most awesome pound for pound activities. Large budgets do not hold a monopoly on large business growth... you can grow massively without spending a lot and I promise you that if you systematically address each of these ideas, and then refine it a little to make it right before moving on, you will literally fly!

Like many other areas, these might at first challenge you in that you do not quite fully appreciate how they are to be applied to your business or that you need a little time to get used to doing it and feel comfortable with it... but persevere, it pays off!

Networking

My watchword is always "Be known in your industry, be known in your area".

They're the two focus points that I want you to work on. I want everybody around you to know you, and everybody in your industry to know you.

Why be known in your industry? Surely that merely alerts the competition! Well there are going to be times when the peers in the industry are good network contacts; you'll hear about clients and jobs, you'll hear about developments, you'll hear about staff, you'll get invited to events where you'll need to rub shoulders with movers and shakers, <u>network peers</u>. No, do NOT be afraid of competitors knowing what you do. It definitely pays to be known in your industry, but for now I want you to focus on being known in your area, your local geography.

In this particular instance, we're talking about <u>getting clients</u> and potential clients, so we want to network or rub shoulders directly with either potential clients or with people who can lead us to them. Remember, we've looked at the profile, "Who normally buys from us and where do they go?" and we also know who else deals with them so networking becomes immediately easier.

Networking, I believe, is <u>singularly</u> the most powerful way to get business. If you can get your message across so that people you're networking with really know what you do, then it can feed you both quality and quantity and you could even base your whole business around it should you wish. So how do we do this 'networking'?

My scientific approach to getting more enquiries from a networking basis is...

Get out more!

Get out more! I don't care where you go. Anywhere! If you get business because you test and measure the response from your contacts at parties, then go to parties! Just make sure it is paying off! You and I know well the stories of business done on the golf course or with a golfing colleague... this is merely networking applied.

So, **get out more**.

Sit down and ask, **"Where can I go where my clients might go?"** Or, **"Where can I go to meet people that would introduce me to my ideal client?"** Or, **"Is there a gathering or social group that many of my profiled clients might be at?"**

There are many organised business groups that I will mention and indeed many more that you can source but look always to connect with either your client profile or others who you can clearly see are able to lead you to your prospect.

And as I have said, there are several networking groups: the FSB (Federation of Small Businesses), the Chamber of Commerce, Breakfast for Business, BRX (Business Referral Exchange), BNI (Business Network International), 4Networking etc. Literally these days in every town there is a group or two of business people who deliberately get together with a business theme attached to a social function. There are lots of independent groups. So look around. Use the Internet for business groups. Ask other colleagues and spread your contact circle.

There will be more network groups than you realise. And those network groups are made up of firstly people who might buy from you, and secondly people who have clients that might buy from you.

There is an old saying, "People like people like themselves". And you, as a consumer, will buy from somebody you know <u>first</u>. Always. You will always buy from somebody you know and trust first (there is an assumption here perhaps that obviously you would *not* buy from somebody you know if the somebody who you knew wasn't reputable or safe!). Secondly, when buying a product or service you do not frequently purchase, if you do not know anybody, then you'll buy from a person who 'somebody you know' knows. You will act upon a recommendation – and that is the core principle of networking.

You will always buy from somebody you know or from a recommendation of somebody else you know and trust first. Why? Because none of us enjoy getting it wrong! And thus we feel more secure buying from somebody who we can get a reference on in as much as, "If they did it correctly for my associate, then they should also do so for me." We feel safer and trust more... and that is an absolutely prime driver in a buying decision. In fact, it is <u>the</u> number one driver of people's buying decisions, so therefore your potential clients have to know <u>you</u> and a lot of other people have to know you to feed the clients your way.

I'll just reiterate that. A prime driver in anybody's buying process is trust... and we relate trust to 'knowing'... so make it as easy as possible for people to 'know' you and help them with their trust issue.

So get out more!

But certainly, you should join your Chamber of Commerce and the like and make an effort to go to all their meetings. It won't work if you don't put the effort in. I have heard many business people moan about what they haven't had from a group... and then when it is examined in a little more depth, they haven't really given very much in the way of input! You get out what you put in! One point though... possibly the most <u>important</u> thing about networking, it is not <u>just</u> about the meeting. It is also very much about what you do after it. It is about the follow-up procedure. Remember, a key driver in buying is trust, and a key indicator of whether you trust someone enough to pass on to another friend their name, is how well you know them. Therefore you've got to develop relationships with the people you've met so that they feel like they know you enough to pass on your name. You have to spend time with anyone to feel like you know them; hence the after meeting work is critical to that growing process.

So <u>between</u> meetings, you make time to see the people that are at the meetings. (I know that's another time pressure but that would be <u>strategic</u> time.)

For argument's sake, you have a garden centre. A lot of your ideal customers are buying general house refurbishment products as they wander around, not just the odd potted plant. In fact, in your marketing attack you're going to try and frame your garden centre to some people as *the* place if they want to make their home feel and look better. That might be exotic, expensive, large, indoor potted plants, or it might be complete, luxury patio furniture, or large, all-singing, all-dancing, barbecue equipment. The challenge then is that you have got to find who these people (your target clients) are and where they go and get more of them to come over to your garden centre. Difficult, perhaps? Well let's see.

Imagine that you know from your profiling and your data capture process that your clients enjoy £40,000+ company directorships, and they drive Jaguars, Mercedes, that sort of car. You might decide that you could meet owners of dealerships of these sorts of car through business networking and decide to work together to attract more clients to your business. Or conversely you might meet with that type of business professional actually directly as they could be fellow attendees at the network meeting.

The point I'm making here is networking will lead you to a lot of people who could very likely become your client either directly or indirectly, especially if you have planned your networking according to intelligence that you have gleaned. Networking can feed your flow of prospects.

Remember, people like to buy from someone who is recommended or indeed from someone they know... so get out more and let more people know you. To really capitalise on this, remember the acronym FUKIT - Follow Up on contacts and Keep In Touch to develop a level of trust so that they refer you. This alone, I promise, will massively grow your business over the next year!

And don't evaluate the network group you're going to based upon the people at the group. All too often this is a reaction of the 'hunting' networker. The selfish 'what's in it for me immediately'-type approach evaluates instantly the people around the group as to their value in terms of prey. Do NOT do this! A fatal flaw! Don't look at it and say, "Oh, I don't sell to any of them." It's not about them; *it's about who they know*. It is about who the group in front of you can lead you to!

And not everybody, at every network group, is going to be your sort, or mix with your sort. So some of the people you mix with, at your networking group, are not going to have clients that match your clients. Some people will not be useful contacts but do not be put off.

You might think, for example, that the lady that just does an ironing service is no good as a contact, however probably some of her customers are actually business owners running successful companies and she is doing their ironing work because they can't be bothered to do it any more! In fact, the ironing lady could very well be a key introducer! So again, look for service providers that do the 'dirty bits'... because for most people, as they grow in income, the less they do themselves. Service providers generally have got a client base of people that are running businesses and buy-in a service because they are too busy themselves... and thus become key introducers!

Just think about the links. Please remember that. Go to all the networking groups you can, and learn to identify the people that deal with the people that you sell to. **It's not just the people you meet at the networking groups, it's who they know.**

Remember, as a buyer, you buy from somebody you know first, and somebody you've been recommended to second. The object of the game is to get loads and loads and loads of people recommending you. They won't <u>all</u> become customers, some will just be strong contacts, but the overall value is massive.

So, for enquiry overload, the number one, best approach is networking – get out more.

My recommendation is to try <u>getting to four separate events a month</u>. Meet with new contacts then meet with them again at a different occasion – perhaps visit them at their work, develop a friendship and watch as contacts become business generators!

Obviously, as you start to ramp up your contacts, you'll have to cut back on some of your activity, but start it by having four events a month. And then you're going to capture the data (remember we talked about that), you put it into your electronic system, and the electronic system drives outgoing frequent contact mailings, which builds up the relationship, and it all gets easier. Enquiry Overload is on its way!

Host Beneficiaries and Joint Ventures

Do you remember we talked previously on doing a 'profile' of your ideal client? Well, once you know who your ideal prospects are, the next question is who else serves your ideal customer? Ask yourself that question. Who else serves my ideal customer, or my ideal client?

Who else do they buy from?

Do they buy a particular range of vehicle, holiday, job scenario? If you're after a consumer of a certain income category, you might link with home improvement companies who are finding people in those categories, e.g. conservatory suppliers or landscape gardeners.

If your client is a furniture manufacturer of high value furniture, for example, then who else is feeding in? Obviously raw material suppliers like the wood, the leather, the fabric. They've probably got designers; probably got somebody somewhere that provides power tools. If they are actually a manufacturer, there will be somebody providing them with perhaps the compressed air, the air guns, nail guns, the glue. There will be somebody providing them with perhaps computer programmes that do the design for the furniture and a recruitment service for new or added staff.

Whether business to business or business to consumer, look at the client profile you have drawn up, listen to your best clients as you go through the satisfaction survey, and they will give you clues as to what else they buy. When you have a pattern of other providers serving that same client then it is a logical step to presume that these other providers have more clients that are similar to your client. Find the other providers and you find another way into your client group. (Take a look at the diagram 'Circle of Influence' that you completed previously for your ideal client and use this to draw out for yourself a diagram showing you all those who liaise with your ideal client.)

Do you see how this will work? You'll find another door into your target client and your new ally won't be averse to working with you because you don't threaten him. I will just add here that I am presuming that your approach and analysis will have identified other providers to your target group that are non-competitive! It really isn't going to be much good to you if you identify someone offering the same or very similar offering as you do!!

Now the point I'm making is that if your client, the furniture company, deals with a leather supplier and when you find out who the leather supplier is, guess what? If you make a relationship with the leather supplier, he will lead you to other highbrow furniture companies. The leather supplier is selling to the furniture manufacturer you're already dealing with, so all of the other furniture manufacturers he's selling to probably have a similar need for your offering as your original client has.

Or another example, if you have a service related to direct mail intelligence, that saves people time and particularly money when they're sending out bulk mailings, and your ideal client, is by necessity a bulk mail house - who else does your client deal with? Well, to function as a bulk mail house, they will have to buy data. They're going to buy print, they're probably at some stage going to talk to recruitment agencies for temporary staff, or telesales providers for follow-up on the advertising mail-out. They'll use advertising agencies to put a design together for what they print. *Lots* of other suppliers feed your client and you could potentially link with these and subsequently be introduced to other mail houses that might become clients.

It really is not very difficult!! Just look to create strategic alliances or joint ventures, where you link with somebody who does not compete but also serves your ideal clients.

Joint ventures, by the way, in my opinion are singularly _the_ quickest way to grow your business. I've said networking is very, very effective and it is, but especially effective when it develops a relationship that becomes a working joint venture partnership. If you can do a joint venture with one of your network contacts... wow!

Do you know why?

The database!

They've spent five, ten, or twenty years building up a client base. If you were to get another three thousand, five thousand, ten thousand clients, it would take _you_ another five or ten years. Do a joint venture with them so that they allow you access to their client data and you've got them in five weeks, or five months! Now that is a turbo boost to your business! Don't struggle organically – get smart!

If the client profiles match, and there's no threat, well then they've got nothing to lose!

So do it. Get out more to make the contact, think differently to make the alliance.

If you want to grow your database, you haven't got to go out and generate loads of enquiries. You go and create some strategic alliances and suddenly inherit!!

If you want to grow quickly and get more enquiries than you can shake a stick at, don't go out and try and grow another three or five hundred enquiries yourself. Doing that organically could take you several years. There _is_ a better, smarter way... link with a non-threatened partner and share his years of client accumulation!! Go and find someone who's got five hundred and speed your growth!

People make business hard! They go about it the wrong way!

You can be hugely more profitable and have a vastly different outcome. Use this technique effectively and leave the others behind!

And please don't forget... don't look at just what you can get... look at what you can give.

An absolutely key ingredient in this process is the trust issue and many business owners quite rightly will guard their client data with their life! It actually is not going to be quite as simple as merely walking up to the new contact, asking once and they will hand it over to you! No. You will have to engage with them and create a trust. It will probably take months and a lot of meeting and sharing... but the truth is, whilst it could take months, it is unlikely to take as long as actually growing the data organically as he did. And whilst we are on this subject, please remember the absolute human mindset of reciprocity that we mentioned earlier. Go and offer to give first and then they will feel obliged to give in return.

Give and you shall receive. (Now where have I heard that before?!!) How about offering *your* clients to the chosen potential partner? Or if you don't have lots of clients to offer in return, how about offering him cash on all sales? Make it two-way please! Make the prospective partner feel like they can win, not as though they are being used. Offer more gain, less pain. Offer benefits with no downside as YOU will do nearly all of the work.

Build the base and then develop the relationships.

If you work strategically at this over the next few months, you could be sitting here in six or eight months' time with two or three thousand more customers at your reach.

Would you like to double your business in a year? If I mentioned that when we first started out, you might have thought I was being a little flamboyant. You might have thought it was sales speak and a bit unrealistic... but can you see now though that it is 100% realistic and totally possible if you approach it using these Business Booster tactics! Go for it!

Like I say – be smart! Make it easier on yourself – do it a different way!

And, the key to all of this is the WIIFM principle, isn't it? What's In It For Me? So when you're looking at strategic alliances, ask yourself **from the other person's perspective** what they will be asking, which is, "What's In It For Me?" They will ask, "Why should I do it? What's the biggest risk?" The first thing they're going to be looking at is what's the risk? What could they lose? How could it backfire?

When you go and approach anyone, please appreciate that the first thought they're going to have is protection. They will obviously be looking after their business interests and although you might paint a picture of potential gain, they will probably have a greater fear of losing what they have already got. For example, they don't know your service or product yet and hence they might well fear that you could let down some of their clients if they are passed over... and this will in turn lead to a backlash onto the partner for allowing you to deal with his clients badly. So realise the potential partner will be protecting his interests first before getting excited about extra revenue that you are offering... but he *will* become excited once there is a level of trust or a well structured arrangement that takes away fear of loss.

Make your approach non-threatening, white flag, preferably giving them something first and make your style evidently considerate to his concerns, and you will win through. My suggestion: allow the potential partner to use your service or product and especially allow them to see your history and talk with your clients to verify that what you say is true and that you will not cause a backlash effect for his business. By allowing this open evaluation of your offering, the potential partner will see that there is no backlash possibility and will then be keen to focus on the gain you have promised... and the gain will always be assessed against an input requirement to see if it is worth it. Thus to ensure success here, make certain your offering not only includes a cash return for them, but that you have correctly thought through the process and have done or will do most of the work to see it through.

Join venture arrangements, strategic partnerships or host beneficiary arrangements... call it what you will, but don't miss out on this prime method of attaining enquiry overload. It is awesome; make it happen for you from today!

Your 'Ideal Client' Circle of Influence - Suppliers

Remember the Ideal Client diagram...

Draw again with an extra depth... i.e. take the 'arm' and list the supplier type, then list where the suppliers might congregate, then list possible venues you can go to meet up with more of them.

This diagram will steer you to actual meeting points!

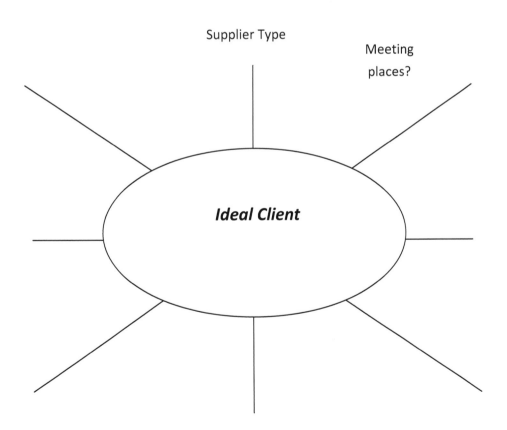

Special Events

What do I mean by special events?

Well, simply put, an occasion that is an event outside of the usual working requirements.

For example, educational seminars, a sponsored golf day, a music festival, race nights, a sponsored cycle ride etc.

Look at how many opportunities there are! You could have a special event created in your business calendar easily - a birthday party, if nothing else.

You could have something to do with calendar events that are going on, you can link a promotion to the Olympics or a football tournament or whatever's going on that is publicly around... a Royal Wedding, the World Cup, anything. You can link to all sorts of events.

There's lots of ways you can do events. Think about putting on a special event because the great thing about an event is, if you do it the first two or three years, it then becomes 'an event' in the calendar, one that the local area or specific target group get accustomed to experiencing and thus it becomes established. There is then a massive amount of press and media exposure to be gained, which we will talk about next, but simply arranging an event will again allow you to mix with those who you are trying to sell to or those who can lead you directly to those who might buy. An event is a perfect opportunity to gather data and to develop relationships that lead to more purchases... And you can get all sorts of people then to pay you to have the event. In fact, this is how Ben's brain works; *you don't pay for the event!*

How can you manage that? Because you do strategic alliances to share the data from the event!!

So the way *I* look at it, the way I'm encouraging <u>you</u> to look at it... a joint venture can be a paymaster, certainly a cost splitting partner. Put a special event on.

Allow me to give you an example... a client that's a large format printer. She's just had a business birthday. I showed her how to invite other people from other companies, so the birthday event didn't cost her anything. But she got 56 people through the door.

Another client, a retailer of bathrooms and tiles, held an anniversary party and he invited loads of guests. I suggested that to make it more attractive we should put on some cheese and wine and get some entertainment in. My client was enthusiastic about the idea, but was initially concerned about the cost of the party. Instead of thinking, "It can't be done," we asked instead, "How can I make it happen? How could we create a special event without making it an expensive event?"

Guess what he did?

A call was made to a wine dealer and he was asked if it might be valuable to him if he met and engaged with a group of higher income business people who pretty much all buy wine for home consumption. The dealer was almost obviously keen and so he was invited to come along and mix with and talk to the businesses' client base and asked to simply bring along a few sample of his wines so that clients might taste it and purchase from him. The same style of approach was made to a catering company so that we could put on some nibbles, and to entice guests to come along we invited entertainers, both musicians and magicians... and ended up with a complete ensemble of ingredients for a social gathering. In addition, we 'allowed' each invited trader to bring along a selection of their best clients and thus my client had a very successful event AND fresh warm prospects to talk to!

My client had a successful evening, even gathering new prospects, with virtually no outlay financially!! An event for free! Now that's what I call marketing your business!

Could you do that? Could you create a special event and work with strategic partners to make it happen without massive cost? Of course you can!! And imagine the return you can enjoy when you get this right!

Follow a simple process: strategic planning, strategic alliance, joint ventures, and special events. Remember, it's not difficult, it's just different.

Now of course, going one step further, if you stage a special event and you choose to share with somebody so that you might facilitate a larger event and not have all of the organisational hassles to yourself, what do you do then?

Well, let's suggest that you do a 'Summer Ball', and you invite all of your clients, your industry peers and some influential people from suppliers and providers. Knowing that some of your larger clients and suppliers often already do special events themselves, you might say to your marquee company that you're looking for the cost to be hugely reduced but that they will get several introductions to really big companies at your event... and then you do a deal at a much better rate for the marquee, because the marquee provider is going to get some very heavy contacts and potential for more business. So he's quoted you £10,000 and you get it for £5,000.

And then you go to your large company/supplier guest and you say, "Look, this party is going to cost me £10,000 to put on but I'm going to invite 300 clients, and other business owners. And that's good for you, for your profile, so please can you contribute out of your marketing budget towards the cost. It's costing me £10,000; can you give me £5,000 towards it?" And they say they will. So your £5,000 from your supplier pays for your marquee hire!! Your event costs nothing!

And that's exactly the sort of technique that I am suggesting and you can manage. You bring in two or three partners, you get an event on the calendar and <u>all</u> three partners bring their own clients. So you swell the numbers which improves your reach, but you divide up the cost which means you don't pay. Is it possible? Damn right.

Do you want to grow your business without cost? Let's do it!

There is no such word as can't, remember? You ask instead, "How can I?"

You just have to think creatively. And they all go together. If you 'get out more', you will meet more people to form alliances with... and together you'll come up with excuses for special events and you'll share.

Let me clarify something for you right now... these are not wild ideas... these are proven strategies. These are techniques that with a little thought, a lot of planning and some dedication YOU can grow your business massively with. Do you want more enquiries than you can handle? Do you want Enquiry Overload? Then make yourself committed to applying these ideas and over a few months or a year you will explode your business!! Go for it!

PR

Would you like more exposure in the press? Would you like to extend your publicity reach easily?

Well have a guess what you do when you've had a special event?

Get some PR from it! Splash it all over the papers, because it's news!

And here's what you do. You say, "Dear newspaper, have you seen that special event that's going on? This glamorous 'Summer Ball' that's being showcased? It is a regular event every year, are you covering it?" They will probably say they've never heard of it, but don't be put off!

You say…

"There are exclusive invites to a select prestige business group (or wealthy community notoriety) and it's the talk of the town… why not ensure you have the news and gossip? Would you like me to make sure you get a press privileged pass?"

You will soon hook them in… I don't think there is a journalist anywhere that doesn't become interested when you offer free food and wine! They will come along and you get the exposure in all of the press! Free publicity!

An event is news!

You have a great event… it gets publicised and so subsequent events are even easier to create and stage because people heard about the previous one! Three years later, people are paying you to attend! You've got an event that publicises your name everywhere, and it's costing you nothing! How cool is that?

So you can create special events, if you've formed your alliances, because you've made contacts when you've got out more. And every special event, you splash all over everywhere because you get some PR from it.

And by the way, I'm not saying just newspapers, but I'm saying press. Industry specific magazines, magazines in affinity groups, etc. Get press coverage, it's excellent.

Why does this work so well? If I gave you a magazine or a newspaper now, if you picked up a magazine or a newspaper now, do you know what you'd read in it? The articles, not the adverts.

So, get yourself in as an article.

We don't read adverts, but if there's a headline that shows a crazy photograph of some guy climbing a brick wall with a bike stuck over the top of it, you'd think, "What the blooming hell's going on there? Some silly stunt by a bike shop! Taking a bike over an assault course, for charity!" The fact is, it got your attention. You duly noted the bike shop and you as a bike shop owner have just scored an awareness victory with no cost.

Be creative. Why not consider linking in with outdoor activity centres, and get a bunch of underprivileged school children from the cities to come out and experience an outdoor activity that your company helped provide? This will definitely give you coverage but also genuinely gives you a worthwhile glow as you can help others whilst still helping yourself. Create a story and splash it all over the media!

We miss hundreds of opportunities with PR. Get people dressed up in Mickey Mouse costumes, get a member of staff to take part in a charity event, sponsor a local cause, or stage a function. There are actually lots of PR scenarios... have you won a large contract recently? Increased your staff levels thus becoming a benefit to the community through your creation of jobs? How about your latest client who just happened to be a distressed former social challenge e.g. a pensioner who was afraid and you gave security to ease their worry? Think creatively then splash it all in the press.

Again look to *give*... help others and then it feels even more worthwhile both to you and the media.

Following on from these ideas, one of my clients gave a kitchen to an older couple who just deserved something for themselves after being model citizens and parents but having gone without for the sake of others... a dream kitchen was given away and covered on TV... imagine that? How much would it usually cost you to have 30 seconds on TV, let alone 30 minutes? Huge pound for pound payback but it also then made local press and radio!! Incredible... but it took an unselfish 'giving' first. So, think about PR as a major weapon in your arsenal!

And just to illustrate how powerful PR, have you ever heard of Ratners? A prominent jewellery chain that was very successful in the eighties? Their owner Gerald Ratner initiated the downfall of the whole empire by saying the wrong thing at a corporate function that was subsequently splashed all over the press. PR articles in the press destroyed a huge successful chain of stores in just a few weeks! Or how about Red Letter Days? The well-known experience day company owes and attributes its huge growth to a PR article in its early days that gave it massive national exposure and from there it never looked back. Believe me, PR is hugely powerful and it must be included into your weaponry for growing your business.

Referrals

Simply put, I guess everyone understands the principle of getting referrals in business... and equally I presume that nearly every business owner would say that they do in fact get referrals, but I want to focus for a moment on actually *driving* referrals. I want you to look at how you can get several of them each week instead of the odd one a month or a quarter year.

Driving referrals, so that everyone who deals with you gets to such a level of satisfaction and closeness that they want to encourage others to be with you, is where I would like you to focus next. Thus the next stage of Enquiry Overload is gathering referrals from relationship building.

You know, on the surface, this is common sense, isn't it? On the surface, every business knows about building relationships and getting referrals because all businesses do... but in practice, how many do you get?

Possibly more importantly, how many do you ask for?

It may sound a little silly to ask such an obvious question, but how many referrals do you actually ask for? And how do you do the asking?

Could we learn a way to ask for referrals that gives you a much higher chance of getting them? And if you did, then could you also *create* opportunities that allowed you to ask for them more often?

Again, let us remind ourselves that there is no such word as can't! Always ask instead, "How can I?" How can I ensure my business gathers raving fans and enjoys massive referrals?

Firstly, let's look at the way you might have asked for referrals in the past, or indeed the way you have heard others ask for referrals around you.

How does it go? Most people's referral asking is, "If you know anybody, you know, that might, erm, want something like this then, erm, tell them to give us a call"!! That's not really very exciting, is it?

A far better question is, "Who do you know who... " and then add a slightly different slant to the end of the question that offers a release from pressure as to the quality of the referred name and its intention to buy.

For example, you have given them your service in HR advice... you've rewritten employment contracts and guided them as to disciplinary procedures etc. You've sold them well and they are very happy. Ask them, "Who do you know in your business circle that also employs several staff and that like you have probably experienced the odd difficulty with staff over disputes or disciplines involved? Who would you know in a business of similar size?"

Now you will probably have got them thinking immediately because you've steered their mind into a specific direction, rather than leave the request open. You have asked their mind to think of 'people they know in similar business situations'. This is *not* the same as asking them 'who they know who wants to buy something'. The critical difference here is that if you ask them 'who they know who might want to buy', their mental programme runs something along the lines of, "I don't want to say they want to buy because I don't know for sure and don't want to get into trouble for steering you wrong so I will say nothing." They offer no help for fear of wrong help. By asking with a twist in emphasis you are, after all, only asking who they know in businesses that are similar... and there's no threat to offering that information. Thus, a twist to slightly ease direct pressure in their mind as to the certainty of the referral buying gets a lot more names and introductions in response.

Think a little next time you are with a client and then ask them a question along the lines of "Who do you know that might be in a similar position?" and see what happens. My promise is that when you get proficient at this, you'll start to hear them reel off a couple of names immediately... and that's a good start!

But I'd like you to get even more than a couple! I want you to get so good at this that your business runs on referrals so let's see how you might improve to yet another level.

My question to really lever referrals is, "Who do you know who you *care* about...?"

Why the twist? Why ask who they care about, and how do we get to this level?

It's easy if you 'Put the Cook in the Kitchen'!

You see, the critical factor is that you cannot ask about who they care about until you've got them in an emotional state i.e. one where they are linked in with feelings, not merely intellect. You need to get them into a caring state of mind. The person you're asking is in *mental* mode, not *feeling* mode, so asking them to start accessing emotions as to who they care about is not going to get them to just switch to that deeper level. You need to get them operating emotionally first and so the best way is to get them *emotionally* linked to what you've done for them.

So the process to get lots more referrals starts with getting them to access emotions and especially emotions linked to your product. I call it, 'Put the Cook in the Kitchen', and here's why.

Imagine that I am a chef and you ask me about my absolute favourite recipe, one that I am famous for and one that I am supremely proud of. Guess what I do? How would I usually react?

Well most probably in my mind I would flip straight into automatic mode, because I'm so used to doing this recipe, and I'll start actually playing the role through as I describe to you the skill at which I create this wonderful concoction. I will start to speak with energy and passion about how great I can make this recipe and I will talk you through the various stages, explaining at each juncture exactly why the process is critical and why the way I do it ensures incredible results as opposed to the way most others do it and just getting average results. If it's a cake, you'll hear me describe how I'll get the flour and I get the eggs, and I beat it up and then put it in the oven, and I make sure it's only this specific type of flour and the specific type of butter at very precise ingredient measures etc. etc. I start playing the role through, because I'm so used to doing this recipe. And if you get me talking about it, I'll start to enthuse about how the mix has got to be right, and how it raises to the right level, and the temperature's critical, and timing's everything. I'm talking about *my* recipe because *I love* it. But I get *enthusiastic and passionate* about it. Then I'm emotionally linked. (You've probably experienced this type of process hundreds of times when you ask somebody about the interest in their life... they easily get 'carried away'! Well I use the example of cooking because chefs are usually very emotional about their creations and the illustration serves to highlight that when you get them to focus on what they love doing, the emotions come out naturally. They almost change into another person as they get going!)

Now the point is, you have now got them connected on an emotional level. So use this approach reference with your product or service. Get your client 'in the kitchen', talking about what you've done for them and how it has helped. Get them to relive the experiences of pain before you solved their problem and get them to relive the feelings of massive relief when the issue was resolved. Stir them into an emotional state linked with what you have done for them. It's important that they feel emotionally linked to what you've given them; they feel you've done a great job. They feel it was saving them hassle; they feel that you've just made them happy, solved all their problems, and they just thank God they've met you! You get them back into the zone of when you gave them good service, and at that point, you ask who else do they know that they *care* about? Because if it's people you care about, wouldn't you want them to feel like you feel? And if it was someone you cared for e.g. like a brother, sister, other family member or friend, wouldn't you want them to experience the same relief from threat or pressure or whatever the original problem was? Yes, you would!!

And when they are in a feeling state, an emotive state, then they'll think, "Oh yeah, I wouldn't want anyone to get the bad problem I had before. I would want someone to feel like I feel now, so yes, talk to this person."

You will find that asking who they care about shifts the emphasis. In their mind you have got them into a different role... almost where they will feel it is their duty to help if they have discovered something that is beneficial and they do really care, then they have a duty to pass it on. It is incredibly powerful! It will give you absolutely massive returns when done well!

It is not easy though. It will take a bit of practice and it takes skill.

The critical part is the emotion part. If I merely ask you on an intellectual level, "Who do you know?" the reply you'll give me is, "Oh I don't know right now. I've got several, I'll dig them out." Nothing comes. And that's what usually happens when folks ask for referrals.

To make me want to give you referrals, get me back in the kitchen! Remind me just how good your service was. Remind me of the problems I was facing before I met you. Remind me how I felt. Remember how I was worried. Remember how I was stressed. Remind me how I felt when you came along. Ask me how you performed your service... did we do that right? And did we do that right? And did we do that right? Yes. And how do you feel after? Oh, fantastic! Great! And *now* ask me, at this moment, who else I care enough about to protect from all of that pain I was experiencing previously and follow it up with a twist along the 'similar business' line and watch your referrals double or treble!!

I promise, practice this and then ask at the right moment and you'll get loads of referrals.

One final thought... we all have similar psychological patterns or mind programmes that when we understand and learn to play along with can be hugely useful in our attaining what we want. I have mentioned them before. One such programme is the need for 'significance'...the need to feel important or recognised. When you understand this core human psychology, applying it to referrals we could appreciate that by giving a referral a person gains a level of significance in another person's eyes thus actually we can even intimate to the client we are asking for referrals that by giving names he will become important to the named person because he has saved them from pain. We can leverage up the feelings that motivate a human. We can actually stimulate more referrals by playing on their need to feel significant.

Try mentioning how it could be highly likely that the person they are referring could be extremely thankful and that they are most likely to think highly of the referrer for passing on the name!

It's fantastic how much you can boost your business when you apply some better thinking! You really will watch your enquiries explode as you practice and refine these techniques!

The Internet

Now then, you know about the Internet and you know that there's lots and lots of 'hype'. In fact you are probably suspicious of all the stories that claim fortunes made form the web, however you are also probably just curious enough to want to know more about it and just greedy enough to want it to be true because then it could work for you!

Well, some good news... it *is* possible to make a fortune from the web. Possible but not simply a question of posting up a few pages and watching the cash flood in! So let us talk for a few minutes about the Internet and what it can do for your business and specifically about how to generate enquiries and sales.

Firstly, do you know anyone that is currently making lots of money from the Internet?

Well I do. I know several... and I know first-hand that Internet income is possible in 'traditional business' not merely Internet marketing where one is sold a 'make millions by clicking here just once' pipe dream!

As I have said, it *is* possible. There *are* a few serious Internet marketers who make literally millions from the web. There *are* a few techniques that they all understand that are critical factors, but what can you do? Let's look at it, shall we?

First off, you need a website! Not rocket science! You cannot make money from the Internet if you haven't got a presence so**, if you haven't already got a website, get one. And, if your website isn't e-commerce driven and database driven, make it so.**

However, assuming that you can see the potential to be gained from the Internet, the questions are, how can we generate enquiries from this source? And how do you get to a stage where there is money being made whilst you are asleep or on holiday or doing something else? Because the idea is to generate not only more enquiries, but more income streams.

Now some people say, "Yes, but Ben, you don't understand. My business isn't like that. I can't sell my business off the Internet." Or they tell me that it's not the way their industry works, people just don't use the Internet or wouldn't ever buy their product/service from a source such as this. "It needs a personal touch because there are so many variables."

Believe me, I have heard all of the reasons why you "can't use the Internet for my business"! Remember though, there's no such word as can't!

For example, you might appreciate how you can buy a packet of crisps from the Internet because that's just a packet of crisps but anything major needs a person to talk to. Well, is that the case? Is the Internet only valuable in smaller more static purchases where there are fewer variables or fewer things that can go wrong?

Let's look back. A few years ago, when the World Wide Web first sprang into our lives, it was a source for information on topics we couldn't easily access... a sort of glorified library with a few shops attached where you could buy simple items. The consumer gradually became hooked on the convenience and numbers climbed... and then the business community realised it held a source of shopper so it started selling in earnest. For example, seven or eight years ago you'd never have bought a car off the Internet, would you? I mean, you could understand how people would buy a holiday but you're never going to buy a car off the Internet. Or you're never going to buy a house off the Internet. Now of course all of these items are offered for sale over the World Wide Web. But in fact, technically speaking, although they don't do the transaction online for a house or a car, you still buy it; you make a decision and you surf it, search it through. It is 100% used as a research and examination tool that is a critical part of the decision-making process.

So you just simply cannot afford not to have a website. The world of buying and selling today is vastly different than it was only a few years ago and our expectations are different too. Every day literally millions of potential purchasers are surfing the Internet looking for help and looking to spend. You must get in front of them. Indeed look internally... look at you. Your habits have changed. Today, before you consider getting into your car and driving to do research... maybe to look at a new home or a new vehicle or a new electrical appliance... you searched the Internet first! AND often times you are quite happy to buy from the web-based provider.

And this is the point. A website should be an income stream, not just a brochure. It should at the very least drive lots of enquiries so that people who have searched you out have then seen something they like, read something they understand and are now attracted to talk with you about the finer personal details of their potential purchase.

It isn't just about business *now* either. It is about your future.

It may well be the case that right now your business doesn't need the Internet because your current clients are finding you without the net, so why bother? Well, any business in this day and age that wants to still be around in three or four years' time must move with the times. It is about tomorrow as much as today.

The point is, and I'll just reiterate this point because some people <u>still</u> say to me, "Ben, you don't understand, our business is different, our customers are not that sort of people" etc... the point is, that the customer of tomorrow might be very different than the customer of today.

When I hear this type of comment I ask, "Are you planning to be in business still in five years' time?" And the puzzled reply is, "Well, yes, but what's that got to do with it?" Well, what it has got to do with it is that the customer of today will die and be replaced and the customer of tomorrow that's coming through is in a world now of Internet. The customer of tomorrow thinks differently to the customer of today. The customer of tomorrow is already acting differently as they grow through. The customer of tomorrow has grown into a world of immediacy and everything accessible when they want it through Internet advantages. So if you want a business of tomorrow you've got to tune to the people coming through, not the people now.

Does that make sense?

If your business is geared around the people that buy from you now, good. But if your business is *only* geared to the buying habits of people buying now, beware because your business needs to be able to cope with the people who are going to buy tomorrow and their buying habits. Research styles will all be different, and they will all be Internet driven.

And believe me, four or five years from now, more and more so.

So make sure you have an Internet presence.

When it comes to enquiry overload, there's lots of things you can do with an Internet site, or with Internet presence, to generate enquiries.

Primarily there is a hope that potential clients will find your website sooner or later but you cannot afford to leave it to chance. Building a website and then not actively spending attention on how you promote it is a bit like spending loads of money on a brochure only to collect the printed pile of brochures and leave them hidden in a cupboard where no one can see them!! Would you do that? No! So never assume that buying a website in itself is enough. It isn't. No one will see into your cupboard unless you drive them to it. You would need to get a printed brochure 'out there' and in the same way you need to get your electronic one 'out there'.

You must initially consider doing all of the electronic aids to promotion that you can. Search engine optimisation, for example, along with correct use of keywords and site links and all of the technical aspects... all the various things you can do behind the scenes mechanically, but you must talk to somebody technically proficient about that.

A word of caution here... when you don't know something very well, it is not easy to decide if what you are being told is the truth or only partially true. Indeed shopping when unsure as to what to buy is highly dangerous and leaves you open to buying the wrong item. I can only speak from painful experience as I have been misled by poor Internet advisors and site builders myself. I spent a couple of thousand pounds with a local contact with 'good intentions and a fair price' only to find that it cost me a lot more time and money than it would have done if I had done it correctly in the first place. My simple advice is that the old adage of 'getting what you pay for' is never more applicable so spend on the most expensive and get the best. Cheaper providers are cheaper for a reason... they may talk a good talk, probably repeating accurate words and even perhaps understanding the theory, but actually leave you very short when it comes to practice and results. Spend a lot... spend on the most expensive, and you will probably be nearer the ideal outcome. You see, site builds all vary. Types of code vary and structures vary... and these are all non-visible to the eye when seeing a finished product, but they are very visible to search engines and can definitely hinder promotion that gets you seen.

Poor build design can seriously cost you money in respect of lost ranking and lost surfers finding you. Better to spend a lot more but get it back many times over from a successful shopping flow. Then search engine optimisation will work when you have studied the keywords people are searching with and when your site is written with correct levels of keyword usage and page saturation etc. For more specific help and real time advice and guidance, go to www.thebusinessboosteracademy.co.uk and inside the academy there is a stack of constantly updated material and direct one-to-one coaching help.

Okay, so you must talk with a professional provider and utilise all of the electronic options available, and I might add this in itself for some products is all it takes to have a massive business... but it is rare that it is that easy! There is only so much you can do from things like search engine listings unless you are spending a lot of money and really paying. Things like pay-per-click and AdWords should definitely be explored, but please do your maths! Make the right word choice and know how many visitors become purchasers before you commit! Especially on lower priced goods.

So, aside from electronic stuff, what can you do?

Well, for example, whenever you have anything printed, everywhere you have your logo, have your web address prominently displayed.

What's in your logo? Look at your logo. Now if you were to print that logo anywhere, for example on a T-shirt, how would you print it on a T-shirt? What would you print? Is it just a name or is it including contact details, specifically the website?

Try this... ensure that if you put your logo onto anything anywhere, part of the logo is a Freephone number and a web address. Just a little tip... make it so that as your logo is drawn, underneath it is a Freephone and a web address. Almost create a badge that incorporates both main contact points in the design and then literally every time you print anything you have given the onlooker a chance to get hold of you in the way that suits them best. They will look for a web address. It is just the way we have become educated and it will help drive enquiries the more it is displayed.

(As an aside, I mention Freephone numbers because I believe it will help you promote your business in two main ways... firstly, prospect clients will be drawn to the no risk of expense when enquiring because it is free and secondly, the non-geographic number doesn't tell them that you are located somewhere where they perceive you cannot look after them properly. Lots of people do use non-geographic numbers, not just 0800 but 0845 or 0870. These are widely accepted by the consumer now. If your phone number is something they don't recognise as local, your prospect might. For example, question where you are based and interpret that as being too far away whereas if it's non-geographic nobody really questions it. They just go, "Oh that's the number." Results are proven to be better if it's non-geographic. So consider 0845 and 0870 but especially consider getting a 0800 Freephone number, it is the best.)

In your logo, always have your URL or web address easily visible, but what else can we do to drive Internet enquiries?

Again, let me cast your mind back to when we spoke about the issues of networking and joint ventures and indeed PR. All of these are profound ways of promoting your business and they are all supreme at adaptation to the web. Your site needs traffic and over and above spending lots of money to advertise and get your web address out there, you can drive traffic in the same way as gathering enquiries offline. Networking web-style is about talking to other business owners and always promoting, "Go to my website and have a look,"-type conversation. *Actively* talk about and push your website as a means to find out about your company and do business with you. Literally mention it whenever you can... do not talk about brochures or necessarily even offer them... merely tell them if they wish to find out about you and your offer, rather than a brochure they should go to the website and have a really good look around.

And extending from this, if you are looking to establish partnerships or joint ventures, then why not try the same thing electronically? Why not talk with other site owners and look to establish reciprocal trading links... a banner click through-type on each site offering visitors the chance to crossover? Links, by the way, not only drive visitors from a chosen site but links also massively effect search engine rankings. One of the things search engine 'spiders' read is the size, or impression of size, that your site creates. If your site has a lot of meaningful links, it goes right up search engine listings. I say meaningful because you can also get your site quarantined if it thinks you have engineered false or meaningless links to non-related sites so aim for lots of links and as you will be linking with businesses that also serve your target audience, then they will be by nature connected and meaningful.

So please look really hard at how you can make links or strategic alliances with online trading partners.

Remember, the principle that you applied to promote you in a network sense was to 'get out more'. The best way to get people to know about your website is to get *it* out more. So, traditional exposures drive traffic to your website.

Without digressing too much, understand we are in an information age. We're all programmed 'to find out first', thus clients of yours are also trying to find out first. Every single one of us must have a website that gives information away.

Imagine if you've got to buy something you've never bought before... an insurance policy, a mortgage, a pension, a holiday home, anything.

If you were to go and buy it, how would you know what you're hearing is true? How would you think in unknown territory?

You wouldn't have a clue. So what's one of the first things you're going to want to do if ever you want to buy something new?

Talk to someone who knows. And probably more than one. You're buying something that you don't normally buy. You're buying something in unfamiliar territory. You're going to want to find out first, aren't you?

Would you buy anything you'd never bought before comfortably without finding information out first?

No.

It's generic human psychology. You are in an information gathering process when you're buying for the first time. In fact, the more the purchase involves potential jargon, potential technicalities and quite a lot of money, the more you're going to want to make sure you get the right data. You as a purchaser will go and find some information out and you'll want 'free reports', you'll want 'buying guides', you'll want 'hints and tips'. You do not want to buy wrong... and gathering knowledge helps you feel that you are making an informed choice thus you're not going to buy wrong. Knowledge protects.

And the person that gives you up front loads of information, lots of help, will engender your loyalty even though you're not aware of that. And if that help is unbiased, if you hear comments like "Yeah, no problem, any time you want to come back and ask me, any help you need ask me," or, "Here's all the information. Hey, watch out for this, don't get tricked. Hey, listen, if you're thinking of it, just call me, but if you don't call me, these are what to watch out for, good luck,"... any of that sort of comment, they all help you feel like they are helping you and consequently ease you towards buying from them.

It's true that this is the process that people go through when they're buying something new, and if they haven't got somebody they instantly call, like a trusted advisor, they will do some shopping around using the Internet. More importantly, your next year's customer *will*, your five years' time customer *will*, your buyer in five years' time is going to be today's student.

More and more people are doing their unbiased research first... because it's the preliminary information before they go into buying mode, and then they'll know what they're asking for so they don't feel stupid, and they'll speak to three people and then providing all those people are going to tell them the truth, because they know what the truth is... well, then one of those three people is going to be lucky, and if you're the one they like, it is you that gets 'lucky'.

But it's got to first match up with what they've already done because then they feel safe, because the two ends meet. So your Internet presence must be a source of the information a potential client needs to become a purchasing client and it must be linked to all possible areas that your potential client will visit. What I am saying then is simply have a 'Free Report' or '7 Top Tips' buying aid on your website as a Free Download. Make sure that it looks highly visible... make certain the title sounds appealing... and make sure that to access this valuable information, they enter a name and email field so that you can talk to them at a later stage and 'help' them with their prospective purchase. Follow Up... remember!!

Okay, after using technology to promote your site and then traditional approaches like, 'Get *it* out more', and 'Strategic *web* alliance links', the third thing you want to do is PR.

Now how do you do PR on your website? Well there are loads of news sites on the web. There are loads of sites which do 'consumer guides', or there are sites with their own web magazines. Why not look for sites that possibly attract your similar audience and offer to contribute articles? You could create news articles as you would traditionally, but use them as electronic news articles and get them splashed all over web pages. The truth is, if you ever talk to an editor of any news based magazine, they all need content. It is a bind when week after week, or month after month, there is a page that needs filling and something of interest has to be found. Contrary to many people's belief, theirs is a constant need so get contributing and promote the hell out of your website!

Create the 'PR event' then; together with an eye-catching picture and an attention-grabbing headline, contribute your article.

And by the way, make it newsy. <u>Nobody</u> is blatantly going to publish an article that is merely an advert with words. Make your PR interesting to the relevant audience. Think from their perspective.

Remember also that the editor's challenge is constant. Good copy is often in short supply – they may use something several weeks after you sent it in if there is a dry news week.

For Internet enquiries, follow the same offline process.

We all have the same amount of hours, we have the same opportunities. Never say, "I don't get the same opportunities." Ask instead, "How can we create the opportunities?" Remember, there's no such word as can't!

And if you can just get that pattern to run every time you have a challenge in your head. Every morning you get up and, as soon as something doesn't quite go the way you planned it, you ask, "What can I do about this? How can I overcome it? Who can I go and talk to? What do I need to do?" And you're quickly running four or five questions. Once you get into that habit, you find that you find the answers.

Social Media

Such is the speed of change in today's modern world that modern news spreading is almost instant with the innovation of what we refer to as Social Media. Now unless you have been living in a bubble for the last three years, you will have heard about blogging, Facebook, Twitter and the likes, and so we simply must look at how this modern phenomenon is impacting your business... and more importantly how you might harness the power of this media to drive your business future.

The world is now so Instant Messenger-linked that major news happenings, such as planes crashing and bombs going off or even bank robberies, that the news media is alerted by the person in the street! The days of the person being informed by the media are over... and the media spend thousands of pounds employing people to just watch Twitter feeds to pick up on stories!!!

Truthfully, this subject warrants several books in itself and so for now I wish only to clarify a couple of misleading thoughts.

Firstly, if you are a person who is reading this and thinking that it's okay but not really relevant to your business or business world... WRONG!! You cannot be further from the truth.

I guess that at first you probably even thought that the Internet wasn't going to take off, that personal computers and mobile phones weren't really necessary and thus a social media is only a fad for the young.

Maybe in some circles it started that way...but it is no so embedded into culture that it cannot go away. Huge corporates are playing the Twitter and Facebook game and so it is too heavily invested in to die.

Thus if they are pushing it, you need to ride it.

Your business must have a Facebook presence. Why?

Because the growth rate of members is nothing short of historical. It's amazing and frightening and mind-blowing. Soon one billion people will be connecting on it!! AND think of the profile of those people? Are they the down and outs? NO!!! They are at least affluent enough to have what we refer to as 'smartphones' that cost hundreds each model! They have accounts for banking and more likely credit for bill payments. This is a buoyant marketplace looking to connect and then find solutions to their problems. To help, have a look at www.facebooksuccesstips.com

Their problem might be weight gain or searching for another love... or it might be childcare or health issues... or it might be employment or income... or it might be fixing their washing machine that morning!!! Everybody has something on their minds! Your job is to be in front of their minds in any moment... and Facebook and Twitter are so in your face that you MUST be in the field of play.

You can have 'pages' which is like a mini website on Facebook... and indeed you can add to that with Google Places and so many other links. Again there is a ton of stuff all dedicated to this subject in www.thebusinessboosteracademy.co.uk and inside the members' area are dozens of highly proven and recommended partner providers so that you can be safe and sure if you need this doing and don't know anyone to provide for you.

You can set up a Facebook and Twitter account for free and you can do it yourself within five minutes, so there really is nothing to fear. You will, of course, have to choose a 'profile name' which may or may not still be available as there might be another person or business already on there with a similar name... but don't be put off. Push to find a name that suits. For example, you might have a business that is called

'Beautiful Blinds', and then as you search you see that some other person has a profile call 'Beautiful Blinds' and so you might have to change to 'Beautiful Window Blinds' or 'Best Dressed Windows'. It won't matter because as you develop your presence, you actually add comments each day where you talk about how blinds make windows look great, how they impact the mood in a room, how they can be made for little money etc. etc. and it is the writing or articles that people read first... and when they decide that they like what you talk about they feel a little connected and at that point they are triggered to enquire if blinds indeed are on their agenda.

It isn't an immediate process but it is a powerful and proven one.

Your task is to start the process today so that without you knowing it someone is slowly becoming a fan in the background and one day steps up with an order. The sooner you start, the sooner you have a new client.

You create the presence and indeed use the presence to drive traffic to your website... and use the pages to 'give away' free 'How to Buy Blinds Safely' guides, and you strategically link all of the forums so that the interested person is gently schmoozed into a comfort zone where they spend.

Add to this mix a Twitter account where you make several comments each day... comments that show your feelings and commitment to your task... and comments that show you as a person with a normal life and thus the reader or linked person 'connects' again.

In short, Facebook, Twitter and a blog are the modern mediums towards you getting your name out there and creating a fan base.

Your mission in business today is creating a fan base, and fans are created when you feed them news and ideas that help.

I have mentioned blogs... so what is a blog?

Again, it maybe warrants a whole book on blogging... here is something that might help www.successfulbusinessblogging.com but essentially a blog is like a modern diary that is 'open'.

It stems from the words 'Web Log' which was and is a simple log book or diary type book that is on the Web as opposed to merely a hard copy book in your library.

Thus a 'Web Log' became a blog and today we are avid readers of other people's diary or blog entries as it helps us connect with people with a) similar issues and pains, and b) solutions to those pains.

You would be well advised to create a blog, and it again can be done for no money. simply log on to a forum such as Google and go to Google BlogSpot, as an example. There are hundreds of free blog forums, so please have a look around, or indeed you can create your one using a platform such as WordPress which is possibly the foremost blogging platform in the world. You can create your own 'site' with your company name and a ton of excellent designs all for nothing, and all in literally less than 15 minutes.

And as for content, you simply comment! I don't mean meaningless chatter about the weather, if indeed it is intended to be a business forum, but genuinely telling brief stories about clients and challenges and how you have helped and want to help more people. Eventually it gets found and shared and you have a fan base of several thousand.

When you invest a little dedicated time and energy into these modern marketing methods then, simply put, the results can be dramatic.

Frankly I strongly advise stopping spending in traditional advertising mediums and reinvesting the same time and money into this type of area. It might be that you pay someone to write and post articles or design pages and add content. Again, all of these services are now available. Inside of the academy, we have trusted providers from as little as £200 a month... but there is no doubt whatsoever that these types of news and social media are here to stay and will only grow. If you don't get on this wave now, you miss out. It is that simple. And finally, we cannot leave this section without a note on YouTube and using video in your business.

Fact: YouTube is now the world's second largest and busiest search engine!!!

Google dominates our world in the early part of this twenty-first century and Google owns YouTube!

Add to this the fact that we are so much into video that every person on the planet almost has a mobile phone with video capture facility!!!

Your business therefore MUST get with it! You MUST incorporate video into your business promotion life.

The good news though is that as it has become such a massive part of our modern world, the prices for producing video are dropping and no longer do you need a corporate budget of £10,000+.

Indeed again there are facilities available where for literally £300, you can have a video... or you can use the video capture on your new smartphone, and point and shoot and upload!! It is good enough!

You see, add a simple video to your website, and it adds YouTube traffic as well as Google traffic! Almost in 15 minutes, you massively improve your ranking and traffic to your website!! For two minutes invested into a point and shoot and upload exercise!

You need not be afraid either. It doesn't have to be professional... and some argue that it is more effective when it isn't 'polished' as we are now distrusting of 'polish' because we fear it masks the 'real'.

Your two minute home video can be uploaded onto your own YouTube channel for free! You can then link it to your emails and your website... and you can embed it into your website too.

Shoot a little video of you solving client's problems... you showing you as a person openly and honestly... shoot a video about your new venture and your new promotion and all of these are adding up top exposure and traffic... and traffic equals sales eventually.

Thus in closing this Social Media section, I cannot urge you strongly enough to seriously invest money and time into this area TODAY!!

If you think that having some help in this area would be useful then please contact the team... www.thebusinessboosteracademy.co.uk and we will help you NOW.

It might be a slightly challenging adoption phase, especially if until now you have always operated in a very 'traditional' sense, but having gone down this path myself over the last 12 to 18 months, I can promise that it is a journey worth taking... and within two or three months, you literally can be on a massively different and more rewarding path to business success!

Direct Sales

Here is an area where many people's initial reaction is a sharp intake of breath and a thought along the lines of, "Oh, I don't want a sales team."

Well, for a moment, allow me to firstly set the scene. Your business growth depends upon clients asking to pay for what you do in ever increasing numbers and probably paying increasing prices over an increasing range of items. Indeed, as the scope all around increases, so too will the requirements for running your growing empire. There will no longer be a facility for you to do everything. It won't even be possible, even if you wanted to do so... thus you'll be hiring others to take responsibility for the growing task list.

Now you will look at that task list and choose which to delegate and where the best areas are for your skills to be deployed... and your strength as the creator of the business might be that you *deliver* the service the best. For example, you might be a life coach and you are definitely very skilled at coaching your clients. However, when you are busy your time is consumed with actually doing the job – coaching, and nothing else gets done. Then when you finish with a client or have a gap in clients, because whilst you were doing the coaching you didn't manage other tasks, such as maintaining a marketing activity or presence, you have a drop in work volume and thus income. This is a classic 'feast and famine' scenario that most small businesses suffer from. To get around this issue of peaks and troughs, you need either to consistently do less coaching, so that your time is equally divided into coaching *and* marketing activity, or you'll need to delegate some coaching work which you probably don't want to do (in the belief that you are the best and no one can do as well as you!) or the third option is to delegate the marketing activity and have another entity gathering the work for you so that your efforts are concentrated on the actual coaching and building your reputation. At this juncture, then you are effectively hiring a direct sales force.

So, please let us assume just a couple of points 1) that you do actually want to grow your business and 2) that you want at some stage to enjoy more money and less stress from the process. To do this, you are going to have to allow others to do more and also force yourself to back off and do less; even in the areas you love doing. As we have talked about already, if you have a business that relies upon you, if your business is only generating cash when you are doing your stuff, then sadly **you do not have a business, you have a job!** In fact, you are worse off! Forget all about the ideology of not being told what to do and being free etc., you are now not even getting paid sickness or holiday pay, and the pressure is way beyond that of an employed role with a demanding boss! At least with a demanding boss you got paid, despite a poor performance sometimes... in this new role you don't get anything, unless you generate it! And very often you can even feel like you're working just to pay other people's salaries!!

So, getting very hard-nosed and real about this, unless you grow a business with a stream of income that still flows without your input, then you only have a job still!

Thus, we must examine how we can increase sales beyond your efforts... and a direct sales arrangement is the key.

Now what I *haven't* said so far is that you need to employ a team of hungry, hairy bottomed animals who terrorise the client into signing and leave a wake of damage behind them at every turn! No! 'Direct sales' does not have to conjure up the doorstep double glazing-style operation, nor does it have to pose a threat to your sanity.

The thought I want you to ponder on is this... just quickly remember the last time you went into your local post office. Tell me, what did you see? Do they merely just offer a mailing service and sell you stamps? No. These days the Post Office is a sales floor where you can buy greetings cards, telephone services, shoe repairs and much, much more. The Post Office staff aren't all trained in different sales skills, but they will directly sell you additional products. They are, in fact, then a direct sales force for the commodity provider.

So, my question to you is, "How can you grow a direct sales force using this illustration as a directional idea?

Ask empowering questions. There's no such word as can't, remember! Ask, "How can I?"

How can I create outlets for my product or service where others can sell it for me direct to the end user? Who do I know? What else does my client purchase?

And now whilst you think along these lines, all of the work we were doing together earlier where we looked at profiling and learning about and from our clients... all of that work pays off here. You can now identify many areas and other places of business where your client goes and where it really doesn't affect the host's trade if they also allow their clients to buy your offering.

Direct sales can be massive and you can have loads of outlets if you think constructively about where your client goes and then create a process where your 'offering' can be passed on without massive skills and time at the other end.

A few examples.

Have you ever been into a garden centre and seen barbeques for sale or conservatories? Do you think that was all a part of the garden centre's business, or do you think it was a direct sales operation by someone else merely operating through the garden centre's premises?

How about when you last purchased a television or computer, and the assistant also offered you extended warranty insurance? Do you think the electrical retailer is also now an insurance broker?

The world we live in is increasingly looking to work together. We will mention some techniques to grow sales in a little while and one of them is this principle in reverse almost... it is add-on products that suit your client. However, all that you need to do to create a direct sales force is to find another outlet or business that serves your client group and offer them your product as an add-on. It generates extra revenue for them from a client that is already in their sights and it generates huge extra sales and a client base for you without you being involved!

You *can* grow a direct sales force, and your mandate from today onwards is to always be asking the empowering questions. "How can I?" and "Who can I work with?"

Keep asking and ideas will flow but essentially there are lots of outlets that will gladly pass on your offering **if it doesn't hassle them and if it gives them something extra**.

Very quickly... I have mentioned this already and I shall mention it again... the main concern of a potential partner here is, "What is the risk?" They will ask themselves, "Is this arrangement ever going to cause me to have hassle from my existing client base because your product or service offering could make them unhappy?" Will he get more pain than extra pleasure out of the arrangement?

And then of course, "What's In It For Me?" The reward scenario for your new direct sales outlet... it doesn't need to be massive because he hasn't really worked for it, but it must be worthwhile.

There should be no paperwork, no training and no follow-ups for the partner... they merely pass on your offering, but there must be some financial gain too, so look at what you can give them. (If your offering is a little more involved or technical perhaps, then we have an answer for that too in a moment!) Again, remember it isn't all about one-off profits here... it could be very valuable in a gathering process but more on that later too.

Sit down now and look at the work you did before reference profiling and where your ideal client shops, and then look to set up other direct sales outlets for your business! Think constructively about what your target prospect has as a challenge in their mind… where they are also shopping… and how you can make it easy for the prospect whilst getting another person arena to add cash to your partner's sales volume.

You will find that with a little effort over the next year, you could establish four or five direct sales outlets pretty easily, and if all of these only do a fifth of what you're doing now, you will effectively have created a business that does what you're doing now without you doing anything!! Go for it!

Agencies

Now I mentioned a moment ago that some business offerings are a little more complicated than merely giving a host a greetings card and letting them sell it for a percentage commission. True, if you're selling insurance or financial products (although most stores these days have overcome that paperwork issue and offer such things), or if you are selling a product with many variables such as home refurbishment products where there is massive choice and only really a sales person with huge knowledge of the range can advise it might not work as easily. I appreciate that having a direct sales outlet for your home redecoration service in another person's shop might be difficult… but not if manned by a member of your staff that you have trained up! Then you are taking advantage of their client flow and their position and because you put the staff in, you represent no burden on the outlet.

However, for this illustration I shall concede that some offerings are more difficult to establish 'direct sales' outlets where you are not involved so here's where we look at agencies.

What then is the difference?

Well essentially, the agency might well be capable of completing the sale but they are primarily a feeder arrangement. As an agent, they offer your product or service but then having got their client to be interested they maybe take a few details, and pass on the work to you by telling the client that someone will call them. A good agency might well take a deposit, depending on the sale, or may certainly take the enquiry to a level of commitment or interest, rather than merely gathering a vague wishy-washy 'might like to look at' sort of non-enquiry. Your agent will be capable of selling the concept, even if the scope to complete the sale is beyond them initially and thus you will be fed half-completed sales. You gain hugely as you enjoy a halfway house where you're fed virtual sales without having to do all of the work yourself.

For many business owners, this is ideal. I have seen businesses grow massively by creating a network of 10 or 15 feeder agencies where every week, each agency passes an enquiry or two over and the original business is effectively trebling in size by merely filling out backend order sheets and filling in the more detailed technical knowledge.

By way of example, I have had a client that had a reciprocal agency arrangement with a related product serving the same client group and they both did extremely well out of it. My client offered a specialist Fire Risk Assessment especially to schools and he linked with a provider of fireproof blinds. Whenever he did a fire assessment at a school, he checked out the blinds and whenever their existing blinds were a fire risk and they needed new compliant ones, he suggested that new correct blinds be purchased. The blind company often merely filled out the order, as the selling or gathering had been done, and my client earned a very nice commission. The blind supplier was happy to pay as they'd had little work to do, and indeed they were very happy to reciprocate and introduce my client for assessment work whenever they approached an institution and supplied new blinds. It worked extremely well for both parties.

So look at your business and ask yourself, "How can I..?" Never ever say to yourself that you can't grow agencies! "There is no such word as can't!" You can grow your business massively, hugely, exponentially by adding an agency or two and a direct sales outlet or two! Go do it and let me know how you get on!

Telemarketing

Oooh!! Now here is an interesting area! How do you fancy having a telemarketing operation?!

As with the 'direct sales' thoughts, many of us have negative visions of telemarketing. Why? Well primarily because we're fed up with having to answer the phone to a scripted person who doesn't listen trying to sell us something like a new mortgage when we're quite happy with the one we've got!! Obviously I am using mortgages illustratively as most products these days have been pushed to us down the phone whilst we are sitting relaxing at home... and indeed the consumer marketplace has suffered more because most consumer-focussed offerings, such as windows, mortgages, insurances etc., have been heavily pushed at us using the telemarketing system.

It's also true though that actually using the telephone doesn't phase us... the equipment itself we will all use readily as you talk with friends or colleagues for hours when you want to. The key is you don't want to be 'pushed'. You want to choose how far the conversation goes and especially dislike it when it is obviously scripted and the person at the other end hasn't paused for breath yet because it doesn't tell him to yet! You hate it when you talk to them and it seems like you don't exist because they haven't been told to listen yet!

But does it have to be this way? Can the telemarketing idea be refined and used effectively by your business?

Yes!

Here's how. Firstly, examine what you don't like.

1.   You don't like being called and then immediately the person at the other end launches into a script where we aren't even asked if it's convenient!
2.   You hate the obviousness of a script... where they sound like they are reading. There isn't a personality and we don't want to talk to machines. Heaven forbid some of the latest offerings where in fact it *is* a machine that 'talks' to you!! Have the creators of that business got no idea what people want?!!
3.   You hate being spoken 'at', where there isn't room for dialogue. We don't even mind being called if they ask us something and actually treat us like individuals!
4.   You hate being called when they have their information wrong! For example, being asked to buy new windows when you've already replaced them all?!!

Truthfully though, sometimes you don't mind being called if the caller is polite, respectful and pleasant and even some of those times you end up buying because actually it was a pretty good offering and you *could* use it.

You see, the fact is you *can* be effective on the phone if you tweak your approach to match that which we wouldn't mind having come at us.

Make sure you train your people on the phone to ask questions... initially, for example, ask whether it is a convenient time or not! But questions create dialogue, which makes one feel involved and the psychology massively works to create more warmth and acceptance... it almost feels friendly!! Heaven forbid!

And then, of course, you need to ensure that whilst your people are trained, they are not obviously reading from a script and do indeed pause for breath! And once breathing, they identify if indeed it is a product or service that the target might ever have cause to use (critical if you are ringing cold data, which I don't really recommend).

So by turning around what we *don't* like, you *can* make telephone use effective... especially when ringing the data that you captured by your marketing exercise, such as competitions, or PR, or networking etc! You see, it all ties together! And that point is extremely important. I am mentioning all of these 'Enquiry Overload' ideas now because if you have done all that we talked about in the first section of this guide, then you can slot these ideas in and they will be massively effective. If you haven't done the data capture system, if you haven't recorded client information and if you are planning to just ring cold, then it is a different story altogether.

Gathering the data and recording in your CRM system details that you can recall to remind the target where you met, what you talked about etc. and all of a sudden the call doesn't feel like a telemarketing call to the recipient. It thus enjoys a much better response and your business grows accordingly. Telemarketing is a vital part of today's business growth, not least because by and large our roads are unreliable and slow, let alone our weather being diverse and potentially troublesome! We need to use the phone to reach the people we need to grow, so getting good at it isn't an option... it's a must!

Telemarketing is not hugely difficult when a little thought is applied. Apply some of these issues as we have discussed and create a message from you to the client that you would like to receive in return. Train your team or yourself to ask questions and involve the other party, not just talk 'at'.

One other thought... it is often said to be hard just getting people to work on the phone. The challenge in "finding telemarketers is difficult", I hear. Well, like lots of areas these days there is a great deal of competition and yes, it can be difficult more so in some areas, however one avenue I have tried and recommend is that of the 'part-time mum'.

You will probably find that a lot of ladies who are newly mums want to do something that keeps them in touch with the world of work - a world they used to live in and do not wish to miss out on whilst being a mum. They want to have other contacts outside of the home and the nursery and they want to show that they are capable... but there are limited opportunities perhaps, especially if they do not want to work at the local supermarket, until they can go back full-time.

Try placing an advert in the local press for a part-time position that would suit a mum with preschool-aged children, and even consider the home worker idea. Today's itemised billing, for example, even allows for every call to be tracked so it is certainly possible to track their labours.

Typically an ideal use for this type of telemarketing assistance is to source enquiries or to make appointments for you or your sales team to follow up, and certainly it is possible to source a great deal of talent within the 'new mum' community that can have a tremendous impact on the sales potential of your business. Again, in this modern world there is a massive 'outsource' community where you can find a supplier for your business and engage them on your terms and equally have them for as little or as much as you wish and always flexible. Indeed, in today's legislative society I do not recommend employing people! Sadly, in my personal humble opinion, the rush to protect the labourer from abusive employers has gone too far the other way and created legislation and rights that restrict an employer from a slack or poor quality employee. Thus I recommend outsourcing all but the most permanent needs of your business. Please consider this as an option... and not merely a more cost-effective option buy possibly because it allows you to search talent from a far wider pool i.e. global and that might mean that you have a much higher success rate once the person is engaged.

Try www.elance.com or www.peopleperhour.com as examples.

Telemarketing then, can and does work, and should definitely be something that you examine from now on.

Exhibitions

Have you ever been to an exhibition and thought it was a pretty good day out but that it must have cost them a fortune to put on that stand?! I have... and the events industry in recent years suffered because it got too much of a reputation for a 'jolly up', a good time for the 'boys' but actually apart from schmoozing a few good clients it brought in no return... consequently events and exhibitions began to get looked at as an expense and a waste.

I believe, however, that exhibitions are an excellent gathering ground for enquiries and a superb part of your overall strategy for ensuring enquiry overload.

So, how do you use exhibitions to get you what you want... more business growth... with little or no major spending!! More growth with less stress and more left over for your pocket!

Here's how.

Firstly Stop, Stand Back and ask better questions! Each exhibition must be considered on its own merits and the idea of exhibiting very carefully analysed. What are you really hoping to get from it? How much can you afford to commit to it in terms of resource? Manpower? Cash? Time? Is it really going to put me in front of the exact potential purchaser?

Assuming that you can identify an exhibition that you think its good to be at...why is it good to be there? What exactly do you think you will gain from it? Will you gain significance amongst the other players or competitors? Will you win the hearts of potential customers by wowing them with your offering and getting into their minds so that when they are ready to buy they will come to you? Will you actually meet people who are immediately looking to purchase your offering and thus can you expect to turnaround some immediate revenue?

Clearly examine exactly what it is that you are after.

Next give some deeper thought to your operational strategy. Exhibiting these days is not merely just about turning up... that's what the mediocre business owners do. Not you! You are a 'guerrilla' and you know the effectiveness of planning... and goal setting, and data capture etc. You are using the exhibition as a micro business venture. You know what you aim to get, you know how to measure it as to whether it was a success, you understand that you need a different approach and you are ready to take them by storm!

So having planned the stand and its appearance, make sure you also plan the activity. Make clear exactly what is expected of the staff... or you, for that matter. What is your customer attraction system? Do you smile sweetly and expect them to march over to the stand, cheque book in hand! More likely (especially now after learning all we've discussed) you will have a sheet for capturing the interested party's details and you will have perhaps used a competition to drive enquiries to your stand... and give yourself an excuse to capture details on your target group! (Competitions are a must! We'll look at them in the section on refining sales techniques but <u>never</u> consider an exhibition without a competition to drive data capture.)

Another idea is to use an entertainer or similarly interesting attraction to draw show visitors to your stand... magicians are good, for example, as is a loud exciting video or 'live' demonstrations. Whatever you do, give special dedicated attention to the thought of "How do you attract visitors to your stand?" and place this high on your list. In my opinion, it is far better to spend a few hundred pounds on an attraction than fancier stand décor.

Now that you are there, you have a steady stream of clients or potential clients enquiring about your service or product offering. Do NOT spend all of the time chatting with them whilst on the stand! Unless you are really quiet, in which case you have either picked the wrong exhibition or are using a lousy attraction method, or both. You cannot afford to be engaged with one person when possibly hundreds of others are floating past. You have paid a lot of money to be there to reach *all* of the people going there, not just a few, so save the lengthy time talking for a later appointment! DO NOT get stuck into a visitor, unless they clearly identify themselves as the hottest prospect this side of the planet with a time frame that says, "It's now or never and someone is going to be lucky today!!"

Your data capture competition system should have a few questions on that help the target 'win' the competition but these questions will clearly filter out the hotter prospects or the poorer ones. For example, if you are after a business that is a start up because you sell office furniture, a question might be, "How long have you been in business?" or, "When do you see yourself starting your business venture?" Or you might be selling a piece of machinery or equipment that is used by established businesses but is not a machine that lasts forever i.e. a photocopier... we all need one and find it difficult to live without but having accepted that many folks will already have a machine, that it will one day need replacing, a good question might be "How long have you had your current photocopier machine?" or, "What sort of copying volume do you carry out and do you see this level changing in the next few months/years?" These types of questions will quickly allow you to filter the good enquiries from the poor ones... and you may even decide to 'help' a really hot potential client win!! (Not that I would ever suggest that competitions are fixed or that I would entertain such an idea!!)

Finally exhibitions do not need to be expensive.

If you recall, we talked a lot about joint venture arrangements and strategic alliances... well what could be better than sharing an exhibition stand or sharing the data from an exhibition with a partner and sharing too the cost of exhibiting and capturing the data? Or how about several partners who all might be interested in the data and the response because all serve the same audience but do not compete. You could end up with three or four alliance partners all contributing to the stand cost, or the competition prize cost, or even contributing the prize!

Allow me again to quote a real example. I worked with a client in telecommunications and it was proposed that they attend a major exhibition. (It was already underway when I began work with them; however we were still able to address most of the arrangements.)

I asked a few questions like, "If your business does well, who else benefits?" In this example, the supplier to my client was directly in-line for more sales, should my client do well as it was the supplier's product that was going to be sold. Thus I asked, "What contribution towards the cost of the show was the supplier was making?"

Then we examined the audience of the show and asked who else might want to be talking to these visitors, but was not going to be exhibiting.

We established a list of other potential partners and we identified a 'prize' that the audience might want to win. What happened? Well we got a 50% contribution towards the cost of the exhibition from the supplier and we jointly involved three sponsors of a competition using three partners who, in return for the data captured, all contributed a set fee each... which was massively below the cost of attending and equated to very cheap data if compared to purchased data. In the end, the major exhibition with a large fully equipped stand that should have cost £15,000 cost just a net amount of £1,000!! Trust me, with creative thinking and correct planning you can do anything!

With the type of creative thinking that I am sure by now you've hooked into, you will see hundreds of opportunities. The approach is one of "No such word as can't", and by adopting this attitude you'll see possibilities everywhere. You will be able to look at, and identify, exhibition opportunities and then execute them so much better than the rest of your competitors and even maintain your presence without major cost!! Imagine how effective your business could be with this type of approach!!

Exhibitions can and do help you grow your business. They will raise your profile. Remember, "Be known in your industry, and be known in your area". They will help you learn about your competitors and establish friendships and relationships that might count for something one day. Exhibitions can launch you into new markets and they can also help with the obvious task of increasing sales. They are an *excellent* weapon in your arsenal and one that many of your competitors will choose to leave thinking that they are expensive and unproductive. Allow them to think that (don't let them read this book!) and then steam in with partners and win the day!

Go on, make an exhibition of yourself!!

Sequential Mailing

Here is a foundation stone of many marketers and one that I have possibly pushed towards the back because for the most part it also conjures up an image of expense. In much the same way as the exhibition process, many folks think that this traditional marketing method needs to be done in the traditional marketing style and frankly today this doesn't work. Consequently it represents, or could represent, a lot of monetary investment and too big a risk on the return.

But not the Ben Kench 'Business Booster' way!

The key components are

1. Intelligence – we have already discussed the need for your business to have, as a core centre, a client management system that also stores information on all prospects etc. This CRM system drives all outgoing material and directs it to those who want to hear about the particular message. It allows messages to be targeted and more effective. Intelligence then is a prime driver.

2. Profiled targets – the natural progression from using intelligence is that all targets are grouped into profiled sections that you feel will best respond to a certain message. For example, if you sell glue and all sorts of adhesives then you might record that many of your clients are tile fitters... and thus along with adhesives they also might need to purchase tools such as spirit levels and tile cutters. Your messages relaying news of tool offers or adhesive specials might well be aimed both at tile fitters you already know, but also tile fitters you don't yet know so you might set them up as 'tile fitters existing' and 'tile fitters prospect'. Thus all messages hit a more receptive ear... and the likely response rate climbs dramatically.

3.   Variety of message – again an example… if you sell menswear, it is no good asking someone who doesn't see the need for a new suit repeatedly to buy a new suit! If they don't see the need, then unless you show them a need or create a need, they will not buy a suit! However, they might see the need for an overcoat, or a scarf, or a hat, or a pair of casual trousers, and so your messages will constantly relay to them all of the range that you offer. You will send one message perhaps about 'winter warming' where you offer scarves, hats and gloves. You might send another offer message about 'special occasions' where you talk about smart shoes, executive shirts and ties that stand out. You might then send another message another time about 'social graces' where you offer casual clothing with a difference to help them stand out and be noticed. The point is, as you can see, asking time and time again about a suit would put off the potential client but constantly talking to them about other things they might use actually looks like you might be trying to help. It certainly helps put your range of offerings into their head and more likely therefore for the prospect to call back and buy.

4.   Follow-up phone calls. Now obviously if you do a multi-thousand mailshot then following up might be a little difficult… but maybe my question would be why are you doing such a massive mail-out? I'd guess it was to get a bigger response… and thus I would suggest that you can get the bigger response that you're looking for from a smaller volume mailer if there is a follow-up procedure. This call will help reaffirm the message that is covered in the mailer and indeed it allows a person to connect in a much more effective manner. I promise you, my friend, that a smaller volume of mail will still produce the return you are looking for if followed up and it will continue to produce as the relationship matures. You will not get build up if you rely upon volume to give

you the return without any further effort, so a key ingredient for now and the future is follow everything up.

5.   A plan! Yes, sorry to be boring again and suggest that before we proceed, we must stop and stand back a little but please, plan your approach, plan the other side for action after the mailer has hit. Plan the conversation, and plan the alternatives and the diary, and just ensure that your whole effort is planned... it will feel less stressful and yield greater returns.

To facilitate a mail campaign then, either by electronic or traditional means, we must use a programme that sends out sequential mail automatically. Doing a mailshot is quite laborious. If a machine does it, it's not half the hard work. You can programme a piece of software to print the mail piece overnight, for example, and then merely fold and envelope the letter another time. Or, of course, if sent electronically it can happen anytime in a few seconds... but please let software do the work!

Now the result is simply tremendous! Imagine if you sent out every week, or every month, for example, 100 messages to a contact who you knew was the right profile... what will happen? The consistent sending out of 100 messages is absolutely bound to give a healthy return... especially if the target is correct and the message well crafted.

It is a fact that, as a consumer, you as a buying 'animal', buy first from people that you know because we like to buy safely, we like to feel trust. It's a huge, huge driver. As we have learned already, essentially you buy from somebody you trust because you don't want the pain of getting it wrong. It takes time to build up trust, so you want to know that company's been around a while, and you probably want to really feel safe with them or get testimonials or something like that... and frequently hearing from somebody and gradually learning about their service or offering helps you build that feeling of trust.

One-offs don't work. <u>You</u> don't buy the first time you see something... unless it is a specific timing issue with an immediate urgent need. You rarely buy on impulse, except perhaps if it's a consumable item like a Mars bar or groceries!

But as the price goes up and as the frequency of purchase comes down, then the buying decision gets more and more driven around, "Who am I buying it from?" Your client's buying decision will be, "Who are you?" So your challenge is to say, "This is who I am." And, as a busy individual, your prospect will forget most of the first input messages because there is so much going on around them. The second and third will only just make an impact because they'll say, "Oh, I think I've seen that before but I'm too busy right now." But the fourth, fifth and sixth are critical. And the seventh is where it all starts to go crazy.

Currently I guess most people activate a mail campaign and look towards volume of one-off mail to produce the results... our process is to gather the data and send out a target message *frequently* to the people we know. And because they know us, the response rates go up. We're not constantly going out to get more numbers; we're working the numbers we have.

For example, if you are in finance, there are a number of ways you can go if you just keep endorsing every 30 to 45 days. Send them a letter that says, "I'm here." The first one says, "We did your mortgage. Just to let you know that we're keeping up to date with all the mortgage trends and we've got these fantastic software systems, etc. that tell us of the latest changes. I can help you when you're not tied into a deal blah blah. Come to X Mortgages."

Six weeks later, you send them, "I know there's a lot of stuff in the news about pensions. Do not worry about pensions; we have a special programme at the moment, which is there to guide you for pensions.

We're not trying to sell you pensions, but if it ever comes up we will talk to you about that and guide you."

Six weeks later, "Look I know there's a lot of talk about buying property. Buy-to-let mortgages are all the rage, and obviously the property market's booming, but actually because we do so much in mortgages, we can also help with advice on buying the right property."

Six weeks later, there might be another message that goes out and says, "There's a lot of people worrying about having health benefits these days, okay. The hoo-ha about National Health Service, you can go into hospital with an illness and come out in a coffin because you get this new super disease, or whatever it is. If you'd like to go private and you're not sure how, talk to us, because as your advisors we also deal with health insurance, blah blah blah."

So your message is constant and always about different things, but it's always you, you, you, working for them, them, them, them. You need to be able to see things that they need. More importantly, things that they need and you can supply.

But you as a business don't just do one thing, so you have an opportunity to send a different message from you, at regular intervals, just to keep the presence felt. And because the buying process is trust, security, trust security, trust security, I as a buyer of your services need to know that you're always around. So just keep talking to me. And it's as simple as that most of the time.

So, gather your data, do your profiling, plan ahead your campaigns. You might write six or seven different messages and sequence them out. If you do that, over the next year your business will boom. Because the more you send out, the more they ring you, and once they start ringing in, that's marketing. That's all you want. You want the phone to be ringing red hot and your doormat to be full of letters saying, "Come and do this for me!"

To help you, I suggest research into software that automates mail. Email is obviously easily automated... you can have a 'auto responder' script on the back of your website that literally sends as many automated messages as you have written and over a pre-specified period of time and so once you have written and stored the messages, the prospect or client keeps receiving them and you aren't working. With traditional mail, the same sorts of rules apply. Your task is to sit and create the sequence and to decide on the look and feel and frequency... but all of this is largely one-off work. Once you have the messages and the designed sequence, it can be passed over for fulfilment to a fulfilment house and you carry on with the management of enquiries and the rest of your business.

You *can* build your business into a massive entity as large as you'd like... just apply these tips and be a little patient!

One last thought... which is better - Email or Postal?

Frankly, I believe the table has turned and email has got to a stage of nuisance for many senior business people to an extent that most of it is either blocked by spam filters or by the office 'firewall' known as the secretary! This is my personal opinion and I respect that email is still an essential piece of the arsenal, but let me just clarify this issue and my reasoning: as an *individual* consumer, you open all your letters. As an *individual* consumer, you open up your emails. If you're not in business and you don't have to do this business email thing every day, you'll open all your email but you'll bin your junk mail. However, if you are a business person that probably is deluged with mail messages every day, then you probably are less conscientious about opening every one and opening them every day. Indeed, I believe that as a business owner you probably *don't* read everything that comes through to you, By contrast however, if it is a hard copy paper letter you tend to put it down on the desk for 'looking at later'... and often it *is* actually looked at, if not read - thus it scores a major point on the remembering / recognition scale.

Thus, I believe that in recent months, the business environment has changed and, due to the volume of messages involved, that emails are now not as effective as traditional mail. The major advantage, of course, with email is cost... it is literally pennies each but this must be considered against the very, very small percentage of opened and read emails... even on targeted warm lists. If you are targeting consumers in a non-corporate world, then quite possibly email is still the winner but I place less reliance upon email in a business to business environment. My suggestion would be a combination, but consider more the 'snail mail' route.

What about postcards?

For a first contact and for awareness, postcards are brilliant. You can have really eye-catching images and clever messages, and if thoughtfully created, they even get posted onto noticeboards! I recommend using them.

By the third and fourth contact they should know you a little <u>and</u> if they are targeted because you've got your data right, you should be sending a message that's relevant to what they're thinking of. So, if the target is thinking of extending their loft, then the first two are just picture postcards and they think, "Oh yeah, I might do that one day." By the time of the third message, it's been in their head for three or four months, and they're thinking, "Yeah, I'd like to look into this."

So your mailer says, "Open this to find out how you can save money by not moving house", or, "Open this to find out how loft space could be turned into cash", or, "Loft space can save you thousands." And then they're thinking, "I'll look at this", and then it tells them in a bit more detail about how using loft space instead of moving house can add value to the house, add de-stress to the house and the family, and add all the benefits. And it's £10,000 or £15,000, instead of £30,000 or whatever. So the third and fourth mailings must contain more information. The prospect might be ready to buy at this stage, but they're certainly not going to buy without information. So think creatively and with sequenced targeted mailings, you can see a huge return!

Postcards to warm a prospect, and mail to educate more thoroughly. Combine, be creative and win!

Business Booster Marketing

What do I currently do? Why do I do this? Do I really know if it works? What else could I do? How could I use what we have just learned? What new methods can I implement with these Booster Ideas NOW!?

_____

_____

_____

_____

_____

_____

_____

_____

_____

_____

_____

_____

_____

_____

_____

Networking Events

1. _____

2. _____

3. _____

4. _____

5. _____

Potential Strategic Partners

1. _____
2. _____
3. _____
4. _____
5. _____
6. _____
7. _____
8. _____
9. _____
10. _____

Events for PR

1. _____
2. _____
3. _____
4. _____
5. _____
6. _____
7. _____
8. _____
9. _____
10. _____

Enquiry Overload

How can I create enquiry overload for my business NOW using what we have just looked at? What can I do immediately, and this month, to Boost my business?

_____

_____

_____

_____

_____

_____

_____

_____

_____

_____

_____

_____

_____

_____

_____

_____

_____

_____

_____

_____

Business Booster Marketing – a quick recap

Okay then, let's look back again at all that we have covered... remembering that repetition helps it to become readily accessible knowledge and consequently knowledge that is actually used. It helps you create habits that drive your growth.

Understanding where you have come from, the foundations that you have laid that have given you an accurate knowledge of strategy and your planned route to a specific goal; let's look at what you have now got. Your data awareness and your newly adopted use of an intelligent system enable far more to be done with far less stress and that in turn produces far greater return for an input of hours and physical labour. You've gathered data and done some profiling. You're using a CRM contacts management programme, and you know your customers. You know who buys, why they buy, how often they buy, what they buy. You know them. And if that takes you two or three months to gather that information, it's the best two or three months you've ever spent. Don't be in a rush to go forward.

So onto this foundation, you have built a programme to generate 'Enquiry Overload'. This is a business method that relies upon a guerrilla-style approach, not upon muscle or cash. Your goal of domination isn't lessened because of your lack of resource; it merely heightens your senses and makes you sharper. Remember the words of Henry Ford – "Don't wish it was easier, wish you were better."

So 'Enquiry Overload' begins with **simple networking**... do you remember the scientific approach? **Get Out More!** Discover the variety of network meetings and then attend vigorously and critically follow-up on the contacts you have made, develop relationships and they can then become both clients and introducers.

The next level then is pretty easy... if the relationships you have nurtured are healthy and you have genuinely been looking for a win-win scenario, then you can introduce the idea of **strategic alliances or joint ventures**. This is where you will strike a deal with your business colleague that allows you to market your product offering to their client bank. This client bank will have probably taken years for them to have accumulated and it should go without saying that they will not carelessly throw caution to the wind and allow you access but it *will* be possible. You should first offer to give and genuinely look for a partner where you can help them, not just where you hope to gain. They will, of course, sense that you are predatory if that is your motive and then they will back away. Don't forget that as an animal, all of us have senses and we 'feel' whether it is right or not... thus they will sense your approach as fair or not and I heartily recommend being open about what you can offer and clear as to what you expect. And don't forget that they will feel at risk if they are not 100% sure as to the level of security in offer that you represent i.e. they need to be totally sure you won't let their clients down and cause them to feel a backlash, so please try to give of your service or product to the potential partner first so that they can endorse form first-hand experience.

When you work at these areas consistently over a few months, you will suddenly find that your network of contacts has grown enormously and business levels with it... and your first JVs are already looking promising... now add an event.

Special events that can be organised between you and several partners... they could be birthdays or award ceremonies or charity functions... whatever the excuse, make sure that you organise them and invite your prospects, as well as some select existing clients, and also invite the prospects and existing clients of the partners. Putting on a special event even just twice a year can add several dozen clients to your prospect list and turn several prospects into clients. There is no doubt that a well structured special event can pay you back several thousands pounds above its cost.

And then of course we talked about **PR**. This can be off the back of the event but actually you need to be looking constantly for PR opportunities. Again they can be all sorts of excuses but the overriding factor is that they are newsworthy... something that people would want to read about, not just a blatant plug for your company. I might even suggest using a professional agency. For a few hundred pounds, they can effectively get you many thousands of pounds worth of exposure... depending on your ambition level and desire for fame!

Then of course from all of this activity and meeting all of these people, the natural follow on are **referrals**. You should be pushing for them and actively asking for them... but only once you know people are genuinely delighted with your product or offering. Put the Cook in the Kitchen! Get them emotional again about what you have done for them and then watch the referrals pour in!

Next we looked at the critical role of **the Internet** in today's business society. Simply put, it is vital and you need to do it and do it properly. Spend a lot of money, do not do it cheap and then watch as your image and reputation grow alongside your bank balance. Closely allied to this and almost taking over is **Social Media**... using Twitter, Facebook and blogging and especially using video such as YouTube to literally launch your business into a whole new audience and lucrative income streams.

Direct sales were next and again we talked about another 'direct to your audience' outlet where sales are made, but not by you. Remember the illustration of the Post Office? It is where someone else sells what you sell, but where they can do so for you with little or no hassles or extra activity. It must be seen as very little extra activity but still giving added revenue, or else there is no reason for someone to be a direct sales outlet for you. It is very possible though, and with thought you will be able to add perhaps five or six outlets over a year... imagine what that could do to your revenues and income!!

Couple this with a few **Agencies**. This is where they are not probably completing the sale as the direct outlet above but where they are definitely covering most of the initial interest and passing the enquiry to you as "these people want to buy" type of enquiries. Imagine if you had three or four of those passing a lead or two a week over! What sort of a difference would that make?!

For good measure as you work through these approaches, add some **telemarketing**. This isn't meant as a 'boiler room' where unsuspecting contacts are badgered into submission but merely where contacts that are 'warm' are spoken to with regularity and where they are offered the chance to sample your service or product. It might be using part-time mums as a source of staff and it definitely will develop a relationship, not burn a bridge. When done consistently and properly, it is a massively effective way to grow with minimal cost.

Exhibitions were then a prime area to seriously grow your presence, and remember the philosophy is not to spend fortunes on the costs of exhibiting... either do a lower level stand or preferably share the cost with one of your strategic alliance partners.

And to top it all off, include **some regular direct mail** communication with your contacts. This will consolidate any contacts you have made and expand on their knowledge of what you do. It should be consistent to the same group of people, not looking for one-off hits but developing a relationship.

The overall compound effect of these will seriously be to double or treble your profits. With dedication to improvement and a focus on the future, not looking at the old way, "the way we always do it," but instead embracing an idea, that maybe the status quo can be much better... the application of these methods on a regular basis will see your business grow exponentially.

Allow me to show you something. Just take a look at my version of a business growth graph here. Most people/business advisors would assume that consistent work means your business will grow in a consistent linear fashion that all of the effort slowly starts to pay off and you slowly see a steady growth. That's not the way *I* want your business to grow. My growth curve is a slower start, then an exponential explosion! Once you finally get your foundations right, this exponential curve goes through the roof!

So don't beat yourself up, as you're trying to do all this work, that you're not growing your business yet. You shouldn't be growing your business yet! Your growth curve *should* be slower, flatter for a while and *then* rocket. Take the time to do the background work. Build your foundations properly, even if it takes a few months. Build a marketing process that consistently uses all of the approaches even if it takes a month or five, and then *know* that your business is going to be massive and enjoyable and valuable to others! Be excited, be very excited!

Expected Linear Growth Chart

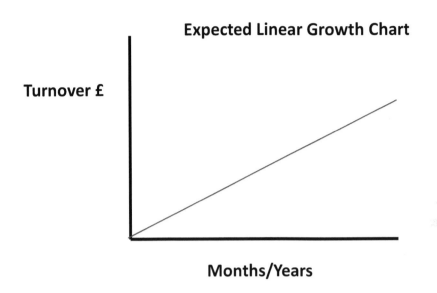

Turnover £

Months/Years

Business Booster Growth Curve

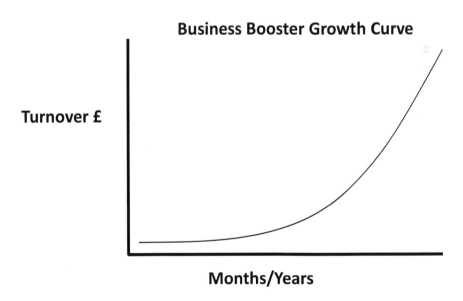

Turnover £

Months/Years

Much work and preparation goes almost unnoticed for months before all of the good work kicks in and you enjoy exponential growth.

Enquiry Overload - loaded again

Next we're going to look at your existing customers. You want to grow your business and I assure you passionately it is not only possible but pretty much achievable by anyone... as long as you follow some newer ideas. Sadly I usually hear advice given along the lines of, "To grow your business, you need to tell more people about it and advertise a lot over a lengthy period..." Frankly this advice, the most common advice I hear being given to companies seeking growth, is blatantly wrong! It is the least cost-effective and the shortest lived. The advice is based on outdated principles grown from an age where every person shopped with different habits and vastly different attitudes.

In today's market with today's society pressures and today's attitudes towards security and other issues, the key to growth is your existing customers. They have already experienced your offering and (if we assume that it is a good one that left them satisfied!) so they will be more inclined to buy from you. They should offer least resistance and be cheaper to find. Your existing clients, *not* new unknown contacts, are where you grow. Your existing clients are the rich pickings but they need to be nurtured... they can't suddenly be made to buy a lot more. And just in case you are in the type of industry where the offering is a more infrequent purchase such as a home improvement like windows, bathrooms, kitchens etc. do not believe this to be a one-off purchase! It is probably more true with higher value purchases that the loyalty bond is apparent and thus whilst the purchase frequency is lower, even representing several years between purchase, these are still clients who can and should come back... they just need nurturing.

Business Alchemy

The external approach most usually adopted by business owners is understandable but that's the wrong way, because your real value is in the people who already know you. And that's why you've got to know them first.

I call it Business Alchemy, your business producing pure gold. You're looking to 'mine' gold from the gold deposits that are already with you, just hidden.

What you're going to do is put a programme together to consistently talk to your existing customers... and sell to them again and again and then expand your client base from within the existing client base through the referrals given by your loyal base.

Here's what you need to do... a very simple yet powerful three step process for making your own Gold.

Example 1. Replacement Glazing to consumer market (B2C)

Name of Client/ Business	Product/ service Replacement Windows Front	Product/ service Replacement Windows rear	Product/ service Conservatory	Product/ service Patio Doors
Brian Jones	✓	✓		
Mary Beadle				✓
William Taylor	✓	✓		✓
Edgar Shoost	✓	✓		
Elizabeth Lunn	✓		✓	

Marked boxes are where sales currently happen... unmarked boxes are opportunities waiting!

How wide can your top line go? How many products or services could you add? Are you currently selling all that they are buying?

If you are not, then it leaves a gap for competitors to sneak in and they might then steal all across and take a client away! Go Wide!!

Example 2. Professional Service to Commercial Markets (B2B)

Name of Client	Service/ product Computer sales	Service/ product Computer support 24/7	Service/ product Goldmine software	Service/ product Goldmine training
AGH	✓	✓	✓	
Walker & Sons				
Tibbs Foods				
Bentley Hicks				
Alan Hucknall				
Simply Systems				

Question: what am I doing to tell them that I do the other offerings?

Make sure you create a marketing message about each of your offerings... or form an alliance with someone who offers what you don't.

Step 1 - make a note for yourselves of *all* of the products or the services that you offer. Break down your offering into *several* areas.

Step 2 - write next to this *'what that means for the client'*. So if your service is advice, which might mean less stress. If your service is a widget, it might make this area reduces cost. Don't list just what you do; list next to it *what it does for them*.

Step 3 - you need to create different angles of approach around each of the aforementioned benefits... reasons to 'look again' at the client's words.

One step at a time... Listing all of the various items or services you offer.

For example, if you sell bicycles, what sort of bikes? What about accessories? What about puncture repair outfits and maintenance accessories, or clothing accessories? Safety or visibility products? What if they take their bikes that they've purchased from you on weekend trips? Do you sell them a rack to go on the car? What about ropes or straps to help it stay on the car? What about waterproofs when they're using it outside away from home? And in fact they're using it away from home, which means they are out for the day, so why don't you help them with flasks and some picnic-type accessories? Or maps? Think about **all** the various things you could offer. Give this some thought. Write it down now as an exercise for your business, please.

I'll show you in a moment why this is so particularly important because, if you go back to your existing customers as in the bicycle trader example, they already know you sell bikes. If you're going to go to them and saying, "Hey, I'm here again," they're going to ask, "Why are you coming back to me? I've already got a bike," or, "I've already had my stationery done, Mr Printer," etc. As a result, many business operators feel they cannot go back to them because you don't know what else to go back with. Usually business owners haven't crafted messages about their other offerings and haven't therefore got reason to communicate. This is where you are going to be hugely different though. You will find a way and besides, there's no such word as can't, remember?

So break your product offering down. Think of each product offering and list your existing clients and **create a simple grid showing which of**

your offerings are bought by which client... or more importantly, which ones are not being bought by each client! **It is the missing gaps** where a known client is not purchasing something you offer **where your opportunity lies!**

Then, step 2 is to create your messages for each additional product offering or a message from a different angle for the same offering. Think of each offering as a *different* benefit to the client, and then get a message around the benefit. Focus a little attention on the message in relation to the client... the key part of this is to personalise the message in their language. We know about features and benefits, but go one step further. *Personalise* the benefits. Make it what that means for you. Put it in their language.

To create Business Alchemy, you need to go back to your existing customers but with a *different* message... and that's the key.

If, for example, you think that you do only sell one product, shoes for example, think of all of the possible uses of the product. Even though it's only one product, try to put different angles on it... sports shoes, leisure shoes, business shoes, town shoes etc.

As an example, pretend I sell bags. You bought a bag, you're my client. Do you want another bag?!

Now if I'm an idiot and I just keep asking you the same question, "Do you want another bag?" you're going to become fed up. But I'm not an idiot so, after you've told me you don't want another bag, I come back to you for the second time asking, "Would you like a fashion accessory?" And then I create a story of how the new chic, man-about-town, has got these type of bags. Maybe with that approach I was trying to appeal to your ego or fashion sense. If it doesn't work I come back another time and ask, "Would you like this really practical, hard-wearing, durable, tough mobile carrying assistant?" (We don't call it a bag this time to try another angle - it's a carrying assistant!) But it's tough and it's durable and it can withstand your rough lifestyle. You still say no.

But each time I come back to you, I've got a slightly different angle. *One* of those angles will suit you. Just keep persisting with a variety of approaches and one of them will hit the buying point of the buyer. You might not want another bag but after a while you see a need for something for a weekend trip or a sports event or a hiking trip and you say okay. In this instance, I just need to be prepared with all of the angles and be ready to keep asking... one of them triggers a buying response.

And of course, if you are in a business that can offer many additional products and services as we have already looked at, then it is a lot easier. You simply list all of the products or services... Go Wide, and then identify those which you sell to a particular client and those which you do not.

It then becomes quite obvious that the Business Alchemy process begins by selling to the existing client something else that you sell but which he currently isn't buying. It might be worth mentioning here that if you are the shoe retailer we were speaking of earlier, and then try adding additional products or services such as socks, gel pads to ease aching feet, polish, protective sprays etc. There really is no excuse!

Link your product into your customer. If, for example, you sell Human Resources advice, it might be that it represents more to me as a potential client as 'reduced stress' or it might be that I don't care about the stress, I only care about the money I might save if there is a potential for industrial tribunal over a dismissal. Or it might be that I don't care about stress or the money, I care about image. It might be that I don't care about stress or money or image, I care about advice delivery. I want it now. It might be that I don't care about stress or money or image or delivery, what I care about is how I feel with *you*. There are a lot of personal angles that can be my standpoint... your task is to make me hear your message in such a way that it hits home. *My* language might be many slants... you need to hit me with all to ensure a hit.

So you've got to try and put a different angle on what you offer because your clients will have a different take. If you go back to them with a series of different messages, you'll get <u>loads</u> more business.

I do realise that at first glance this could be difficult. It is another of those areas where I recommend you take time out before reading further. The creative mind *can* come up with lots of ideas and listening to your client comments in the survey we mentioned a while back will make things like this help. It is a bit like holding up a baked bean can and asking your team what it could be used for. The immediate obvious answer is 'baked beans' and indeed it might take a few minutes before other creative ideas flow... but it could also be used for a water scoop, a small flower pot, one end of a string telephone, a musical instrument... and lots of other silly things! It's just a question of getting the juices flowing with ideas, and in much the same way, try thinking of lots of ways your client could interpret your offering as filling his 'need'.

Sadly too often business owners miss the 'gold' because they merely say to themselves and their clients that, "If I want anything else, I'll come back... I know where you are." In truth, this just leaves paying clients to wander off and be looked after by another trader. If you believe that because I have purchased a bag from you once that I will immediately remember you for a briefcase, suitcase, sports bag or a rucksack, then you are mistaken. When I as a consumer walked into your store and bought my first bag, I only had that one issue in my mind and even though the other sorts of bag were on display, my focus only registered the sort I needed then and there.

This is because of a recognised condition or function of the brain/eye relationship called Reticular Activation System... essentially where the mind only registers consciously the vision of that which it is programmed to be aware of. For example, like me you probably remember playing a game as a child looking out for new car registrations when travelling... or even now as adults when thinking of buying something new like a new car, when you are looking out for them, they seem to be everywhere! They were always there, of course, in the same number but you just didn't see them.

Well that is how a buying mind works... it only sees what it needs at that time thus your responsibility when trading is to go back to your clients with a message that highlights products or services other than that which they bought first time. (You will of course only be able to do this is you have embraced the data capture disciplines we have already discussed!)

I didn't know you did that!

It might also be that you've got a range of products and you have sold them only one and they perhaps don't know all about your total range, and the danger is that you might walk into their office one day, see them using something new that you sell but didn't sell to them and you hear those immortal words, "I didn't know you did that!"

How many times have you heard that? Have you ever gone into any of existing client's office and you've seen something that they've just bought that you could have sold them?

And that's so common, isn't it? **You must never allow it to happen to your business! Could it happen now? Is there a slight chance that your existing clients do not know all of your offerings?**

Many times, sadly that is the case... and that's why we hear those words too often, because at the moment, as we've said, businesses don't go back to their existing customers. The thought mostly held by business owners is, "We can't go back to them, and we don't want to upset or annoy them." The usual voiced belief is that of, "If they want more, they'll come back to me."

It's not right. The human mind doesn't work like that. As a consumer, you get swathed with what's important in your life. You forget about what I or anybody else has sold you. You don't consciously stop buying from me.

I'll give you an example. Imagine you and your partner have gone out for a meal one night and you have an excellent experience. The restaurant food was superb, as was the service and the wine and at the end of the evening a total package representing marvellous value. You say to each other that it was wonderful and that you'll go there again.

Then what happens? Well time slides past, perhaps a couple of years during which you've gone out with other friends whenever the situation arose and even gone out for other meals with your partner, until one day someone else suggests you go out for a meal and when you're with them they say that they know an excellent place to visit. They lead the way and you find that they have taken you back to the place you'd experienced together a year or so before. Now, in the last couple of years as we said, you have gone out to other places. You didn't stop liking the original place. You didn't deliberately avoid it, you merely forgot about it.

Imagine if you were that restaurant owner. Imagine if you had communicated with them after their first visit on regular occasions and by doing so maintained a presence in the mind of the couple dining... maybe they would have been back within the last two years instead of spending their monies in other establishments. Maybe.

Simple frequent messages and invitations, perhaps even crafted around themed evenings or topical calendar events, might have increased the spend in your restaurant by three times... and if you did that consistently with all of your clients, how busy would your restaurant be?!

The illustration serves to remind us that *your* clients need reminding. As a consumer, your client is focussed on what is most important to him... possibly family matters or immediate business cash matters... whatever it is, it doesn't mean they have fallen out with your business, it merely means they forget.

And then one day somebody else comes along offering them something similar to that which you offer and they think, "Yes, I could do with that," and they completely forget about you because they're engrossed in their world. You as a business owner would lose out after having sold them something in the first place merely because they have got so many other things on their mind that your business offering was pushed out.

So you can't afford to let your clients forget about you. You've got to go back to your existing customers time and time again!!

Here's a fabulous question: Am I selling all that they're buying?

Try asking yourself that about each of your clients. Are you selling them everything in your genre that they are spending money on? If you honestly look at their name on a list and then think of their potential spend in your area of business, does the volume of your sales match the volume of their spending?

I have mentioned to you a few pages ago timely reminders about the Tortoise and the Hare... which one was 'faster' in the approach, but which one wins? You know well how the real cycle of life works. Nature tells us that we must plant a seed, then nurture the seed, tend to it, water it, shield it from dangers and then we watch it grow and finally harvest it months later... and always remembering that not every single individual seed produces a shoot and a harvest. Many fail to produce, but the process works when followed with a whole packet of them.

Business, my friend, is no different even though we live in a world that pushes for immediacy. It will not last if it happens fast. Work internally and patiently. Remember, this is 'different, not difficult'.

I won't labour it any more, but I think you've got the point. Please realise that growing your business isn't, "Let's do a marketing campaign to get more customers". That is **not the way** to start. Look inside first, not externally.

Business Alchemy, the ability to produce pure gold, is derived from powerful, yet simple communication with those who already know you. Talking to your clients to make sure you take off them the money they spend in your field. Internal focus and nurturing relationships with existing contacts is your key to massive success!

Looking at Loyalty

Following on again in a similar vain, here's another great way to increase enquiries. Look at a loyalty scheme.

Ask yourself, "How can I create a loyalty system? What can I do to incentivise frequent purchase?"

Another great question that can help you go to the next level is, "What is it that makes people buy frequently?"

How do you find the answers to these excellent questions? Well as talked about earlier, asking existing clients is always a very smart move... but in addition, Ben's response is that the best place to find answers on buying behaviour is 'look inside'.

Turn around and say to yourself, what makes <u>me</u> go back to a place time and again?

(You know, I'll keep telling you to be good at questions. And if you're good at questions, you start to ask yourself a series of them, and then you come up with great answers!)

So, ask yourself what can I do to create a loyalty system? Loyalty is supreme. Why do Tesco and Sainsbury's, and Shell and Texaco, and British Airways and countless others, all have loyalty schemes? Is it because they don't work? No, it's because they *do* work.

Create a system of reward that entices your clients back again. This could easily be linked in to your data capture system that by now you will have begun to use. For example, asking them to join a frequent buyer programme that gives them 20% discount of their first purchase if they sign up... and then you have a way of communicating future offers and thus developing the relationship, and they have something that's worth their while both now with 20% off and the future as they always benefit from first offer on new lines or special invites events etc.

If you own a restaurant or a retail outlet especially, then it should be absolutely a given that from today onward, as a newly energised creative thinker, you will create a data capture system that is also a loyalty scheme. Ask everyone who purchases to become a member of your scheme and offer an incentive. You then have a known database and the chance to develop a relationship... it really is not difficult! Simply put, whatever business you are in, from today onward, create a scheme, capture data, communicate regularly and watch your fortunes change.

You might not get 100% of your clients to register but anything is better than the nothing you have now!

And if you're struggling for an incentive, try giving what *you'd* like to enjoy receiving! Get creative, it's easy!!

Competitions to Beat the Competition

And on the subject of getting creative, use competitions to beat your competition.

We've all got competitors. So what are our competitors doing? Very rarely are they innovative. Very rarely are they finding ways to change the face of the planet. They just use discounts and sales.

By being innovative, creating things like competitions, you will win. Why not think of a way that you can put a competition together *right now*? Possibly a competition that suits an objective, e.g. use a competition to drive staff to increase sales, such prizes to do another X thousands of pounds in a month. And make the prize bigger! Greed moves people!

Lots of people try competitions, for example, referrals. "If you pass referrals, you get £15 or £25." And then they are disappointed with the result. So why not give me a £2,000 luxury holiday? I might get you some referrals then!

Competitions can be simple. A client of ours drove numbers into his garden centre over Easter with a drawing competition over the Easter period. He got the kids' picnic tables in a side area, and they just got drawing! The prize was a £10 children's folding chair. He left it until after Easter to judge it, so the winner comes back again to collect the prize, he takes the photographs (obviously) and it went into the local paper (PR!) Very successful.

Another group of parents dragged into a shopping environment, more PR, fun – everyone's happy.

Try targeting youngsters if your client is a family. There is always another way in!

That's what McDonald's have done, isn't it? Get the kids to go!

But you *can* do competitions frequently. Here's a tip if you want to stir your creative juices to boost your marketing: use your calendar! Get your calendar and look at all the dates in the calendar. You've got Valentine's Day, St George's Day, and St Patrick's Day. What else have you got? Mother's Day, Father's Day. There are loads of opportunities!

There's even an American link with Thanksgiving! There really are loads of occasions for you to make a play upon! There'll definitely be five or six dates you can use. Plus, you've got your sporting calendar. Wimbledon? World Cup football? Test Match cricket? Grand Prix motor racing? There really are lots of 'excuses' to hang a marketing campaign or creative competition upon.

And then you look at your calendar and ask yourself, "What about news events?" And by then you have your year full of fresh initiatives that keep you and your team buzzing and give you a constant reason to communicate with clients and to make conversation leaning towards their purchase or your offer, or anything that assists your business.

Please look at your calendar and it'll give you loads of angles for marketing initiatives. And then please put something together!! Try it! Imagine if you had a whole year planned ahead with fresh monthly initiatives... how would you feel? Excited? Energised? Optimistic?

Probably. You would feel always lifted because you had something to talk around and there would always be something happening to drive enquiries or sales.

Competitions are great but remember, use competitions with a prize that's worth winning. Make it a massive prize and just Stop! Stand Back and plan a little the maths to ensure that it works *before* you action it. As a word of caution, a few years ago there was a promotion done by Hoover involving free flights... they had not planned it correctly and the take up was so high it almost crippled Hoover and caused a lot of bad publicity as consumers were being told they were not going to get their flights, so use big incentives but get it right first!

You can give away a thousand pounds cash or a two thousand pound holiday, for something as simple as referrals, but you just make sure that it's a period of three months or four months for the competition period, and everybody has got to give you at least five to qualify for entry into the prize draw. Now if you've got two or three hundred customers, and you get five referrals off a hundred of them, five hundred referrals should get you probably, at decent closing rates, two hundred deals, because you close higher on your referrals. So work it out. What would you make on 200 sales? Enough to pay for the prize? And who said you had to pay for a prize?! Why not link with a prize giver?

A competition might be tied towards a specific product line. For example, if you are a garden centre owner, it might be tied towards sales of patio furniture or big barbecues. If you are in the stationery or print business, a competition might be driven towards all those who buy complete stationery packs, or stationery packs, calendars and flyers, or driven towards colour brochures that are at least 12 pages thick. Whatever your business or your choice of what needs promoting, whether it's a product with higher margins or to move stagnant stock.

If you are in IT, it might have been that your competition is driven towards numbers of PCs or complete installations. Think about it. Plan it. Use a prize that's big. The secret of competition is a big prize. We're all greedy. We'll talk about emotions later. Greed is one of the most powerful, it really is. Use greed.

Think abut how you structure it too. If you're linking through a dealer network, dealers have principles and staff. But the value of the dealership is the number of accounts it has, clients it serves, and the number of accounts is gathered by the staff. So, you're dealing with the dealer principal, yes, but his value is based on the activity of the sales force. So, to get the dealer principal on board, we have to give him a prize, but to get the people to make the dealer principal valuable, we have to incentivise them as well. So use a two-tier structure.

You can use competitions to gather fresh data. We've talked about that previously, but just approach the press or media outlet carefully and structure the competition properly.

For example, data collection. Make sure you structure the competition so that all responses come to *you*, not the newspaper or magazine, because then the newspaper won't have an issue under the Data Protection Act and giving you data.

I did one competition with a bathroom company and we gave away a bathroom suite. We ran the competition over several weeks with 'teasers' to announce it in advance. The press outlet put half a page display in that shows the swanky new bathroom, and you make sure that entrants collect a coupon or similar from each issue to enable them to enter.

If you look at it from the point of view of the newspaper or magazine, what do they want to do? Sell magazines or papers. So you put a teaser programme together so that the person has got to buy the issue for four weeks or whatever. Or the paper or magazine promotes it for four weeks, so that more and more people buy that one issue, something like that. But your argument to the press people is, "We're giving you a five thousand pound bathroom suite, that's going to drive sales of your newspapers, so I'm not going to pay for your advert." You approach them and say, "If you want to drive more newspaper sales, let's work together. Here's a ticket to help you do it. I'm giving you five thousand pounds worth of incentive".

You are going to have to test and measure, suck it and see… but the point I'm making is if you have not done competitions, or you do them infrequently, just do them more often. You can use competitions for *lots* of different things as we have mentioned… and structured correctly, they can get you hundreds of new clients and cost virtually nothing. Try this please… just try to do one or two this next year… and when they are done, learn from them and improve and do them again. Your business will rocket with just a few of these strategically created throughout the year.

Selective Sponsorships

Now I'm not a fan of spending money! I guess you already knew that!

In small business land, those 'national splash' sponsorship deals don't apply. You can't afford to start chucking twenty and thirty thousand pounds or more to create what the ad/media people call 'brand awareness'. When you're Coca Cola you can, or McDonald's, but not when you are you.

So, to create 'brand awareness', you've got to be much more creative. And that is frequency, not necessarily one-off mountainous posters. If you sponsor a local football team, for example, you could get a number of events throughout the year that are public, as well as every week your name blazoned across a shirt and perhaps around the ground they're playing on. So, for say a thousand pounds, or two thousand pounds, which is not a lot of money, you could have five or six public exposure events which probably would equate to quite a good return on your money when compared with the straight cost of advertising. The crucial key is whether the audience viewing the league are your client profile. If not, if the football league has an audience who don't buy your product, then you've just *wasted* your cash. Your name might be known, but by the wrong people.

Singularly this is the biggest issue... the name awareness concept is only viable if your name is being made aware to the prospective purchaser of your offering. If your business is selling a service purchased by business owners themselves, such as office cleaning, then brand awareness-type advertising or sponsorship in a local shopping mall might just be a poor use of your hard-earned cash!

It is possible though to find a 'match'. If you're selective in your sponsorship, you could get a massive amount of mileage. For example, if you were to sponsor a polo team, all the people that play polo probably have access to a few quid as it is not a poor man's sport, and if your offering is luxury garden landscaping, price range five to twenty thousand pounds, well it might be a good match. Again, it's all about profiling. Sponsorship can be very attractive if it puts your name directly in front of your key target buyer. For example, you might sponsor an award ceremony or sponsor a special event but in return you get a high profile and probably an opportunity to meet with your direct target prospect. In an audience of 150+ people, you should be talented enough to generate more than one or two enquiries which should handsomely return your sponsorship cash.

And the other thing is, I don't know how good you are at negotiating, but sponsorships don't have to be monies up front, do they? You could agree an amount for the season, payable in easy chunks. In fact, you could even make it performance related; "If you do well, we'll give you an extra five hundred. If you don't do so well, hold it back."

You could negotiate a sponsorship as a reciprocal arrangement where you allow a sponsor for your work wear or vehicles in return for exposure on your materials to their audience. There's lots of ways you can negotiate a sponsorship arrangement, but you'll never get one right until you try doing one in the first place! So go out there next week and look for your prospect's influencer and try a sponsorship arrangement to be exposed to the right people.

And like we were saying previously, create your logo so that it incorporates a phone and contact web address because anywhere that anybody is pictured with the sponsor's name on the shirt, you can stimulate direct response.

Advertising for FREE – Piggybacks

Now I may have mentioned that I don't like spending money, and I may have mentioned that advertising rarely pays off and consequently I suggest caution when thinking of spending. However, advertising for free is always a no loss option! Why not try this?!

Here's how: get your suppliers to pay!

If you sell goods for other suppliers, why are you paying all of the costs to advertise?

Indeed, if you sell goods for other suppliers and your business grows as a result of the advertising, then surely their business grows too as you'd purchase more of their goods to satisfy your growth! And if they are going to win, why shouldn't they pay?!

Let me tell you something. All of the companies that provide you with products, the manufacturers, have a 'co-op budget' – a special fund set aside for spending on co-operative projects with their distributors. So, ask them for some money towards your costs! You're selling their product, they win. You're creating brand awareness for them, they win. You're creating a database for them and a future market for them to market to, they win.

Ben's approach is always to try not to pay for anything! Don't say you can't. Ask instead, "How can I?" Don't say, "I can't do adverts, I can't do a mailshot, I can't do a flyer promotion." Ask instead, "How can I?"

If the challenge is finance, ask yourself the question, "How can I pay for this? Who can I bring in to joint venture it so that they share the cost?" Just keep asking questions. If it comes to an advert and you're selling somebody else's product, like if you're in IT serviced support and you sell Compaq or HP or Microsoft, ring them up and say, "I'm doing a big campaign, it's going to cost me two thousand pounds. I want four or five hundred pounds towards it." And then ring your other suppliers you deal with who offer complimentary products to the first supplier asked and do the same with them.

Think for one moment. Whenever you do business, does it involve buying something in? Do you have to pay a supplier in order for the product or service to go from your business to your client?

If so, then list these suppliers now and make a point of calling them and suggesting they share some of your promotional cost! After all, if they have competitors for your business, if you could get the service or product they provide from another source, surely they would want to hang on to your business? And if they value your account, then they really will not mind helping you as it will only help grow their account. Ask them for finances! Get your adverts for free! But always at least get a contribution towards your cost!

And don't let it stop at adverts. Why not ask them to contribute towards a large programme of events or a mailshot followed by a competition and a special event for the prize ceremony?

Remember, there's no such word as can't, ask instead, "How can I?" Keep asking, keep looking for ideas and they will flow... and you will soon be flying!!

And all you've got to do is ask. So advertising can be free.

Five Top Tips

Okay, so let's look at what we have covered and where it's the best to start. You see, I have worked with a lot of busy business owners and they get all excited about the millions of ideas that start to flow through the head and then get all confused because with so many great ideas, where do they start? "What shall I do first?" is a common question.

So, for you, my friend, here is a top five. If I had to break this down and give you something that was absolutely a <u>must do</u>, a sure fire start with this and proceed along with these, what would I say?

1. Give something for free

What can you give for free? What <u>do</u> you give for free? Greed is singularly, aside from lust, identified as the strongest human driving emotion. People do all sorts of things for greed. People will leave a beach in their shorts, and be taken on a promotional tour of a holiday residence for three, four or five hours, to be mildly abused, and dumped, because in the first instance, they were offered some duty free! They will waste hours for a seemingly small free gift! It is not unheard of for people to risk their homes and relationships on gambling forays or dodgy business ideas all because of greed... so get your clients greedy!

If you look outside of your industry and you see what's worked for others, maybe you'll find an idea for you. I've used the illustration just then of a timeshare scenario but you could say to yourself, "How can I do that or emulate that in my business?" Pull it apart. Look at the mechanics. See what could be redeployed. You might ask yourself, what's the component part? Well, there was an offer, a sensible, easy pitch, perhaps some friendly, smiley bubbly people, and it was a combination of things. But the objective was achieved; a potential client sourced from a marketing initiative and placed in front of a sales person.

So, look at something that's worked phenomenally, and say, "How can I apply that to me?" And you'll find an answer.

But greed is King. So give something for free. Do you give anything for free at the moment?

And in today's information age, especially give information. They say we live in 'the information age' so your client is hungry to find out more before they buy – especially if it's a big ticket purchase. Your client has a mixed bag of buying emotions which we are going to look at shortly, but it is true that they will want to know they are doing the right thing in buying from you and the best way for them to know this is by researching. Give them a hand with their research and then you'll also invoke that good old 'Law of Reciprocity' we talked about earlier. (Remember the inner feeling where if someone gives you something then you feel almost duty bound to give them something back... for example, when you receive a Christmas card from someone who wasn't originally on your list and you feel obligated to quickly give them one after all! It is incredibly strong, this inner drive!)

So always give 'hints and tips' or 'buyers report' or a 'free consultation', so that you help them buy from you.

A word of caution though. If your product offering is in fact information, you can't give everything away in your free report! Offer a consultation and a free report, but make the report verbal. Show them you know your business but don't give them all they need to improve things without paying for your services!

Give it verbally and people will forget, but they interpret it as you're giving them all your knowledge and they remember that 'you know your stuff'. It has the same weight, but saves you.

There is a caveat to this. There is a rule of thumb that says if it's free, it has no value.

So you've got a potential contradiction here. You see, if you give something away free all the while... if you as a buyer have got something that you know is always there, and it is always free, you don't dash back for it, do you? Because it's always there.

If it's always free, do you really give it credibility and value? So you've got to be a bit careful here, but building value into something, so you're giving perceived value is the skill. So, what you need to do is attach a value to your advice. Don't say, "Free advice." Say, "A thousand pound consultation yours for free." Don't say, "Free service." Just say, "Free maintenance valued at five hundred pounds annually." You might invite them along to a seminar where you will explain all that you offer... but explain that this seminar is usually priced at £300 (and maybe even charge them a nominal £25 as a reservation... it builds massive value and stops a lot of false bookings!). So give for free but be wary of it representing little value.

Is there a difference between free and complimentary?

Give it free and attach a value, okay. Then you've got a lever.

Try also putting a hurdle to it, a qualification. For example, suggest that they can qualify if they currently spend £X annually on your offering or currently have used Y (a competitor of yours) as their supplier. And then, it becomes in their mind something they've got to have and is worth having free, and then you're in.

Give them a chance to sample your service. It doesn't *cost* you money, it *makes* you money!

Computer software is a great example. Give it to them for three months so that they're used to using it, and can feel the benefits and would thus feel the loss when it's taken back!

Try it. Give people your product as much as you can. The best thing in the world, if you get them to buy it, is to let them use it and get used to it. We have called this a 'Puppy Dog' close for many years in selling because everyone understands the analogy of having to look after a puppy for a few hours/days and then just when you have adapted to it and got used to it, the owner returns and takes away the puppy... what do you do then? Yes! Go right out and buy a puppy because it was actually great having it around! So let's adapt and be creative. Use this 'getting used to it' approach and see how many of your prospects want to give it back!

2. Give a guarantee

Next, closely linked into that, number two, is 'Guarantees'.

What do you give as a guarantee? What are your industry guarantees? Could you improve on it?

Again, I stress this is a critical component of your selling process and should therefore be a major point in all of your marketing. Guarantees are interpreted by the purchaser as giving them 'safety'. Remember when we spoke about some of the core human psychologies and inner drivers? Well one of the overriding inbuilt needs is that for survival... a hangover from our early days, some might say! However, wherever it comes from it is a fact that it is there. We look for safety... we avoid risk. Thus a guarantee was created to say to the shopper, "This is not going to hurt you, buy now with confidence."

It still says exactly that, and whenever you shop as a consumer the potential for risk will always be a factor... and most usually you'll be swayed away from purchasing something if it feels less safe. Think about it for a moment. If you were to buy a car, for example, you would recognise the security of a main dealer perhaps but appreciate too that you will pay more for the vehicle than with a private purchaser... the risk though of buying private, the thought of, "What if it goes wrong and it isn't covered by a warranty?" is massively strong. So much so, of course, that a great number of people do not take the risk and they buy from a main dealer to give them that security even though they know they are paying considerably more for that luxury. It illustrates perfectly the simple, yet profound buying process over risk and security... and the perception is that a guarantee takes away risk of it going wrong, thus a guarantee is a must. A must that many will pay more to experience... so cover your product or service and put your price up!

The caveat of giving guarantees is that you must make sure you've structured it correctly. So, give a guarantee on your work, but for example with print work, guarantee your *print* work, not the final article, so that if there are spelling errors then these should have been picked up by the client when they proofed the artwork and signed off for you to print. Or another example, if you are a service provider, such as a life coach or bookkeeping service where perhaps the service is less tangible to measure right or wrong, the recipient of the service basically needs to be happy and to feel totally satisfied... and simply put you should make it a 100% satisfaction guarantee. If they are not satisfied and you have them tied into a contract, they will only moan, begrudge paying you and bad mouth to any potential future clients. It's far better, in my opinion, to have less emphasis on contracts and more emphasis on satisfaction. Whatever you provide in your business, the bottom line is to make sure the client purchasing has a risk-free scenario. Give a guarantee that says to them, "I will make sure you get what you want form this purchase and if you don't, then you have a money back guarantee."

So, just give a guarantee. If it is a product, this should be fairly easy to work out but have a look for how you can still go the extra mile... see if there is a way where you can guarantee that the client gets satisfaction even in a scenario where the product you sold hasn't gone wrong. If for example, the client purchased the wrong product, see if there is a way you can offer a return of his money, even though it was not your fault. This type of approach may 'lose' you one sale now, but will probably gain you several more over the coming months as a client finally finds someone who adheres to good old fashioned values!

If you're selling a service, as this is less precise as to working or not working, then obviously you've got to guarantee results. For example, if you're selling me a service on the basis that it'll save me money, then you pretty much have to make sure it does so, or else I am going to be extremely unhappy. I'm saying that I'll spend money with you and if it 'does what it says on the tin', then I shall be glad to have done so, but if I don't save money with you, I want my money back. Especially, as in this case and many like it, where I as a purchaser do not really appreciate how you can save me money. I am not truly confident as to what you know that I don't... I mean, "I have been doing what I do for years so what exactly can you show me that I don't already know and thus how can I save money?"

With a great many service offerings, the client purchasing doesn't really know the benefits and he is taking your sales pitch as a reason why... but is not 100% convinced until he experiences the result. Sceptical purchasing such as this, the initial introduction of a service or service provider, requires a greater removal of risk and thus a stronger, fuller guarantee. So you have got to give a 100%, rock solid guarantee, because we don't like risk. If you do not feel you can do that, then I suggest you stand back and evaluate exactly what you are offering and examine your own arguments as to why someone should buy it from you. Somewhere along the line, you are either missing a factor that can be endorsed as a guarantee or selling something with questionable ethics.

What about living items? Plants or animals? Can they be guaranteed?

Well, imagine yourself as a consumer. You wish to purchase a pet for a child or a plant for your partner. On first glance, you are happy with your purchase but after having it a short time, it dies. How would you feel? Would you perhaps feel cheated by the store? If you went back and they denied responsibility, blaming perhaps the way you cared for the purchase, you'd feel pretty indignant. You'd perhaps accept the purchase as dead end and walk away, but you sure wouldn't buy from there again and you'd hardly recommend friends to the same ill-fated experience. So now think of the same experience as a store owner and then see what would be best for growing your business – a happy client who got an unconditional return/replacement service regardless of whose fault it was, or a disgruntled client but maintained margins on one item only. If you sell anything, even living items, underwrite the offering. Give rock solid, unconditional satisfaction guarantees. Clients and referrals will grow dramatically. Plants? "When you buy plants in my nursery, they won't die and if they do, I'll replace without quibble."

Absolutely give 100% rock solid guarantees on everything.

And broadcast it in all that you say and do. Loud and proud.

People buy because of security; people don't buy because of fear, so take away all the fear.

And before we close this one off, I also recognise that some products are a little harder at first glance to guarantee. For example we worked with a client who converted loft space into a usable room. He first questioned this guarantee issue saying that he couldn't guarantee satisfaction, as if they said it wasn't to their satisfaction he couldn't undo the work. Perhaps it was a little more challenging. You have to put a bit more thought into it, but when you start talking to your clients there will be a list of fears that they have that are making them hesitant to purchase... so learn these fears and create a guarantee to protect from them.

For example, one of the fears they might have is that when they've done this loft conversion, they can't use it or it's too noisy. They've heard from their neighbours who boarded out the loft themselves that when the kids went up there to use it as a playroom, which was the idea, it was so noisy that it didn't work. Or one of the fears might be that they're thinking of building a loft conversion for the father to go up there and do his work, but know that currently in the loft space it's so cold that it's too cold to be up there half the time and thus are afraid a loft conversion won't work. In either case, you'd have to understand thoroughly what they wanted from their loft conversion but having taken the time to listen and learn properly, you would be able to guarantee that they'd be satisfied because you'd take steps to cover specific areas raised and explain comprehensively beforehand all of the potential limitations and drawbacks.

So, this is why it can only work once you've done the legwork at the beginning. The foundation work we started with is critical. Go and talk to your customers. Find out what they really, really like and more importantly find out what their fears are. What would they improve? You'll find your clients will tell you when given a chance and when you know it from the client's perspective, you can come up with guarantees that help them feel safe enough to buy every time.

Find out what their fears are, and address them in your pitch. "We guarantee this will be soundproof, so that you're not going to hear your kids. We guarantee that this will be warm, so that you can work up there in the winter. We guarantee that this will be sufficiently lit." So, pick up the arguments of your clients, find out their fears, and talk their language. It's no good knowing your business from your side, you've got to know your business from their side and give guarantees that your client believes in.

3. Joint Ventures/Host Beneficiary

Third in our list of MUST DOs is joint venture arrangements.

To reiterate the power of this, I just want to mention once again that most businesses take a period of several years, up to 10 or 15 years, before they have large client banks to work with. If you make a solid fair relationship with a complimentary provider of another offering and manage to work his client base, then you could have short circuited the growth process by those 15 years! So, I ask you simply, would you like to grow a business in a fraction of the time?

There are a few caveats to this process, as we discussed. The fear of reprisal should the venture not work out is a massive one and obviously no business owner is going to walk straight into a liaison without safety nets. You will need to nurture a relationship, give the potential partner total confidence in your product or service (so that probably means giving them a chance to use it/own it for free) and probably offer them something first before they are receptive about them giving to you. (Remember the Law of Reciprocity!) In addition, you will want to show them about your character and your ethics and trustworthy nature and all of these will take time and a certain degree of closeness.

Do not be misled here. I suggest that correctly structured joint ventures are massively powerful and can quickly grow a business far faster than an organic growth, but I am not saying they are absolutely simple to create and that there isn't any effort or patience required. There is, but it is well worth the wait. Whatever you do, please make sure this is included in your 'go forward attack' as of now. Why not give yourself a target of creating two this next year?

So, look at your diagram of influencers to your client and think of people who also interact with your customer and then look to approach them as partners in joint ventures. Ask, "How could I help them? What can I give them? What will they be fearing and how can I remove that risk?" You'll soon have powerful answers and unlock this magical door!

I will tell you this... beware the first time you go up to somebody and say, "Oh yes, it would be great for us to work together,"... you might well get a door slammed in your face! Most people are not enlightened, and you won't be good at your presentation. The natural tendency is that they think, "What are you after?" So you've got to think carefully about your wording, and be prepared for the first two or three people perhaps to slam a door in your face… but just keep going, it'll pay off in the end.

4. Competitions

Okay, if you can only fit in just a few of these Business Booster marketing ideas, then of the top five MUST Dos, here is the fourth reminder – use competitions.

We've talked about competitions already, but the way I approach everything is **"Don't compete, create"**. So use competitions but don't compete with your competitors, if that makes sense. Beat your competitors by being creative, find out what the other people who do what you do are doing, and do something different.

Be creative. Now, I'll give you a tip on creativity. We've all got a creative muscle. We don't use it very often but it's there and if worked and allowed to express itself, it actually grows and strengthens. However, if you struggle to release this potent power, then allow a gathering of your team and introduce a few beverages… a couple of glasses of beer, a couple of bottles of wine, a couple of spirits, whatever… get a group of you together and just have an hour or two throwing around crazy creative ideas. Make it a light-hearted thing, have a recording device recording it, and you'll come up with creative ideas and competition thoughts that can blow away competitors. Obviously I am not suggesting that getting blind drunk is the only way! I am merely suggesting that often the creative instinct is held back because of an embarrassment or a lack of confidence… and as we all know, alcohol lowers the 'nervous' threshold and it is possibly more likely therefore that an idea that otherwise would have remained internal and private will be voiced by the creator.

And somebody will say, "You can't do that, oh that's silly," or, "Try it, because it might not be that silly," or, "Let me tell you about a 'silly idea'."

Imagine one day a hundred years or so ago. You're in a group of friends and someone says, "Why don't you invent a gum that people can chew?" How silly is that!! I mean you've already got fruit, chewing tobacco, bread and normal foods and even some candy, so why would anyone buy gum to chew?!! What a dumb idea! Such a dumb idea, in fact, that merely a generation or two later in only one country of the world, we had a problem in the UK of removing this discarded 'dumb idea' from pavements and streets after people had chewed it and chosen to spit it out! Around the UK we spend £980,000 on gum removal to the extent that it's one of the biggest blights of councils at the moment. But, I mean, whoever came up with the idea of chewing gum?! What a silly idea!!

So no ideas are silly, are they? I mean, Bill Gates came up with the idea that every home would have a PC and somebody said, "What a silly idea!" Be creative. Encourage the creative muscle to strengthen by being open to all ideas from all people, even if they appear 'silly' at first... but beware, putting all of this together will give you one fantastic, amazing journey... and it'll be great fun!!

5. Additional products/ services

Fifth in the top five MUST DOs is look to sell additional products or services. Business Alchemy, remember, is about selling to existing clients and not merely selling them (or trying to) something they already have purchased. **Business Alchemy** is about filling in the gaps and covering all of their needs.

Now again, allow me to expand just a little bit here. Many people have said to me that they choose to specialise in a very narrow delivery band and do not want to expand their product/service offering. As you might have guessed by now, I am absolutely in favour of specialising and I have said to you that, especially when marketing, the more you focus your marketing message on a narrow area and specialise, the greater the chance of success. However, once you have the client won, you will need to cover more than one base... you don't want to hear that infamous, "I didn't know you did that," but more importantly if you actually do not do something related to your existing offering and it is something that a client is likely to also purchase, then you run a massive risk of allowing them to be won over by another competitor.

You see, for example, if a client of yours who is buying a website buys a site from you but, as you have chosen to specialise in *only* creating sites, when he wants to purchase a fancy HTML flyer for an email marketing campaign, he goes elsewhere. Then in conversation, now or in the future, the flyer producer asks about the website and mentions that he also creates websites and that why doesn't the marketer let him take care of all of his Internet requirements under one roof and then he'll get continuity etc. This becomes a very appealing argument and very often results in the loss of the website client for the original website producer.

If you do not offer a range of complimentary offerings that your client is likely to purchase, you will lose a lot of your clients over time as they will be swayed away by competitors offering a comprehensive service. Link in with partners to provide what 'you do, not do'. Whatever you do, do not allow your clients to wander off.

So, there you have it. I believe passionately that you have a grounding here to rocket your business forward, however, as I have mentioned lots of times already, please do not race ahead with merely a reading exercise. Please take a few moments out now and **write _down_** some **ideas**. Why not create for yourself in each of these top five areas a task? Maybe design a competition, decide on an extra product or service offering, list a few potential strategic partners and then revisit your guarantee and your attention grabbing offer to examine how more of a 'Free Offer' and 'Risk Free' purchase can help your clients. As mentioned before, please connect with me and my team and let us work together to manage implementation www.thebusinessboosteracademy.co.uk

Section Three

Business Boosters Selling

Selling the Sizzle

"...turn on the power of your imagination, add a heap of commitment and watch your future unfold."

"Some men see things as they are and say why? I dream of things that
never were and say why not?"
George Bernard Shaw

Selling The Sizzle

Okay, so now we're coming to the end phase... not that there is ever an end to the learning and developing of yourself or your business, but for now we can say we're approaching the final section of this development lesson.

We've covered the foundations of simple basic business construction - albeit foundations and basics that most business owners only talk about and know about but rarely do - and we've covered extensively many marketing or enquiry sourcing techniques... and on those you're busy gathering and attracting enquiry overload, but if we don't convert them to paying clients we're no better off. We're just busier. Selling is still (and always will be in my book) the prime key to your cash mountain. Selling is the key to likeability and selling is the key to your finances. Selling is the holy grail of success... so let's get good at sales.

At this point, I might interject a comment. There are literally thousands of business advisors out there ranging from banking employees and accountants turned business advisors to coaching franchise owners and well meaning friends and, frankly by far the majority of them have little or no experience of creating a successful business! One thing is for sure they rarely possess enough sales skills to set their world alight and often express total business success as attributable to marketing.

The general answer when asked how to grow a business is about the advertising or promotion that you will need to do and even when they have a more guerrilla mindset, they talk about promotions; they rarely talk about refined *sales* skills.

Now, far be it for me to moan about others, but I strongly believe that a **refined ability to sell is the prime skill**. I know from experience that when you are excellent at selling, you can usually market well because the majority of marketing is about the message, rather than a delivery method, and if you sell well then usually you're good at constructing the message. Indeed, if you sell well you can earn cash to pay for skills in other areas, such as systems and the creation of business 'foundations', as often these skills are fairly readily available... which is not the case of sales skills.

In today's driven society the scarcest resource is very often sales talent. The rest can be bought but great sales skill is just not out there to buy! If you want to make yourself invaluable and if you want absolute paramount security in life, then learn a few 'edge' techniques when it comes to selling and you will never fear. You'll always be in a position to walk into a great job, but more likely you'll never need to as you'll have the key ingredient to making your business fly.

Yes, I have to stress for you, **selling is No 1**... so open your eyes, pin back your ears and let us look together at a few insights to take your already good business into a different gear.

And, by the way, I am not saying here that selling is about stereotype personality characters. It is not the case that you suddenly have to be the confident cocky loud person who is always pushing themselves to the front, or that you have to be quick with words and have slick answers. No. Selling is not that at all. You may know those who are like that but it is a little eighties now... today, sales is about relationships and people skills but these are learnable and can be equally evident in quieter, less wordy persons. You need to be able to sell, but you do not need to change your character!

Having said all of that though, in truth this is not a sales book. This is designed to be a guide to building your business into a massive enjoyable business and it recognises in doing so that selling is a vital ingredient to achieve your success. Selling skills, techniques and all of the myriad of questions, replies, situation variables etc. could fill a library but certainly another separate book, thus my thought here is an overview of some basics.

Here are some selling steps that will tweak your growing business, especially in light of all that we have so far discussed and may in themselves shed just enough light to make you shine and feel great! Here goes:

The Game Plan

First of all, every sales process should have a structure to it. I always refer to it as a 'game plan', and every sale has to have a 'game plan' to give the process correct structure. It is probably true that what you do is pretty structured in as much as it follows a pretty similar pattern, and indeed it is probably also true that you are orderly and diligent in your approach as you would not deliberately sabotage your chances of succeeding... but I believe that it can be improved upon. More importantly, I know that some 'tweaks' will not hurt you to implement but will show you a massive extra reward.

Does **'massive extra reward for a few minor tweaks'** sound interesting? Good! So let me give you a structure for a sales process.

And by the way, I appreciate fully that every sales process could be argued as 'different'. I know that the process of selling financial services in a heavily regulated environment is a little different to that of selling timeshares in a pretty anarchic environment. I know that selling to the consumer in the home is different to selling to a business in the office and indeed that selling smaller ticket items differ in process to selling larger investment items as, for example, the sales cycle is a lot longer. I have experienced them all, but actually they aren't that different, so please resist the temptation to say, "Oh but it doesn't work like that for me," and try instead to ask the question, "How might that work in my field?"

The point being made is very simple. There must be a structure to every sale and I know this game plan works. In some sales processes and environments, sticking accurately to the 'game plan' has a more marked immediate impact… if you're selling to a consumer in the home, for example, it becomes absolutely critical. If you're selling in a business to business environment, frankly it is still pretty crucial. It may be a multiple visit sale, but it has to have the same ingredients. One might argue that smaller items, frequent purchase items, are not in the same scenario because the threshold for potential 'pain' is so much lower but any sale that represents a purchase of an amount of money 'worthy of consideration as to whether it is the right move or not' definitely needs this attention to the process. For larger cost items, infrequent purchase items, it's an absolute must.

Before you and I get carried away though, what I believe is a great idea to help is for you to look firstly at what you do now. And I'm sure you know what you do, but think on it for a few seconds… and having done that, what I'd like for you to do very quickly is write on the page included the various stages that you can identify as stages when you are selling to a client.

Think about when you are in a face-to-face meeting or engaged in a phone call with a client you have not met with before (or at least have met only briefly before) and in a meeting that is designed to be the call that results in a completed agreement to purchase. Just jot down what you do… it will help as we look at my 'game plan' in comparison. PLEASE DO THIS NOW!!

My usual 'sales meeting' goes like this:

_____

_____

_____

_____

_____

_____

_____

_____

_____

_____

_____

_____

_____

_____

_____

_____

_____

_____

_____

_____

_____

_____

_____

_____

_____

_____

_____

If you've done that, thank you. Now let me tell you what I usually see.

Number one: you are immediately engaging the potential client in a greeting. The, "Hello, how are you? greetings take up a few moments, perhaps a relevant immediate conversation about the parking or the promptness, if either are the case, and then you move onto 'small talk'. This is general chat about the weather, the roads and the journey there, if applicable, or the day you are having perhaps. This, I would say, lasts usually about 10 or 15 minutes and then... well, then what? Usually it is a mutual thought or even a verbalised thought that is something like, "Well, we'd better get down to it," and so the meeting becomes a sales process. Discussion begins and revolves around, 'what you are there to do'

Obviously I am generalising and obviously I appreciate that this isn't designed to be either minute or word accurate but is that often what happens? I know from asking hundreds of sales people that it is. Well, I'm going to suggest that it can be improved upon. Resist the temptation to argue that I am not in your environment and that you have been successful in your field for so many years; therefore you must be doing it correctly! Please, bear with me and consider the slightly different approach...

Meet and Greet

First of all, there's going to be the obvious 'meet and greet', that virtually happens every time. The point here is that 'first impressions last'. It's no secret that a first impression gives us a feeling of how we should deal with somebody in front of us. Image is absolutely everything and 'perception equals reality'. What the client thinks when he/she first sets eyes on you is going to influence what follows. Dressing, talking and organising yourself in a certain way can give the impression of being more professional and in demand than you perhaps are and this is especially true of a face-to-face sales call. Your clothing, your manner, your posture and your grooming all make a visible impression even before you have opened your mouth. (Indeed, your car also speaks volumes about you so be careful how you invest in your mode of transport and keep it looking clean, tidy and legal!)

You need your prospect to see a winner. They must sense confidence, order and professionalism. They cannot be allowed to see the pressure you are under or the financial strain you might feel and they certainly can never be allowed to know that you are not very busy, if ever any of these are the case! You project non-verbal success... and you arrive promptly appearing calm and prepared. Indeed, I sincerely hope you don't just *appear* prepared but in fact that the lessons we shared when discussing preparations are well and truly ingrained as habits. You should have prepared thoroughly, including looking at their website reading any and all relevant news articles and researching their industry a little so as to talk about anything that may well be topical for them.

Remember, it's often the little things that have biggest impact. You might have an empty diary but you never say that. You might only be an 'I', but you talk 'we'. You might be nervous as hell on the inside but you do not show it.

Another point to remember here is that the most powerful sense that we've got, that all humans have, that we rely on the most, is our sense of visual input. So any impression we get, any image we see visually, gives us a strongest impression. We might <u>hear</u> what they say, and know what we <u>feel</u> about them, but what gives us the first strongest impression is the <u>visual</u>. We get a visual 20 yards away; we haven't spoken to them yet. We trust what we see. The visual sense is the strongest sense, so be very, very aware of your visuals.

So, the first stage in the sales process is the meet and greet. The first time you meet them, the first time you talk to them. Say the right things, look the part, be professional, be smiley, be happy, all obvious stuff. Grooming, cleanliness, hygiene, and although that sounds too basic to bother to write, you would be amazed at how many times I still see sales people or business owners arriving for a sales meeting with dirty shoes, old shirts with worn collars, ties with dirt marks from having been tied a lot and washed not a lot! Please don't allow your image to let you down.

Okay, so you've done your meet and greet. Then what do we do?

Well in my game plan, instead of having a few minutes of 'small talk', I am going to introduce a section called 'The Warm-Up'.

The Warm-Up

I'm going to call it a 'warm-up', for a very specific reason.

If I ask you, "What can you do with a lump of really cold plasticine?" you say not a lot. I ask "What happens when you warm it up?

That's right. It's workable, malleable.

People are no different. You are no different. Look for a moment at yourself when you buy. Think about this, just briefly, when you are looking to buy something. You probably have this big barrier up; resistance. "You're just getting a quote," is what you tell yourself and probably the salesperson. You're probably a bit stiff, a bit reserved.

Now look back at the times when you've bought something. You may have started off a little cold, but by the time you left, you were happy, joking, relaxed!!

Think about the times when you've met people, and the first time you met them it was a bit starchy. But after you'd been with them for a while, you loved them, they were great.

Think about the times when you've sold, or not as the case may be. People you don't sell to? Oh, they weren't very nice, they were arrogant pigs! Awkward, difficult, whatever!!

People you *do* sell to? Lovely people, they were! Isn't that strange?

There is a direct correlation to liking people and sales success, or people liking you and sales success. A direct correlation to liking or warming to someone, which means you've got to 'warm' to people. And I use the word 'warm-up', because we use a language that describes things without us always making the connection between the two. (We recognise the link between the words but often we have spoken the words without thinking of the meaning.)

Warming things up makes them bendy, soft, workable. On the other hand, if you're going to have a starchy client relationship, it's not going to be as workable, so you're going to get fewer results. To get the results you want, you've got to be very good at creating good people relationships. You've got to get them 'warm'.

Whether we like it or not, if you're good at it, you get more success. And the most powerful thing you can learn is the skill of opening yourself up and opening other people up. You can't work with closed doors. If your sales approach is "professional and technical and thorough," and we've "shown them everything," that's cold! It doesn't deal with _me_; connect with _me as an individual_ listening to you, as a person. If this is your sales process, you will struggle. You're not going to get sales, you're going to get one in three, one in four. If I am your prospect, I want to be *personally* recognised and loved before I respond.

It might be the 'professional way', used by others in your industry, but being 'professional' should not limit you to being starchy and correct. Professional is about doing the job in the *right* way and achieving the correct result. Too often it is those who portray the stiffer image as though it is the correct image, that perform at lower levels than is possible but are reluctant to change their approach for fear of being viewed in a less important manner. To me, it isn't about importance, it is about results. If you want to be important and try *to command* respect and then carry on being cooler but if you'd like to *be important because your results are outstanding* then try to be a little warmer. Throw off the stiffer, 'correct professional image', perhaps akin to the stereotypical accountant, for example, or the lawyer, and be warm and welcoming. It might be worth adding that traditionally these professions have been averse to selling, as it was something that they did not engage in thus the very image of a 'professional' emanates from a non-sales environment.

Singularly the most important weapon in your arsenal is your personality and getting people to like you. So, you've got to spend time warming them up.

I recognise that it isn't always easy for that to be achieved. There are some people who find it difficult to relax and let you warm them and indeed there are some who find it difficult to relax and do the warming. I don't know you, but I do know that it can be done *by everyone to everyone* if a little *more technique* is applied.

Traditionally 'sales' has focussed on closing and I am asking a lot more attention please to *opening*. As I have already mentioned, the key is a different technique and a lot more intelligence. It isn't down to personality in quite the same degree, as has always been assumed. Yes, those with more outgoing personality and more confidence might have a head start but they are not certain of victory. You can win too... so let's look a bit closer at some helpful techniques.

During this phase, you will do certain things to help your sales process. For example, during your warm-up you will be doing fact finding. You will be digging for information and chatting around topics that indicate the buying position of the client. I know you will actually be doing this 'fact finding' already and probably in a formalised manner with a 'fact find' sheet or similar. I am suggesting differently; I am suggesting specifically that you merge your finding out of information into the 'warm-up'... you ask many similar questions but in a more random, seemingly unstructured, manner and without the visible reminder to the prospect that you are writing this down and in fact working them.

Talk about emotive topics

Possibly even more critical here though is the *topic* of the questioning. I believe and indeed have seen that too many sales calls are conducted with a minimum of 'chat' and pretty much straight into the 'work' section. Even the chat is about topics that relate to the 'work'. The conversation whilst amiable is skirting around the issues to be discussed for the sales pitch. I am suggesting that you become very good at *other* topics... especially topics that really stimulate interest in the listener's ear.

Don't talk about the weather or the traffic... they feel like poor imitations for conversation and merely act as a filler for an amateur. Talk about things that the client or prospect enjoys. Get them chatting about common likes... and then listen for clues in their answers as they open up.

Again, allow me to state clearly that I do not mean forced conversation about something that is not of interest to the listener whilst you try vainly to get them 'warm'. This will feel like what it is! You have seen, as I have, sales reps that try to 'chat' and they do a poor job and you're saying to yourself, "Get on with it!" No, I am talking about moving the conversation into topics that *interest* the prospect and ones that also give you clues as to how best to proceeds... and this is vital as part of the game plan.

Can you think why?

For example, imagine if you're just chatting, and you're saying, "So, tell me about your week? What sort of week have you had?" It will feel like fairly pleasant but pretty normal and average filler talk. Probably it won't elicit much emotion or indicators as to their decision influencers. You need to hit on conversation that possibly sparks the prospect up.

Nice Motor!

If you're just chatting away, and you notice they've got a nice car outside, and you ask about it and they begin to enthuse... well then you have a different outcome potential altogether. They might be a 'petrolhead' and be excited. They might be very proud that they have a new slick car that is special to them. On the other hand, of course, they might be of the opinion that a car is merely a work horse and nothing they want to chat about. The point is that by asking and watching their reaction, you'll see clues. But be aware that if they hook into a motor conversation, you need to be equipped to handle it! Don't stir a topic that you are ignorant in because immediately they get going and start to share, and they will want feedback of enthusiasm from you in order to feel good about 'spouting off'!

Great tan!

Again, just conversationally you say, "You're looking relaxed. Have you been away recently?" The conversation feels easy and probably they will not mind talking about the holiday, even if they might still view this as pretty normal filler talk... and if they haven't been away, they will enjoy the compliment... but the truth is, all of these areas of conversation open up huge clue areas as to the personality of the prospect. The answer is actually telling you a massive amount... which we will expand upon in a little while.

For now, the realisation is that the conversation must be centred on emotive subjects and not work-related topics. Two prime things happen as a result of doing this. Firstly, they become relaxed and 'warm' as they talk about a topic that they are emotionally involved in whilst also giving you a chance to possibly gain common ground and, secondly, they forget that you are there to talk business and their resistance level drops.

It might be that you see some pictures on the wall and say, "Ooh, that's nice. What's that?" or you see a trophy in a cabinet or an award certificate on the wall. Conversation flows in a pleasant manner relaxing the prospect and 'warming' them to you but you're also gathering information. You're not doing a formal 'fact find' section but you *are* finding out important facts. Again though, you must offer enthusiasm to them and show clearly that it is a genuine interest and conversation because they are suspicious and conditioned by past experience that usually sales people off filler talk and don't really care!

However if you do this, then already you are doing better than the more normal '10 minutes filler talk and then into business' approach.

You might ask, "What is the difference? What is all of this information you are talking about? We're just talking about holidays and cars!"

Well, you're gathering all sorts of information. Think about it. Are you gathering information that might help you to build up a picture of the prospect's potential? Probably you can already build up a picture of the prospect's financial situation, or his stress levels, or his business levels, but you have appeared to be chatting in a conversational manner. You have not appeared to be formal and 'getting down to business', but you've gathered clues that will help you in winning the business.

What's the difference? Well, if you've gone in and spent five or ten minutes talking, and had a cup of tea, you will have begun to make a friend. If you are genuine (and I'll assume you always are), they will have begun to warm them to you, you'll be *connecting* as a person. If you then say, "Well, let's get down to business," or something equally blunt, then there's almost a pregnant pause, isn't there? And you've just reminded them why you're there and the defensive barrier goes up again.

The buyer gets the defensive wall back up. Remember they might be trying to find out information, not actually trying to buy, so they will be on their guard to keep themselves from buying just yet... so when you're selling in that sales situation, don't suddenly go from chit chat into, "Right, into business now," because it tells them, "Prepare"!

Caution! If you've got sales aids, like worksheets, you've got to be very careful how you use them because the minute you start getting a selling form out, it tells them, "I'm working now". It means, in their language, you are there to sell and they interpret that as, "Be prepared, protect, and be safe." And as the sales process is all about a mind game, you cannot allow them to be in control. You call the shots. In sales, if you start using props, tools and questionnaire sheets, you effectively start telling them straightaway you're there to do a job, and that increases barriers and reduces your chances. You *will* need to use them and there are situations where they can be effective earlier but as a general rule, use them only once the client or prospect has truly warmed to you... and even then use them intermittently so that you can switch back and forth from 'sales mode using tools' to 'friendly visitor talking and showing an interest'.

So, when I say put the fact finding into the warm-up, I mean make it warm, make it casual, and make it conversational. Become brilliant at asking a range of varied stimulating questions that maintain interest and keep them engaged but that also feeds you tons of information about how they think, how they feel and if they are preparing to buy. The information gathering is critical but it is information possibly of a slightly different angle to that which traditional sales formats seek.

Usually a sales person's 'Fact Finding' is about the prospect's usage of the product or service and their business scenario... it is, as we have stated, work-related, not client person-related! Your mission from today onwards is to become more person-related and I shall share some ideas as to how to use these 'facts' once you have uncovered them!

If you do this well, you will see a massive increase in response and you will actually enjoy all of your calls a lot more... even if you don't sell every time, you will have more fun every time. One thing is for sure, if you work at this human conversation connection skill, you will make lots of new and fruitful friendships that will always be beneficial someday.

Are you good at it? Perhaps not. Get better at it. Try it. Practice it. Watch what happens. Really be aware of what's happening on the other side.

Sales people usually are only conscious of what? What _they_ are doing! Sadly, most sales people are just heavily concentrating on themselves. In their mind, as a salesperson, they're thinking, "Right, I've done that, and now I'm going to do this." And all they are conscious of is what they are going to say. It's always me, me, me! I've got to sell this, I've got to say this, I've got to do this. My message to you is Stop! Hold back a little! Turn around; think what the _customer_ is going through. That is more critical... if the client or prospect's mind is going the right way, you will end up with a sale even if you are all mixed up!

So remember this, please. Primarily the customer's mind is looking to protect. The prospect is probably trying *not* to buy or at least not to buy just yet. So just be very wary. When I say 'warm them up', I mean I want you to spend a lot of time warming them up. Preferably, 45 minutes or more! And there are a few things, I'll give you as tips, which will seriously help you achieve this rapport.

By the way, if you think 45 minutes or more is a long time and that you or your clients will have a challenge with this, I promise you that by far the majority of the time, you will not upset a prospect if you have done the bonding well and you will be rewarded more often for your diligence than you will be turned away for your slowness. The point is, of course, that if you do it properly, you will make friends and it will be enjoyable for both parties and the time will fly by. As they say, "Time flies when you're having fun." If it is a struggle, you just aren't good enough and you need to work on your non-business conversation skills!

'Warm-Up' - techniques that help

I have said how important this warm-up is and it is not an area that is without structure or planning. It is a highly skilful part of the sales process and consequently amid the friendliness it has a mission... three, in fact.

The warm-up has three primary objectives:

- To establish trust
- To create rapport
- Find out information

Becoming excellent at warming people to both you and warming them into a more relaxed state, as we have said, is a supreme skill. It might appear simple and often look easy... but a Master will be able to achieve this with a person that initially resists and the Master will manage to open the most closed of people... and still come away with a sale when many other so-called professional sales people would have left a long time earlier.

And there are a couple of specific ways to do it which help you. Two great techniques that, if you focus upon being very good at, will help you 'unlock' your clients or prospects and genuinely it will all feel a lot easier.

These skills? Learning to 'Swap Secrets' and 'Tell Stories'.

Telling Stories

The first and possibly the most effective technique is to tell stories. You must become deliberately and proficiently good at telling stories. When you get *very* good at telling stories, they won't know if it's a made-up story or real and happening, being relayed, but it doesn't matter.

Here's why storytelling is a massive skill to enhance.

Critically it stems from how the mind works and utilises consciously what is stored subconsciously.

Think about this for a moment... what does the word 'story' mean?

Well, when did you first hear the word and 'learn' what it meant? Remember a time in your life when you were *most* accustomed to hearing stories. When was it? When exactly? Think about it...

Yes, it was when you were a child and usually around bedtime!

This is important because early on in your life, you learned a word, 'story', and you learned with it a meaning... and that meaning was that 'story' meant safe, comfortable, relaxing, non-threatening.

This is supremely important. Please understand this because it illustrates how language patterns are so embedded into each of our psychologies and impact how we act or react. The word has a meaning which is embedded from its earliest occurrence... and when you use a certain word, it triggers the memory attached to that word when it was stored and learned. Thus in this case, 'story' invokes a safe and comforting feeling and induces trust and a relaxed state.

Thus your prospect's mind will automatically find that meaning and relax a little when it hears the words, "Let me tell you a story." Now I don't want you to go all Val Doonican on me, but words such as that or, "Let me relay a story," will definitely relax the subconscious mind of the listener. Indeed, to enhance the impact of your words, try pausing deliberately for a second or two after saying the word 'story'. This allows the listening brain to register the word, search and find a meaning, and then act according to that stored memory meaning which in this case is an instruction that says, "It's okay to relax." Thus effectively by being incredibly smart and deliberate, you are controlling the mind of the prospect and making them relax so that you can get your message in... which brings me to the second most wonderful fact about this technique.

We are all aware of the power of stories to educate, aren't we? For example, when did you learn the meaning of 'Crying Wolf'? Yes, when you were told a *story* about a little boy who foolishly cried wolf when shepherding... and we have remembered ever since the message in the story!! How powerful is that?! The Tortoise and the Hare? David and Goliath? There are a lot of examples that serve to illustrate that stories are powerful in message conveyance. You know from your early conditioning that stories often have a meaning or a message in them, thus you are already programmed to listen for a 'message' and your brain is at its most receptive when it hears the trigger word 'story'! How powerful is that?!

So, storytelling is massively effective in holding the listener's attention *and* at getting a message across. Indeed, many of the great messages of all-time have been wrapped up in fables or parables and many of the great teachers from Jesus to Ghandi use them to communicate effectively. Why not associate yourself with those type of peers? It really is a powerful technique when used with skill. Your practiced and skilful word usage in just this one example will steer a prospect into a very receptive state and thus allow you to get your message across and automatically improve sales chances!

Here's a caveat... Tell stories, yes, but perhaps even more effectively, make your stories third party That is a story that doesn't directly involve you... you are merely relaying what someone has told you or what you heard about.

Why? Well, if the client says, "I went to Scotland and it was fabulous," and you say you also went to Scotland, wasn't it great, fantastic? You might well strike a chord of commonality and begin to bond... after all, it is quite probable that you both like Scotland. Then 20 minutes later, the client says they were looking to buy a Jaguar and you say, "Oh, I was looking for a Jaguar." The client's now thinking, "Beware!" It's feeling unrealistic... alarm bells ring. The third time they say, "We went to Corfu," and if you say, "Isn't Corfu great? I went there," they'll be feeling as though you are merely saying this to be on their level and it will feel false. The client will be thinking, "Everything I say, he agrees to. That's not 'real' or likely so he must be a liar." There is a probability that maybe you have one thing in common, at a stretch possibly a couple, but three feels unlikely and alarm bells ring.

In fact, you can perhaps imagine how you might feel or indeed remember a time when you had a visit from a salesperson when it happened... it doesn't feel real! It feels fake and signals alarm bells that the rest of what the salesperson is saying might also be fake.

So, critically, you must use a third party in your matching and storytelling scenarios.

Play that scenario again. If they say they went to Scotland, and you say, "I've not been to Scotland. It's a place I'd really like to go. A friend of mine, Ashley, has got a log cabin up there. He goes up there three times a year. Plays a lot of golf, mind. Doesn't matter if it rains because it's all fully equipped, it's fantastic. You should see some of the pictures. So whereabouts is your log cabin?"

Totally different feel when you introduce a third party. Your client will relate to the story without thinking less of you. Indeed, if your story is slightly inaccurate, they'll blame the third party for telling you wrong, not you for lying to them! It's very powerful for rapport building!

So, use third party stories. Get good at creating stories, or probably I recommend get very good at listening and *relaying* stories.

I always remember many years ago I was trying to sell to a BT telecoms engineer and it was the first time I had met anyone who had that occupation and so I applied my full attention to all that he said about his occupation and I learned from him many of the challenges he saw as a BT employee working in a telephone exchange. I listened and probed and found out a lot... I actually got a sale from him, but more importantly I had learned and memorised a lot of what he talked about... and purely by coincidence I came across another BT employee only about 10 days later. I suddenly was able to recall my experiences with the previous exchange engineer and very quickly I was asking intelligent questions and creating a rapport with my new prospect. I established very good common understanding and opened the new prospect up very quickly primarily because I had learned some stories about BT and the issues faced by employees. I succeeded in getting another sale! It worked for me and to this day I remember the instance because it taught me well the value of all that I am passing on here. Please make an effort to *listen* better when clients are talking and *record in your memory* more of what they say because it will help when you relay a story and you will bond even better with future prospects.

Swapping Secrets

Okay, what then about swapping secrets?

Why is 'swapping secrets' so powerful? What do I mean? Do I mean really tell closely guarded confidential information?

Well again, let's look at the psychology involved. What *is* a secret? What does the word really mean?

A secret is something that is shared with you not for common broadcast. Therefore if it is shared with you in such a way it almost certainly implies that you must have a little extra standing in the eyes of the person who tells it to you, which in turn then is read by the listener as a privilege and, almost without conscious recognition, it makes the listener feel special and valued... certainly valued above many others because after all, not everyone else has been told. When you tell a secret you imply, "I shouldn't be telling you this, but I feel that you are above many others and are deserving of a little extra treatment."

And because of how we have all learned, we all have a label of understanding attached to the word 'secret' and that label triggers a feeling... and the feeling is usually a good one which means that simply mentioning the word can trigger a very powerful feeling of trust within the listener... and when selling, this has massive power with a prospect if done correctly. Indeed, allow me to share once again a key human psychology... or at least one of the six key component psychologies - the need for 'significance'. Remember, we mentioned it previously? Well every human on the planet needs to feel significant to some degree and 'secrets' imply that I am significant in your eyes. Very subtle and extremely powerful!

Combine the two together, stories and secrets, and you have an immensely powerful psychology to gain the trust of the prospect... and if you handle it properly and are deserving of it, then you have over 70% of the sales battle already won. How fantastic is that?!

So, when talking with a prospect, you might be talking about a delivery issue, or a bolt-on extra, or a client asks for special payment terms, and you tell the story of how you had a scenario a couple of weeks ago where another client thought they'd got it all set up, and at the last minute the product wasn't ready to go live because they hadn't actually got everything ready for their delivery. And you share the 'secret' that actually there is a gap for a special delivery! Or they could have the bolt-on extra because this other client let his go, or they can have special payment terms due to this other poor client falling at the last hurdle.

It's just a genuine story, and in the end it was a bit of a pain, and you got over it. But it was a story that was more believable because you added a 'secret'. You've told a story about someone else that had a problem last minute. And he's thinking, "That's believable, I sometimes have problems at the last minute."

So, you are using just a little extra bit of skill to create an environment where the potential client feels safe. You use a story to illustrate a situation, and you add weight by telling a 'secret'. It might be, for example, a scenario relating to a previous call you were on and the prospect had a challenge with a payment issue, or it might be delivery, staff shortage, or storage levels or anything. Whatever it is, the client in front of you relates to the situation and believes your story and then the secret allows them to get something they could not otherwise have got.

You can tell this kind of story to try closing a sale too. For example, you say, "You know, I almost forgot to tell you this, but I was with somebody a couple of weeks ago and I was kicking myself when I walked out. It upset me really. I was in with my prospects chatting away, and it was really going well, it was going to be a good deal, and I didn't get it! And it only occurred to me as I was driving down the road that I hadn't mentioned about payment terms. Anyway, when I'd arrived back at the office, he'd rung the office and asked if we could do terms. It was just the timing of monies that was holding his company spending back. He was unsure as to how he could juggle so he had been non-committal. He'd rung in and asked if we would arrange everything for him now but invoice next month, and do you know what? I never even thought of asking him. If I'd just have asked him at the time, of course we can do it. I learned my lesson." Then you pause to allow him to absorb what you've just said.

You've just told him that if payment is an issue, there's perhaps something you can do.

If now with this client there possibly is a concern about how he can pay/affordability, he'll feel less awkward mentioning it. By telling him you had this issue last week and you could have got over it, he feels comfortable to come clean and admit his circumstances.

You *flush the situation out*, by creating a story about a similar situation. So the client feels safe to admit their real scenario. And whilst I have used an example of money, it can be anything. The power of using this technique skilfully is incredible. You will find you can get objections out of clients before the client was planning to throw them at you and you can then deal with it in *your* time, not in confusion at the end of the pitch.

When you get masterful at stories and secrets, you will engage your prospect and keep them entertained and the whole process will not feel like a sale or feel like work, but in fact feel like a pleasant meeting and mutually beneficial arrangement between two friends. It really is supreme.

Here's an exercise that helps you master this.

I suggest that you take a few moments out before reading on and <u>make a list of all of the excuses that you hear</u>... a list of the obstacles or objections that you feel are in the way whenever you do not sell. Make a list of all of the reason why people haven't bought, and then just try and <u>create a story around each</u> of these examples so that whenever you are with a client and feel like you are going to hear a negative and that they are slowly trying to say, "No," you can tell them a story to try and flush out the challenge they are hiding. Make an effort to create a library of stories around both negative and positive experiences. Create an account for larger or smaller issues and have a series of different stories lined up so that if ever you have to revisit a prospect that you didn't close in to a sale on a previous occasion, you have a different story to illustrate your point.

This is not fake or false, it is merely preparation. Make the stories actual accounts and relay real client scenarios... but get used to **illustrative language and stories that wrap up sales points or client pain points**.

Take a few minutes now and give this some attention... and then play a game with yourself and practice telling a secret. Be good at this and you will open more prospects up to you and when they are open to you, you will find out what is holding them back or what their concerns are... and when you know these you are then in a fantastic position to overcome them... or simply bail out early if indeed there is a condition lurking beneath that you cannot overcome, at least for the time being.

Notes

What are the common excuses I hear when potential clients do not buy?

_____

_____

_____

_____

_____

_____

_____

What stories could I create to 'flush out' these excuses?

_____

_____

_____

_____

_____

_____

_____

What 'secrets' could I tell to make them feel at ease?

_____

_____

_____

_____

_____

_____

_____

One final thought on 'secrets'. The word 'secret' conjures up in your mind a pre-programmed image. It's not a 'secret', for example, if you're loud and open about it, is it?! Rather you only _feel_ it to be genuine if it is passed over in a hushed, huddled manner. In fact, it usually means someone beckoning you closer so that others can't hear... so please remember this when using the words. Be congruent and be more powerful. Lean forward, lower your head and your voice and signal them to come closer with a gentle hand gesture when telling a secret to them. You will be amazed! The listener has a pre-programmed understanding and thus anticipated action when hearing and _feeling_ the word. You really will see people lean in to you even without them knowing it!! It makes it so powerful!! Be congruent. Play the game and win!!

And these types of techniques are all really, really subtle, powerful things. But the effect is total control. Now, are you going to be able to sell more to people that you're controlling, or less? Exactly! So take the time now and make it pay off in future!

Character and personality clues

As you are aware, we are also gathering clues in this warm-up area. However, for many sales people, currently meeting with potential clients everyday, they are not recognising vital character traits and missing massive clues that can make the task a whole lot easier. Too often, focuses as we have said is on the work-related information and not person-related information and so right now allow me to share some person-related information ideas.

You see, being able to recognise personality traits and differing character requirements can suddenly make you sooo much smarter!

Here I believe is where you can really gain ground with a little more awareness. If you can spot a few key clues and then include variations in how you present, you will sell to the prospect with greater ease.

You and I know that rarely are two people the same but what exactly are the tell tale signs that help you decide exactly how they are different? Is there a list you can look at to tick off pointers so as to clearly identify people types?

Well you may be familiar with some basic psychology and have perhaps brushed with some NLP (Neuro-Linguistic Programming) at times or possibly you haven't but for a moment allow me to share my thoughts with you as to how these sciences can directly be applied to your sales career for dramatic impact.

Essentially the human mind directs actions according to programmes that run through it e.g. if you've had a scary moment in your early childhood in a swimming pool then you may well have a mind programme that tells you that you are afraid of water and now you operate and choose to act in accordance with that programme by not going swimming.

The action that to you seems perfectly reasonable seems completely ridiculous to another person who discovered only the massive delights of splashing around and having fun when they were younger, and swimming pools touched their lives, and who now love every chance they can get to have fun enjoy the water. Two complete opposites, who is right? Why do they both act the way they do?

Inside your mind, you have a programme that decides upon whether to take an action or not according to two polarities, Pain and Pleasure. Your mind will in a nanosecond run around its memories and scan through all old records and try to ascertain whether taking an action can be judged to be painful in anyway or whether taking an action can be judged to be pleasurable.

Each possible action triggers a scanning process and based upon the programmes installed in that mind, the result will steer one way or the other. For some people, the actions will call up memories that showed when this or something similar was done in the past and it caused pain and thus the message coming back will be one of, "Don't do it"... and for some, the message coming back will see no memories that warn it away but instead memories or programmes that tell it this usually causes good feelings, so go ahead.

Everybody's pasts and circumstances have been different and thus everybody's mind programmes are different but for many of us there are patterns. Broadly speaking, many of us will assimilate quickly into one or the other of those two polarities and then act according to the message coming back.

Thus some people act according to a message coming back that says, "This has caused pain in the past, so don't do it now because it could cause more pain"... and some people act according to a message that says, "It was good before, so do it again and it may well be good again." The first person being a 'Pain Avoider' and the second being a 'Pleasure Seeker'.

Your task when asking someone to take action is to make sure that the proposed action fits with their programming. If you are asking a person to act but his programme tells him that historically similar actions have caused pain, then they will be strongly resisting acting in such a way again. When you are selling, you are going to massively struggle to move someone over a perceived threatening situation if they naturally are programmed to avoid pain.

And as we just touch this, please, let me ask you a question.

I am planning a special event later next year where I shall invite people like you to come over to my retreat in Spain and indulge in an awesome week that will take their life to yet another level. A week in the company of world respected top flight specialists that will 'fix' all areas of your life, so that you run like a highly-tuned engine.

Do you want to come to Spain?

Okay, so just ask yourself that question. Imagine me in front of you asking and offering that opportunity and it is very real. What is the first thing that runs through your mind?

There will, of course, be lots of things running through your mind relevant to that brief question, but can you quickly identify the first and most instinctive response inside of your mind?

Or, imagine in your environment whenever you ask someone if they would like to do something with you or use what you are offering... what is the first thing that usually comes back as a question?

Yes! Usually it is, "How much will it cost?"

Why is that? What is it telling you?

Well instinctively the mind of the person you're asking runs a programme that says, "In the past when I have wanted to go or have been offered something, it was a cost... and that cost meant I had to suffer to make ends meet or indeed suffer comments from others in my life... and those memories relate to a pain and thus I don't want pain again... invitation-type questions usually come before a cost and a cost means some pain for me in either finding the monies or in embarrassment because I can't..."

The response around, "How much is it?" is a response indicating that their prime driver is avoiding pain. They are a Pain Avoider. They will only move forward when the level of pain is reduced.

You see, when I asked you that question about a week-long course, you could have immediately asked yourself excitedly, "Who is going to be coming over? Where in Spain? What will it cover?" etc.

You could have asked or commented about the fantastic experience and have focussed on the pleasure or gain from the week… but your first reaction, or at least most people's first reaction to such propositions, is one of, "Where's the pain?"

Now if you can quickly see this fitting into place and making sense to you… let's take this one stage further.

If you appreciate that most people avoid pain as their first reaction or response… what do you usually talk about when selling? When actually presenting your offering was is that you normally run through in an attempt to encourage people to come your way?

Yep, the benefits!! You are trained by other people's sales training and past experiences that the way to sell is to highlight all of the benefits and then, when the client sees just how fantastic your offering is, they will move across. WRONG!!!

For many people, the trigger isn't pleasure! For many people, they will not move because of benefits… they will interpret *the move itself* as pain. They have a programme that tells them 'change' hurts, or 'spending' hurts, or 'new' hurts! They are programmed to avoid pain and so will not move as 'moving' in itself represents pain!

Unless you find yourself in the fortunate situation where the prospect in front of you has basically shown his or her desperation and that they are already suffering pain where they are, then you aren't going to get them moved. Especially if where they are, they currently feel quite well looked after. More likely the prospect in front of you is comfortable… they maybe don't use your product or offering at all and thus have got by without it, so why change? Or they are using it but their current provider isn't really hurting them, so why change? You're trying to get them to go with you 'because yours is better' and they don't respond by being drawn to 'better'.

And this, my friend, is why most sales do not happen. **The sales programme does not compute with the buying programme. You are talking a different language!**

So the challenge or question is, "How can you identify the correct programme to use so that you talk in their language and see action?" How can you identify whether your prospect is motivated to move forwards because of pleasurable benefits, or learn if they are motivated to resist because moving forwards or buying usually represents pain that they wish to avoid?

Which 'way' do they go? That is the crucial question.

Remember a few pages back and I mentioned that you were looking for clues, and we talked about gathering information? Well that almost meaningless conversation about holidays, homes, careers and children... it is all rammed with information that tells you what programme they are running!!

Imagine this: a client you are visiting (and get chatting to!) has been in the same firm for 18 years and he has lived in the same area of town for 18 years as the home and the job came together. His wife has worked in a local store since the children left home. He drives a new car, but it is a 'sensible' car, not a flash or sporty model. He holidays twice a year now because they can afford to, but they go to the same place every time because they have an apartment there.

Any hints yet as to what sort of person this might be? Do they avoid pain, would you say, or seek to gain pleasure? Go on, have a guess!

Absolutely!! This person is probably a Pain Avoider, as he hasn't put himself through any possible stress situations over the years... he has resisted the chance to move home, stuck with his employer through thick and thin and not chased glory and ambition, and they have survived a lengthy relationship and drive sensible cars... but knew because it is then always reliable and go to a known and familiar place for holidays!!

And in the past, you'd have heard all of that! You've made great conversation and friends, and then suddenly switched from conversation to selling and gone into your pitch! You'd have heard the clues and missed the signs... you'd then have talked the wrong language and probably ended up with something like the prospect saying, "I will let you know." He liked you but didn't feel triggered to respond. You'd bonded but then missed when you fired sales arrows. He was a Pain Avoider and you spent all of the time talking about benefits and how much better he might be if he changed!

Or another scenario. You are in a sales meeting and you see the prospect is a recent occupier of that position... just two years and in conversation you talk about career prospects and they tell you they are looking to progress hopefully within the company, but are not ruling out the possibility of leaving. They tell you about their new company vehicle that they chose according to a budget and they struggled to get all of the extras in, so paid a little bit personally for the satellite navigation and all-leather seats. Then you listen and they have had great holidays... they make a point of going away twice a year because when you work hard, you deserve a reward!!

You've been there, haven't you? You've heard this type of conversation!! And then you have switched into selling and it has remained friendly, but somehow you missed the deal!!

This second person obviously is the sort who seeks the temporary high of pleasures. They will enjoy 'new' and 'different' and 'standing out from the crowd'. They will want to buy 'faster, louder, shinier' things. They will support new technology and added whiz-bang bits! A pleasure seeker will want to see the sexy bits, so don't bore them with old tried and tested. They will be less into the fact that everybody has it, and more into the fact that they will be one of the first to have it and they will need to be made to feel a leader, not a follower.

The truth is all of the conversation in your 'warm-up' is riddled with clues... and when you can learn to identify the character and style of your prospect and **then switch your presentation accordingly**, you will win through literally most of the time. Forget old sales closing percentages of one sale in every three, four or five presentations... it can be one in two or even sometimes one in one! Listen a lot more, learn to spot the clues and then you can fire your arrows correctly to suit them.

A Pain Avoider might want to see stability in your company or proven longevity in your product. They will look for slower presentations and more solid representation of evidence to support the verbal. They might also want to deal with people on their territory, so visit them and they might also want to be given time to think momentarily whilst you present, so pause a little.

Very definitely, the Pain Avoider will not respond to your telling of all of the extra benefits... he or she will respond to pain or danger. Your challenge here is not to *pull* them across but to help them be pushed... create Pain with **not** moving across. Attach pain to their existing or old ways. Show them a painful future for missing your offer. They need to move away from pain so your technique is not 'pleasure pull', it is 'pain push'.

I know we have only touched on this and I know that it will not be always so black and white... sometimes a person can be a pleasure seeker in one area of life and still hold back in others. I fully appreciate that this is a topic worthy of deeper study. I would love to expand on it and certainly if you are interested (www.thebusinessboosteracademy.co.uk) then take a look inside the Academy - there is a lot of very specific help there for you.

My question though is, can you see how making yourself a little more aware of the programmes that your prospect is operating with and then adjusting accordingly will give you more success? The alarming truth is that until now, regardless of this insight, you have probably been bonding very well with people and indeed asking many of the questions and getting people 'warm'. I respect that you have probably achieved well already and can already sell your chosen wares... but imagine how much more you can now enjoy when you apply a little more science!!

Try this please. Take a few moments now to just assess the people you know or who you deal with frequently. Just quickly ask yourself some questions about their lifestyles, holidays, cars, gadgets etc. and see if you can see patterns. Look at colleagues, bosses, team members or neighbours... ask yourself about how they chase new things or accept steady styles. Look for hints of where they allow risk and where they close ranks... it's fascinating when you start to see it... and when applying this refined skill to growing your business, then believe me you will very quickly start to unlock people. You'll hear comments from them about how good a salesperson you are, how you make people feel like they can trust you and how they 'like you'.

All of this is indicative that you have created rapport with them and matched them, which means you've spoken their language; you haven't frightened them off being a salesperson who threatens pain! Play with this and get good at it, my friend, and you will absolutely fly in your life!!

By the way, it works in *all* human interaction areas, so if you see a potential mate or object of desire and you want to win them over, study their character traits a little and then offer them something in *their* language – it might be they aren't pleasure seekers, so don't automatically assume they will be swept of their feet with your promised glory!!

A closer look at people characteristics

Who do I know and how do they 'work'? Describe their lifestyle... length of time in home residence, number of years in same job, marriage, etc. (Write down a name of a person you know well and then write some characteristics and see if you build up a picture of what dominant programme they run, Pain Avoider or Pleasure Seeker.)

_____

_____

_____

_____

_____

_____

_____

_____

_____

_____

_____

_____

What type of programme do I think they run predominantly?

_____

_____

_____

_____

_____

_____

If I were to sell to them, how could I best use this knowledge? What style of sales approach might be more successful? What might I say to produce the 'action' I want?

_____

_____

_____

_____

_____

_____

_____

_____

_____

_____

What am I like? How do I respond to 'push' or 'pull'? What characteristic do I display mostly? What does it take to trigger me to spend?

_____

_____

_____

_____

_____

_____

_____

_____

_____

_____

_____

_____

_____

The Presentation

Once you've got somebody 'warmed up', what do you then do in your sales process?

You do have to move on and talk about your product, so at this stage we'll just call it 'presentation' - the presentation of your offering to the prospect, which by now is friendly and open to what you need to say.

What are you going to present? Think about this now for a few seconds... what are you going to present to this client?

To most sales people, that seems like a silly question because they are simply going to present all of the offerings the same way as they always present. "I will present all of the offerings because that is what is needed to sell! Indeed, how could you do the job if you didn't say it *all* and do it all correctly?" and so that is why they are now very good (almost word perfect!) every time at explaining *all* of the benefits and *exactly why* the client should see them as benefits, and to make this perfect they have structured it all around a very neat PowerPoint presentation!!

(Phew!) But you get the picture!! How many times have you seen that?!

Be honest, are you going to do it the same way as always? Do you usually present the product or service you are selling in pretty much the same way every time? Be truthful, do you?

Let me ask you a quick question... are you the same character and personality as your neighbour or your brother, or another man or woman in your profession? No.

Is it likely that all of your prospects are the same character and personality as each other? No.

Is it possible that all of the companies or clients that you approach suffer from exactly the same challenges or 'problems', and that they all need exactly the same solutions delivered in exactly the same way? No!

So why are people taught to present in exactly the same way to everybody?!! Surely to goodness, it is obviously going to score sometimes and miss a lot more often! No two people are the same, so why should two sales presentations be exactly the same?

Knowing now what we talked about a few moments ago, think about your presentation in a new light. Your presentation must be individually tailored to suit the client in front of you!!

Truthfully I know why this isn't done though... because most sales people in most calls do not *know* the person in front of them! They've merely had a polite general chat for a few minutes and it was a semi-warm polite and time filler-type conversation! Thus when they present, they cannot make it personal enough and consequently have to try to cover all bases!

WRONG APPROACH!!

To be more sure of winning the game and to be a happier, more successful salesperson, you must be able to talk specifically to the person in front of you and to ensure 100% that your offering is exactly what they want... not pretty close, not some of it but not all of it, but make it *exactly* what they want... and you're only going to be able to do this if you have really bonded and skilfully gathered all information possible in the warm-up.

It may well be that you have found out over the last hour that the number one driver for your prospect is 'delivery'. Yes, it will have to be competitive in price as he won't stand being ripped off (and you'd never do this because it is suicide for future!) and he doesn't want to have a lower specification, but primarily he is focussing on one point... delivery schedules and actually keeping promises! Maybe he has been let down on many previous occasions and lacks any real faith in people like you in your industry... so you have to assure him that you are different, and the only way he will test you is in a delivery reality.

Now, knowing all of that, would you still do a full presentation? Or might you perhaps show briefly your product/service and ask if he is happy with the spec or design... then after getting a confirmation in a matter of moments on this issue, you merely ask, "So just to clarify the situation Mr Prospect, can I ask you, is delivery your main concern and if so, are you in fact saying that provided I can deliver as I have said, then you are happy to go ahead?"

Whatever the situation, if you have bonded well and found out the key driver, then the actual presentation may well be nominal. Even when the full presentation is required, you need to be not 'talking at' but 'discussing with'... and that means asking far more questions, but your prospect will not mind answering when they are feeling connected.

You will have heard many trainers talk about asking better questions and indeed I too will endorse exactly how critical superb questioning skills are, but also realise that if you merely ask questions but haven't bonded, it will probably feel like interrogation from the prospect's perspective!! Be careful! Make a friend first!

And before we move on, please let me mention one final point in how best to make winning presentations... the timing and structure of the call as a whole. Remember, **"A sale is made with emotion and justified with logic."** Emotion is what drives the sale; logic keeps a sale in bed.

Look at the way you present and see if it's logical or emotionally linked and then look at the next graph.

When you spend time with people, emotions are raised, thus we've got time on one axis and emotional link on another. In any interaction, the longer you spend with people, what happens generally?

The more you get to like them.

So, your sales process, if graphed, should be a graph that the longer you're with them, the more the emotional connection is established and the line raised. Sadly, what happens with a lot of sales presentations is not correct. Usually they have a process whereby the salesperson spends time with the prospect and 'warms them up' and then switches straight back into sales mode.

The presentation thereafter actually is logic based and then at the end of the process, the client is asked to buy. By looking at this in a visual graph format, you can see in 'Graph 1' that by the end of the process, the emotional level is in fact cool again as the sales process was logic based.

Graph 1

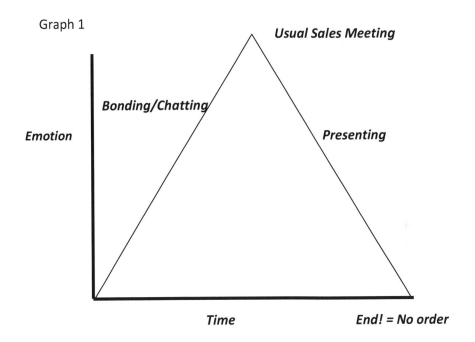

Usual Sales Meeting

Bonding/Chatting

Presenting

Emotion

Time

End! = No order

Graph 2

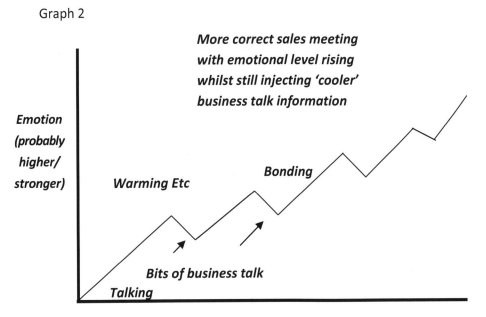

More correct sales meeting
with emotional level rising
whilst still injecting 'cooler'
business talk information

Emotion
(probably
higher/
stronger)

Warming Etc

Bonding

Bits of business talk

Talking

Time (probably longer)

Thus although it made sense, the client isn't moved to act and the usual response is, "I want to think about it". This is because emotion creates movement or action and in this scenario, there is no push to act. It made sense and they understand but don't feel compelled to act.

If, however, a more strategic approach is made, as in 'Graph 2', then you can see that the whole sales visit is made up of emotional content interspersed with reasons to buy. Thus when the process is ended, the client has all of the reasons in their mind but also feels on an emotional high and is ready for action.

This is a tricky and skilful process but believe me it is the difference between lots of presentations where you hear, "I want to think about it," versus clients signing up and you earning highest incomes. If you spend a lot of time planning and learning so that you consciously implement a different process, then your efforts will be rewarded, I promise. You are deliberately mindful of each section of the sale process and you stage it so that emotions are maintained at a high level.

Make a sales call warm and friendly, and interject the necessary facts and figures. Do not make it a call of two halves!

Credibility

Okay then, after warming them up well and creating a friend, and then after presenting and covering the salient points so that the client is satisfied, one issue you've got to build in always is credibility. (And just be sensible and check! Before moving on, ask the client, "So just to clarify my thinking, Mr Prospect, are you happy that my product/ service will satisfy your need?")

Credibility is the assurance and confidence provider that lets the prospect know that they are safe. Remember, please, that the core triggers for choices are Pain and Pleasure, and your client will be probably more risk averse than a pleasure hunter. In other words, he will be looking to protect himself first... he will not act unless he feels there is no risk to him in acting (buying) and so credibility is a huge issue.

Are you safe? Can you deliver? Will the product be all that you have said? Will your company live up to your promise? Will your after sale service be adequate to meet his needs? What about the future? Will you be able to grow with him, or will you be less interested when he stays small and you grow?

There will be a myriad of thoughts and potential risk fears running through your prospects mind... showing how you are credible covers them.

So, what do you say or do here? How do you demonstrate credibility?

The answer is actually very simple. Let them know by both showing evidence produced by your company as to your security etc. For example, possibly you might be advised to show how large a company you are in turnover as this might be an indicator or be interpreted as a safety factor **and** by showing them something that might have been produced by your clients who your new prospect can relate to.

Testimonials and Case Studies

Do you use testimonials of existing clients? Do you boldly gather them and share them as a forefront of your message? Do you consistently tell prospects how well you also looked after Mr Neighbour, who is in a similar situation to them?

Well again, I assure you that when you do, you will massively help your pitch and improve your results. Your testimonials should cover clients' comments, as well as illustrate variety. In addition to be believable, I recommend putting full client name and, if relevant, business name on display... we've all seen testimonials written on promotional literature and thought to ourselves that they could just as easily been a complete fabrication (or maybe it is just me that is cynical!), especially when they merely use a quote in punctuation but the only name is JB in Glasgow!

A good habit to cultivate is that of gathering great quotes that highlight the safety of a purchase and endorsing the fact that purchasing is the correct decision, and then use them fully. Splash them on everything, even your business card... they are extremely powerful if they are believable.

What the prospect needs to know is, are you safe? Can they trust you? Will you let them down, or will purchasing from you make their life easier? They are possibly associating a Pain to purchasing your offering and you must remove that association. Testimonials help.

You've got to put a credibility story around your pitch.

And remember also; take some of the shine off! Do not say, "We're brilliant, we never make a mistake." Admit to a small faux pas to show honesty and humanity... but please make your shortcoming an area where they are not primarily focussed! And then when you relay a testimonial and show case studies, they already have a belief in what you say being true. To assist you, try saying you are extremely good at what you do by using other people's words. What you perhaps should say is, "We're brilliant, here's a client's story, and look, they are like you." When you do this, it's not *you* saying, "I'm good,"... it's another buyer.

Nobody will ever buy if they don't trust you. They might be sold on the product, but if they don't trust you, they'll buy it from someone else. So you need to have testimonials and case studies. By the way, do you know the difference?

A testimonial should be a line or two from a satisfied customer saying how pleased they are with what you have done for them.

A case study is something that you can show that tells a story of how your offering impacted a business or person and the new prospect can relate to that story as it being a similar situation to their own. For example, a brief story of how a client was suffering from a 'problem' that is quite possibly an issue for all in that situation or business and then they found you and used your product and then their lives improved. It briefly shows a 'before' and 'after' in word form.

These types of case studies are incredibly powerful and I cannot endorse the use of them too much. In fact, I recommend that you have to hand a series of case studies that highlight all potential scenarios you might face during your sale process. What you are effectively saying to your client or prospect is, "Here's a similar situation, an example of a client with 'a problem' not dissimilar to yours, and we resolved the situation with what I am offering. If we can do it for them, then we can do it for you."

And wherever you can, make it visual. Videos are so much more powerful. Use it, especially for testimonials. People believe what they see! In today's society, we are all primed for corruption and almost expecting lies before we give the benefit of the doubt, which is why referrals and network contacts are surging ahead as the key business growth tool... but because of this distrust, using a video image of a client relaying to the camera how satisfied with your offerings they are is supremely powerful.

The watching prospect may well even know one of your clients giving the testimonial, especially if you operate within a fairly small geography, and I promise you it works fantastically. Capture great testimonials on film and use them whenever you present. Try this: say, "Don't take my word for it. Listen to what our clients say..." and then play video testimonials.

Because I know how supremely powerful these are and I can vouch for their effectiveness so much, I ask now that you please take some time out here to make a set of case study-type stories for your business. Create a list of all of the main benefits of your offering and then create a story of someone who purchased from you and thus effectively resolved their challenge. Relay the benefit in a story, and it will appear as if someone else is telling me how good you are and not you.

Wherever you have real examples of a success in your sales history, make an effort to get this testimony filmed. Capture a real client saying, "It was good, it worked," and show it all the while. The investment of a few hundred pounds will net you thousands back!

What next? Pricing!!

Yes! At some stage, even though you have wowed them and made a friend and all of that, you are still going to have to tell them a price and go for an order! So, the sales game plan – meet and greet, warm-up, presentation and credibility – now leads to a pricing stage where you need to show them obviously how much it costs to purchase from you.

Now there are a whole heap of techniques that can add weight here, depending on your industry and the environment of the sale. You might, for example, be in a 'Business to Consumer' sale, such as a home improvement, and you use a discount structure to capture a sale.

In this case, you'd be starting with a high price at which you rarely sell and you would negotiate downwards towards a more normal selling price... and it would be a bit of a game making, the prospect work for the levels of discount.

On the other hand, you might be in a very formal 'Business to Business' environment negotiating contracts for hundreds of thousands of pounds, where the margins are naturally very small and there simply isn't a lot to play with. Whatever the scenario, you will need to put down a price that hopefully doesn't scare the prospect right out of the room!

My advice is for you to have been price conditioning whilst talking and presenting i.e. mentioning prices that are perhaps slightly higher than your selling price at periodic intervals all of the way through the presentation, so that if there is a problem with the money you find out early and can adjust it before you get to the time to show a price. Or indeed price conditioning, so that you can make a plausible story as you go through as to why your figure that you're casually mentioning may not be accurate, in order to justify a more accurate price that when you write it down, might be quite different to that which you talked about.

Whichever scenario, the pricing stage needs attention. Do not get complacent. Apply a little effort and forethought to how a client might react or what they are perhaps expecting to see in pricing terms. Indeed, often it isn't about *how much*, it is more about *how you pay*, so again use payment options and have them already worked out. It can be very expensive if you are in such a hurry, or feeling possibly excited at clinching a deal that you make a mistake when pricing!

Consider also that possibly the prospect has other items on their agenda when it comes to spending money and whilst you are focussed on your offering and are continually batting for your purchase, defending the price etc. **it might be that the issue is not actually how much your product is costing, but more about how they fit in the other things that they are trying to buy**.

Notes

Which client stories can I relate as 'Case Studies'?

_____

_____

_____

_____

_____

_____

_____

_____

_____

_____

_____

Who could I approach and ask for a testimonial?

_____

_____

_____

_____

_____

_____

_____

_____

_____

_____

Many times, in either a Business to Business or Business to Consumer environment, the prospect is trying to purchase other items at the same time e.g. you're trying to sell them a new all-singing all-dancing copying machine and they are seriously interested but they're having to upgrade computers at the same time, and whilst they do this it might also require a little alteration to the office layout. All of these things are impacting the sale of your copier but it is quite possible that they haven't told you as they deem it to be their issue, not yours. In such cases you might be struggling to gain commitment and indeed they might be trying to look at cheaper options contrary to what they have previously told you. None of this would make sense without the knowledge of their bigger picture, but it might be a major component of the sale process when you are at the pricing stage.

I'd recommend learning to ask each and every client at the early stages of your sales process about their future plans... flush out the other items early so that you aren't confused and frustrated later on. This situation is surprisingly common and many, many times sales people get frustrated and even angry at a client's hesitation because they just aren't getting the full story... don't let that happen to you.

So, make sure you are properly prepared and that your pricing stage covers options, especially payment terms so that they can still manage the other items on their agenda.

Closing the Sale

Here's a juicy topic! Closing the sale! Isn't this what thousands of sales managers have harped on about over the years as a skill you should be learning?!

Well, the next stage of the sales process after pricing is quite rightly going for the closure so that you can walk away with the deal in the bag. The close is a topic that has spurned much debate and old sales practices have lived on where pressure is applied and sharp questions are used to almost intimidate the prospect into a deal.

Don't get me wrong, I am a huge fan of closing the sale and not an advocate of being wishy-washy, leaving it open for the prospect to 'think about', but there is a right way and a wrong way to do it. The truth, of course, is that if you have done all of the previous bits right, then a sale should in fact already be closed. It is actually a natural flow because you have given them what they are looking for and made it available in a style that suits them perfectly, because you listened and asked great questions that helped the buyer arrive at a situation in agreement and thus a signature is the correct evidence of this.

However, if you haven't really bonded then you might have a lot of work to do. If you haven't been asking 'better' questions and found out all of their challenges, and if you haven't dealt with their fears about moving in your direction, then you will be in for a real struggle here. The close is an area where attention was previously focussed and where clever techniques were developed primarily because not enough attention had been given to the other more important areas earlier on in the process.

My belief is that to be a better and more productive salesperson, you concentrate on opening, not closing.

Having said all of that though, I also recognise that a great many people in a selling situation do not do themselves any favours because they simply are lousy at asking for the order! I have witnessed a salesperson skirting all around the question, "Would you like to buy it today?" saying such things as, "So, what do you think? It's pretty good, isn't it? Sounds to be just right for you..." and never actually asking for an order! You still need to close!

If you are feeling confident that it is in fact all that the client has said they are wanting and if in fact that the price and the terms have been agreed upon then really it is a natural step and you simply ask for an official order number or a signature. Use a sentence such as "Ok, so shall we go ahead with it then?" or "So shall I need an order number for your process or should I simply fill out a contract and push it through with your signature on it?"

I also believe that you cannot start closing too early. It is pretty certain that if you ask for an order the minute you walk in the door, you will hear a, "No," but if you ask in the right way with a smile on your face, you will not offend the client but they *will* get the subconscious message that you are serious about your role.

A quick handshake accompanied by a cheeky smile and a, "Congratulations on your purchase!" will probably spark a comment from the prospect along the lines of, "I'm not buying anything, I'm only looking," but you haven't offended them because of the big smile on your face and indeed it will have shown you have a sense of humour, which is an endearing quality. It will have planted a seed though about your intentions and you will then get a chance to follow that up at each section of the sale.

I even suggest that you can ask several times in the sale process for the order... you do not need to wait until the presentation is done, or wait until the pricing, or the close sections. You can ask the prospect at any stage, especially after you have answered a query they have that indicates their desire to buy.

The Rule of 8

You may be familiar with the theory, but apparently many studies have shown that there is a magic around the number seven. It is a good idea to use a seven in your price, for example... and indeed we are all familiar with the Pareto principle of 80:20. There are many analogies perhaps that we can draw upon but essentially the studies show that the majority of sales happen when the vast amount of 'sales people' have given up asking. Simply put it is a game of resistance! And I don't mean 'Bullishly' pushing on and even being offensive and bullying... I mean simply persisting in asking and offering them good reasons that they should go ahead.

Think about this for a moment. Pretend either with someone near you or with an 'imaginary you' that you are buying or potentially buying something... maybe something someone has offered to you something such as a air conditioning unit in the office or a newer vehicle... whatever it is, think of all the reasons why you should *not* buy it.

Try it now. Just **think of an object that you *could* buy or has been offered to you, and then think of all of the reasons quickly why you should <u>not</u> buy**. Please do this... think of a potential purchase and then think of reasons why you won't buy.

Okay, if you did that in a few seconds, how many reasons did you come up with?

Often you can think of three, four, or even five pretty quickly. Effectively though, this is where most people dry up. Your clients are the same.

They can come up with four or five good reasons in their mind as to why they *shouldn't* go ahead... your job as a salesperson is to come up with more than that for why they *should*!

And essentially that is all selling is about... making them want it and giving them enough reasons for them to act. Compelling reasons... reasons that mean something to <u>them</u>, not just arguments you usually use in your sales pitch.

Remember, we talked about creating rapport, finding their pattern and then listening to their reasons. Well if you come up with more reasons in their language than they thought of as negatives, you will sway them.

Even money is an obstacle that can be overcome. Again, remember we talked a while back about conditions or objections... rarely is money actually a condition. Sometimes maybe, but mostly, people can find the money if they really want to... your job is to make them really want to! (Haven't you bought something in the past that you couldn't afford and shouldn't really have bought? You did though, didn't you?!)

The magic number is eight. Think of eight possible objections... remember all of the excuses clients have offered to you in the past... (Probably again, you'll list about four or five!) And think of all reasons to overcome them... then keep going when in a sales presentation. Do NOT hear the word, "No," as a, "No,"! Hear it as them saying, "That's not quite good enough. Give me another reason..."

"No Means 'Not Yet'. Give me another reason to say Yes." That is all they really mean when they say, "No," to you. It isn't "No, never." It is just, "No, not yet. Based upon what you have told me so far. That might change though, if you add something else into the equation. It might become 'Yes'."

320

Again then, please take a few moments right now and list all of the reasons you can come up with or adopt into their language so that you have an arsenal of eight, ready to fire and wipe out their five or six. Go back to the list you made with reference to stories that 'flush out' objections and make sure you are prepared.

Remember, it is in this type of preparation that winners are made. Everybody else out there says to themselves that they know how this is done... and then they revert to the old way when in front of a client, fail to get an order and blame everyone else but themselves.

Truthfully, selling success is more about this type of preparation as we discussed very early on. Remember the 6Ps, and especially when closing or creating the right environment for the client or prospect to say yes. Consistently giving them reasons to say yes (that stem from *their* language patterns) will overcome many of today's, "Leave it with me," responses. Closing a sale is possible on visit one if it is handled correctly. Practice now and win next time.

I know you want to be the one that stands out... Good Luck!

Consolidation

This is an area where nearly every sales person I have met seems to slack, except on the clients they have massively gelled with and where they are already friends, and it feels almost like a social call.

Consolidation is a vital ingredient to be included, especially where you have made a sale to someone who perhaps hasn't really met you before, and then bought from you because you did a good job. This type of relationship is still immature... it needs reassurance. The client who has just spent money with you feels vulnerable. His mind programme is still trying to tell him of all of the old pain when he bought and thus he is still possibly struggling to feel at ease with the choice... and when you cut and run, he starts playing records of suspicion in his mind that suggest you ran off because now he's been caught in a sting and you ran before the truth slipped out!!

Again, I dramatise but you appreciate my point!

Please, after getting an agreement to proceed, put all of the books, laptops and bits of paper away and sit back and talk again about the client! Talk about children, the evening or weekend agenda, the cars or bikes or holidays, but go back to the 'warm' feeling and make him once again feel rapport and connection. Then when you have had 10 or 15 minutes doing this, you can leave and he/she will remember the glow, not the sting.

Sounds simple, it is simple... but it is also critical. Lots of sales agreements cancel within a couple of days... and if this ever happens to you, it is something you can reverse if you seal the deal with 15 minutes, glow again, perhaps even over a second cup of tea or coffee. Make conversation about non-work, non-deal topics. Leave as a human, as a friend, and deals will stick in future!

And you'll feel happier! You just might enjoy each day more!

Okay!! That is a simple outline of a sales process. It works, try it.

Nothing is rigid. Nothing will stay exactly the same. Sometimes you will have a deal without really feeling like you have gone through a structure and sometimes you will go all of the way through the structure and not get a sale. That, I am afraid, is the wonderful richness of life!

Concentrate on *them, the prospect...* make your focus the client and the person, not your product or presentation, and you will fair better, I promise. One question I am often asked though is, "How long do you think a sales game plan, the structure of a sale, should take?"

Okay, let's assume that it's a high ticket item, like five grand or above.

Well, I'll tell you an interesting fact. I've measured this (because I test and measure), and, by and large, if there's a sales threshold level of say three to five thousand or above, you will want two and a half hours and more... especially if they are spending their personal money such as in a sale to a consumer or to a small business owner where the person is directly spending their own money. I would suggest that you'll never want less than two hours because you just are not going to get enough rapport for them to spend that money in less time. (Again, I am talking about selling to a 'cold' prospect. If it is someone who you already know well, then it will be less because there is already some trust in the bank account and some credibility attained.)

Simply stated, rarely will a person spend his or her money quickly on larger amounts. They will want to deliberate and feel sure. Your job when selling is to give them long enough without extending into a second visit. If it goes to a second visit, the emotional level will cool and a sale is far less likely.

But just so that you're aware, every sale still has a structure to it. The size of the money involved, and whether it's their money or not, will impact the process. If it's two hundred pounds, to a person that's really not that bothered about smaller sums of money, it's a fairly instant decision. If it's two thousand to a person who only spends that amount of money once every three years, it's a big decision.

Some sales demand a second visit. For example, financial services or investment products require that you go away and do research to ensure best advice for the client, and so your dynamic is altered, but please remember that 'a sale is made with emotion...' and thus the emotional level is going to be at its highest when you are first there.

Even if you have to leave because that is a requirement, *get an agreement on the sale before you go. Get a sale agreed in principle* subject to you coming back with the scenario you have painted before you leave. Do not just leave and say that you will sort it out and come back. It *is* still possible to get a sale in one visit and I am saying you must try. Do not leave until you have an agreement... their emotional level will cool down between visits and you will come back to an analytical cold environment that will result in a, "think about it," not a, "Yes!"

And when you revisit, remember please that 'a sale is made with emotion' and even though you got an agreement to a sale 'subject to certain criteria' on the previous visit, there has been a few days or a week or more since they said that and all sorts of circumstances may have changed since then.

Indeed, one of the main reasons I always advocate a first visit sale is primarily because when the emotion has cooled down, as it invariably will, there is always something else to spend the money on. Like all of a sudden the car will break down, or the kitchen will fall to pieces, or the main bread winner will break a leg and need fourteen weeks off work!! You know the rule... Sod's law says if anything can go wrong, it probably will! So, please press for a sale on day one and then remember when it is a second visit requirement, get them 'warm' again.

You cannot revisit exactly the same topic but you could continue along similar lines. For example, if they were talking about the children and some of that conversation centred on the behaviour patterns of the teenage son or daughter, or even a younger child, you can pick up the thread of the previous meeting by enquiring as to how eventful the days since your last visit has been.

You can soon re-warm the client and they will soon flow again into the warmth of the previous encounter when you re-establish common ground. Then, of course, you gently remind them of the agreement they made with you, regarding the proposal and at this point you might say something like, "Good news! I managed to secure…" and you are then back into a warm presentation where you left off the last time.

I stress though that a second visit arrangement *will still* require some 'warm-up' because they will have gone cold in the interim… they are not yet lifelong friends!

So, there we have an overview of a selling process. However, before we close of the subject of selling, let's look quickly at a hot debate topic of Objection handling.

Objection Handling

Okay, that's the structure. That's the sales process in short. What about handling objections?

It would be unrealistic to look at selling without looking at objection handling, as you know that many sales calls will be less than perfect prospects and thus how can you close a sale if there is an objection or two to face? Well, strangely some people in sales fear objections. They think, "Oh my God" I don't want to get an objection." In fact, they think that if they keep selling and keep telling them how good it is, maybe they won't get any objections. Me? I love them! I love objections because they tell me that the client is showing an interest in the product and reacting to what is being said.

The important thing to remember is that if you get objections, you *can* cover them. In fact, you can cover several and still make the sale.

Think about the selling process this way for a moment…if there are no objections, then the prospect isn't that bothered, are they? If the prospect cannot even be involved enough to come up with an excuse, then they are more likely to just pacify you to smooth your process along and then calmly say something wishy-washy at the end like, "Leave it with me," or, "I just need to think about it." No, you want an objection every time and you must learn to love them and handle them as a key to a sale.

There's just one key thought here… how do you know if the objection is real? By that, I mean that for most people during a buying process they're trying not to buy or at least mostly not now, only when they want to, hence very often they come up with an objection to stump the person selling and thus keep them in control.

For example, "I can't buy it today, because I need to get some prices," or, "We're not going to buy, we're just getting some quotes."

So, please remember this. The first time you hear an objection, it is <u>always</u> a fear reflex. And usually the second time too. The client has seen other sales people before and because the other sales people have been amateur, the client has learned that they can escape from the sales 'pressure', be protected and never spend their money if they come out with an objection. Usually their objections cause the sales person to back down… but the objection is rarely real.

So please understand that firstly this is merely a defence mechanism. The client is programmed to say things like, "Yes, we'll just get a quote," and, "Yes, but we can't buy until I've seen my granny," or, "You understand it can't be done until there's a board meeting?" or "You understand all of these other reasons why I couldn't possibly go ahead today?" etc. And what they are telling you is that they have a 'programme' in their mind that believes that if they say such comments to most sales people, the sales people in question reply, "Okay, here's a quote. Call me when you're ready," and leaves! It gets rid of the sales person! The prospect is 'safe'.

The prospect has a pattern of associating pain to buying and thus they push pain away and get rid of the salesperson. It doesn't mean they cannot use or don't want what you have to offer.

But as I have said, please remember that nearly all of the time when you first hear an objection, even the first two times it is <u>not</u> an objection, it's a <u>reflex</u>. It is a *fear* reflex.

They are just trying to protect themselves and scare you away... it is not actually a real reason and thus it should not be handled. By that, I mean simply that if they say, "Oh I cannot make any decisions today. We are just getting prices at this stage," they are used to this approach encouraging the salesperson to shorten or skip the real selling process and thus they don't have to face their fears of buying... but it is *not* necessarily the case that they must defer the decision.

They may well be able to decide... so <u>do not confront</u> their statement with comments like, "Well then what time frame did you think you would be looking at? This offer I told you about is only available for this month," as this will merely solidify the 'objection' and once you have helped them do that, they are obligated to stick with it and you have made it far worse.

Remember that it is only a fear reflex at this stage and the way to handle this type of 'reflex' is to say, "Yes, no problem... absolutely no problem," and just carry on regardless!

Now, you've acknowledged it, ignored it, and moved on. The first time the client notices, you've not bitten but they aren't quite sure if you have ignored him or if indeed that you have acknowledged it and it really doesn't create a problem. The second time the prospect says, "Yes, we can't buy today," and then he adds, "I told you that because obviously we're going to have to have some time to think about it." He's trying to get you to listen and back down. You simply say, "Yes, yes, that's not a problem. It's okay." Again, you've acknowledged it but are seemingly doing nothing about it!

And then the third time it comes up, he says, "Well you'll have to just leave us a quote. I told you that we can't make a decision today." And you say, "That's fine, that's not a problem. Out of interest, dear client, did I say that we've got to make a decision today?"

And then you might quickly follow up with, "What I do know though, Mr Prospect, is that you wouldn't want to make the decision today because it would be absolutely terrible if it was the wrong decision, wouldn't it? The point is, what we really want, is to make sure that we get this *right*, don't we? We need to make certain it's the *right choice*."

At this point, the prospect cannot actually disagree because you have made a totally valid point... and so he agrees that your action is the way to go. You then say, "That's what we'll do then," and carry on.

You've completely taken him off track. He's thinking, "What do I say now? What do I say now?" He's floundering because he thought he was going to get rid of you by saying, "Not today, not today." You've now turned it round to the fact that he just doesn't want to get it wrong. But he's agreed to just make sure he gets it right.

I promise you. Please, if you give this some real thought. Next time you're in a sales situation and people start to give you a 'reflex', think about this and understand it's just fear. You'll just say, "Okay, absolutely, no problem," and then you'll completely carry on. And you'll see in their eyes, you'll see a bewildered look on their face. It will only be for a split second, a momentary look of confusion, but it will just tilt them off balance! Because they're thinking, why hasn't this put him off? And you'll almost see it! Please play this game, because when you start to get excited about it, you'll love it.

When you throw someone's brain pattern off, when you break the pattern and you ignore them, and they were expecting a reaction and they were geared up for a certain set of circumstances… when you break that pattern, you'll see their face go blank. Watch, just watch, and they'll be lost! You'll see their eyes go round as they ask internally, "What do we do now?" It's ever so subtle and ever so visible when you're looking for it. But the first two times somebody says something to you will be a reflex, so you just ignore it.

And by the way, when I say, "Ignore it," I don't mean ignore *them*. I mean simply do not begin to address what they have just thrown at you as an objection. Do not give it credence. Simply acknowledge it as though it isn't a problem (which they will possibly interpret as, "It isn't a problem because you weren't expecting them to buy now anyway.").

Now, the third time an objection is raised, if it's <u>exactly</u> the same as has been mentioned twice already, then it must be dealt with. For example, "I told you we can't buy tonight, because of my Granny," well then I'm going to have to accept that this *is* an issue to deal with and hence I need to ask a little about it. For example, I might ask, "Tell me about your Granny, dear client, she sounds like a wonderful lady." And then I might hear, "Well she was, but she's poorly at the moment…"

And, of course, you need to know the rest, so you'll say, "So, joking aside, dear client, tell me, what role was your Grandma going to play in this transaction?"

Now the prospect is going to tell you the information that must be critically linked to the transaction, in their mind at least. Again, in this example, they might say, "Well Grandma's paying for it, but unfortunately she was going to write a cheque and now I've got to wait until she recovers."

Now that sounds genuine. Indeed, how do you overcome this?

Firstly, you must try to appreciate *exactly* what is being said. Is the prospect saying they have to have Grandma present? Or is it that Grandma needs to agree with the purchase? Or is it perhaps to be framed as a timing issue?

You need to hear exactly what is really being said. You need to qualify the objection. Try saying, "I see, dear client, that's understandable, not a problem. I'm sorry to hear about your Granny. Just to help me, I'm sorry, just so that I'm clear; your issue is a cash flow situation. It's timing really, isn't it? Because what you are in fact saying is that if your Gran was here now, you could have written a cheque, but she's not, but when she is well again it'll be alright, it's just the timing. Is that right?"

What's happened here?

Well, cleverly you've switched the emphasis from 'possibly no money' to 'timing of payments' and he agrees with the fact that the money is there, in theory.

Now, you still carry on... because he's just almost agreed to the fact that the challenge is only timing. You should clarify a bit later on and say, "So, Mr Prospect, when do you think all this will resolve itself, in terms of time frame? How long do you think it will take?"

The prospect says, "Oh, I don't know, six to eight weeks?" At this point, the prospect is thinking that he's just bought a few weeks, because after all how can you expect him to proceed without Grandma's money and Grandma is out of action for six to eight weeks. This isn't how *you* frame it though. To you, now the issue is much more positive.

You then go one stage further, but it sounds a harmless natural follow-on statement, when you say, "Basically then, what you're saying is that you're happy with everything, and if it can be delivered in six to eight weeks when you've got the cash flow, then that's the way to do it?"

The prospect thought he had bought some time and effectively you've turned the time issue into merely a delivery and postponed payment issue... which still allows for a decision to be possible! If the prospect agrees with this statement, you have an order.

And don't think that this approach feels 'pushy'. It wouldn't be pushy if this was spread over half an hour or so... you'd feel it was pushy if it happened as fast as we've just talked it through, but if you're just making it conversational in everything else you're doing and talking about it, it's fine.

Ask yourself a question. Do you want to know if he's serious or not as a buyer? Isn't it better to find out if he is wasting your time?

So what's wrong with pushing it just enough to find out? If you don't push it, and the prospect *is* a dreamer, and you spend three hours because you don't want to front it, then it's a waste of three hours. How do you feel? You feel angry. Whose fault is it?

Your own!

"No!" does NOT mean, "No"...it means, "Not yet, tell me more." (Give me another reason to say, "Yes.")

Remember, remember, remember, the objection does not mean NO. It merely means, based upon the discussion we have had so far, based upon the options I currently have and the information I currently know, then I can't say yes, but give me more information or more options and I maybe can. It does not mean, "NO, never,"!

In this example case, if you had been in the situation and heard an objection twice and decided the prospect was not worth pursuing, it would have been your fault. You didn't ask questions hard enough up front to just determine exactly the situation. Or had you have steamed straight in when they first raised the objection, it would have become fixed and acknowledged, and would either have become fractious or solidified more, as to go against it with a course of action a few moments later, which would have been embarrassing for the prospect.

All I'm saying is that in simple terms, most people in hearing an objection think, "Oh well, he said he can't go ahead, so he can't go ahead,"... and I'd say that thought is wrong, it's a lie, it's a complete fairy story. Of course he can go ahead.

And even the second time when they say, "I can't go ahead." It's probably wrong.

Try this also. Another technique to help you deal with objections is to play their words back to them as a sort of questioning in an "I'm confused" type of reply, "Can't go ahead?" When you do this with a surprised sort of, "Nobody has ever said that to me. What does it mean?" look on your face, you will flush out any reasons the prospect has that they see as contrary. They will feel that they have to justify their statement because of the surprised look on your face. Their brain interprets the look as needing explaining to help you understand and they will justify their statement and in doing so tell you what really is in the way.

It's a superb technique! Pass their statement back to them and they will say, "No, we can't go ahead *because* my Gran is poorly. She was going to pay for it but it's going to take weeks for her to recover. I just can't do anything for a couple of months,"... and there you have it - the real or actual situation. One you can deal with, gradually overcome and thus end up with an agreement. "I see, I understand, thank you for sharing that with me. As I see it, the issue is timing so please allow me to work with you..." and then proceed to sign them up but with different payment terms or delivery details.

"No," did not mean, "No!" Give more information or options and it becomes a, "Yes."

Worst case scenario is that, "No," still isn't a <u>can't</u> buy scenario. It's a, "I can't buy <u>today</u>."

Now which outcome would you rather have? A "can't buy, but I can buy in three months and you know about it," or where you'd have just accepted his objection and gone away and found out that in four months' time, you arrange to pop back and someone else has sold it to him?

"No," means, "Not *yet*." It says, "Tell me more... give me another reason to say yes." "No," does not mean, "no." There's no such word as can't... ask instead, "How can I?" Remember?

I promise that an objection is a *good* thing... when no one cares enough to object, they don't care enough to buy either.

Okay, so briefly please do a little work to help this be effective for your business progression. Applying this thought to your sales process. Take a few minutes now and write down any common or major objections you hear and learn to handle them in a different way. Think about it. There'll always be a monetary objection. Sometimes there'll be a timing objection, but what else will there be? When people say, "No," to you, or, "I can't buy because..." what do they give you as reasons?

By the way, if you're getting stupid objections, guess what you do? You change your process before you go in the door! Get into different doors!

But let's assume, for the purposes of the illustration, that you're doing your job right and your prospecting is based upon accurate information (you see, I am assuming by this stage is that you've done your foundations, etc. that we've talked about) and you've now got people lined up that you should be talking to, that are good targets... they're only going to say, "No," for a limited number of reasons.

They might say, "No," because, what they haven't told you is that they don't believe you can give the right level of service. They might say, "No," but what they've not really told you is that they'd rather deal with somebody bigger. The impression you've created is small, and small to them means unreliable... you can't give the back-up. Or they might say, "No," because the offering you've presented is big and loud and brash, and they've read that as expensive, even before you've got to the price.

Or, they've said, "No," because they're not the person that can say yes, and they don't want to admit it. Very often, you get people that play the role of, "I'm looking after this, give me all the information. Oh yes, it's down to me." Then when you ask for the order they'll go, "Well it's got to go to the board obviously!" They didn't really have the power *but you didn't flush it out either.*

So please take a few minutes and think of the objections you hear frequently. I don't care if you find three or ten, but please find them and use this simple approach. You <u>practice</u> and you <u>prepare</u> properly, and you <u>rehearse.</u> If you think you're going to get an objection about something, use preamble in your setting up, which will be cleverly disguised in the warm-up, and use story techniques as we've talked about: "Oh, you know I had this situation the other day..." Tell a story and smash the objection before it comes out and focus on objections meaning they just need a good reason, so keep giving them reasons why they *can* buy after you have heard them state their reason why they can't.

It might be you are perceived as a small business and that is a negative in their mind... so come up with positives like 'more agile' or 'quicker to act'. It might be that you are perceived as cheap, so explain how other major corporations only raise the price to pay for the marketing overhead, not because the product offering is any better, so why should the client be penalised? It might be that you are perceived as likeable but not a serious contender, so you'll have to show them some teeth!

Whatever you feel you come up against, sit down now and write a list of objections, what the client might be thinking when they raise that and then some stories and counter approaches to knock them out.

It works massively so please get good at this… and by the way, when you do use these techniques, it becomes great fun!

One final thought… don't handle them all!

Leave some objections that you know for sure you can overcome, like time and money, in the air. Do <u>not</u> close all doors of escape in their mind. Flush out the ones that are going to be a bit difficult, like corporate image, who they'd rather deal with etc. but leave something for their mind to cling to because as long as they feel safe, they'll play along.

For example, flush out anybody who thought that they were going to deal with another company, just because of image, by saying, "You and I both know as professional, mature people that it's all about product. I mean, you've got to get the *product* right, haven't you? *You'd* never deal with someone down the road just because they were politically correct or their image was seemingly better, would you? I mean, if you knew or suspected that the product had flaws but on the surface they appeared large and successful, you would concentrate on the product offering, not the image, wouldn't you?"

Use cleverly loaded questions to direct proceedings your way.

Remove minor objections, but 'real' reasons, like money and timing, you leave in. Why do you leave them in? Because you can take it out at a later stage when you have an agreement 'subject to' the hurdle you have left in.

You leave in an objection (that you know you can deal with) and basically ask them to buy. Say something like, "So, Mr Prospect, based upon what we have discussed, am I to understand that you *would* be happy to go ahead, were it not for the obstacle of timing?" The prospect says, "Yes," and you confirm by adding, "Of course, *if* we were able to make it happen sooner/later, then I would be shaking your hand and welcoming you to the fold, wouldn't I?" and then come up with a plausible reason why you can remove the obstacle by telling perhaps a story 'about a client of a colleague who ordered and placed a deposit but then backed off at the last minute due to a health issue', and so that might mean that there might be a gap in the schedule that is about to come up and maybe you can get this secured for the prospect in front of you!

When done correctly, you now have a client who agreed to purchase subject to certain criteria, but who agreed when he felt the criteria couldn't be met. Then when plausibly, you meet the criteria and remove a hurdle, the prospect is left with no escape route except purchasing (or that of admitting he was lying!). Essentially, please believe me, most clients *want* to buy, they just need the right excuses... and you doing a special favour by trying to get a delivery schedule altered was in fact a reason good enough for them to justify to themselves the reason they purchased now. Remember, they purchased emotionally but they need to 'justify with logic' and this was the logic of a schedule that could only be very rarely altered.

And remember to stall a little before asking, "If I could... would you ...?" It'll work, I promise! Have fun.

A word of warning! If *you*'ve got a programme in your head that says, "Sales is nasty, sales people are slimy, sales people are pushy. I don't like sales people. I don't like to be sold to," then you might rationalise what we are talking about now as tricks and you might think they are dishonest and that you are not willing to try this. Well so be it, however allow me to mention one tiny matter... you <u>must</u> sell in order to make a living and I would NEVER suggest telling lies. I am merely suggesting that being inventive and skilful actually helps the client buy... and when they buy, they will thank you if you are offering something that genuinely is a good product or service. So, if you believe in what you are selling, then all of this is actually doing the prospect a favour!

If you try <u>just</u> being consultative, if you try <u>just</u> presenting, then you will make fewer sales and your competitor will take your prospect. The client might end up with a lesser value service and a less than honourable company all because you felt you were helping them by backing off! That is wrong! It is your duty if you genuinely believe in what you are selling to be as skilful as possible to help them buy the best they can get... yours.

And always be friendly. Always be operating in the client's best interests.

A good idea, in fact, is to watch children. Learn from the masters. They 'push' but don't really offend. They just keep going and come up with such great questions and answers, don't they?

If a child says, "Can I have an ice cream, Dad?" You might say, "No," but what does a child do?

Do they give up? Never! What do you do when you're selling?

If you do give up, stop. Children ask, "Can I have an ice cream?" You say, "No." They ask, "Why?" Now when was the last time you asked, "Why?" Someone says, "No, thank you," and you go, "Oh, okay!"

When was the last time you asked, "Why?" Because you think, oh I couldn't possibly ask why, it's rude. Is it hell rude! It's the key to your future. Ask him why!

Children ask why. And you say, "Because you're having your tea soon." And what do the children say? "Well it won't ruin my appetite. I'll eat all my tea!" They just shoot your argument to bits!

So you say, "No," and they ask again, "Why?"

And then you say, "Oh but you've got your friends round. They can't all have one." And what does a child say?

"I'll eat it out of the way so nobody knows!" They find a way round, they don't give up!

You say, "No, you can't have your ice cream. You'll get all of a mess." They say, "Promise I won't. I'll be tidy. I'll clean myself up. I'll have a wash! I won't get messy!"

Kids are the greatest! They're brilliant sales people. But here's the stinger... you have been a child! You just put a lid on your box when you grew up.

You are a natural sales person inside... the only thing that's happened is that you've blocked it off because of conditioning of life. Life has conditioned you to stop.

Allow me to illustrate. Do you remember (well, perhaps not actually remember but be aware of!) in the old days of street entertainment there used to be flea circus shows? Now, we all appreciate what a flea is and one might think how did they manage to make a flea do tricks? Surely the flea would just keep jumping and jump away! Well, to train a flea they just placed it in a box, and the flea jumped continually and banged its head on the box lid, until it had learned or conditioned itself that jumping high hurts... and the flea then stops jumping high. It became conditioned and thus forgot how to jump high and remained captive thereafter. The box is removed but the 'conditioned' flea remains. In a similar fashion, we humans are conditioned by those around us and we get used to someone else's lid on our life.

The **box on the lid for the flea** says, don't jump higher but *you can* jump higher. You could sell anything and get anything. When you were a child, you've merely adopted this 'flea in the box' mentality because of the experiences and people who have influenced your life this far. **Take the lid off and jump higher! Start telling yourself you *can* sell and you'll be the best sales person in the world... you were once!**

Buying Psychology – The Take Away

One last idea to share with you to help you become a master sales person - the 'Take Away'.

Now, I am not talking about a curry and chips on a Saturday night! I'm talking about a process whereby you encourage the prospect to get excited and create desire for the product or service you are offering and then take away from them (using a reason you can later retract) the option to purchase after all.

Again, let us remember a key psychology of the buying process... winning. We, as consumers, like to make 'deals'. We always feel really good about a sale where we think we've got a deal.

Think of this as a scenario: If the sales person says, "You shouldn't really have that." You say, "Well that's what I want." Sales person says, "That doesn't really come with this." And you say, "Well I want them together."

That's how we work. That's how we buy. We push for a little more if we think we can get it.

So, play games, because it's all a game. In your business, make sure you create 'options' and 'packages' then during the selling process show nice little bits that they want, and then say, "But obviously that's only in Package A and you're talking about this Package B."

What do they want then?

They want the bits in Package A, but with Package B! They want to win! But actually you've won because they're committed already to buying!

You simply say, "I don't know if I can do that. But if I could, would you like to buy it that way?"

And what you've done is you've switched the emphasis that the psychology is based upon from, "Should I buy or shouldn't I buy?" to, "Can you?" Nobody likes to be told they can't!

So play games with your sales. Create options and packages and play games. And deliberately offer them something you know they'd like, but then say, "It's not in your package." Just watch, just play games.

Allow me to give you an example that you can probably easily relate to.

You are shopping for a new coat in the colder months and you happen to be in a store where you see a coat that you like. You try one on and it is a little small but the sales person suggests that the one in the display window might be your size... so off they go and return a few moments later with a coat 'from the window' that you try on. It fits superbly! You are just admiring the way it fits and the salesperson says something like, "It really does you justice. It is just a shame that we don't have your size available."

Your immediate reaction is to question this and remind the salesperson that the one you are currently wearing *is* your size.

The salesperson then says, "Yes, but that is the one from the display and we are not allowed to sell the one on display. You cannot buy that coat."

At this point, what usually happens is a rising feeling of injustice and mild anger where you point out that it is absurd that you are not allowed to buy one when there is obviously one of your size there, as you are wearing it. You become indignant and demand that you be allowed to exercise your right as a consumer and you suggest that they as traders are mildly misleading the consumer.

And by now, of course, what is happening is in fact that you are *fighting to buy*!! The salesperson used a technique where they got you warm to the idea, then used a 'take away' whereby you were feeling indignant and actually then instead of you deciding whether or not to buy, you fought for the right to buy!!

It is brilliant psychology and goes back to a core human psychology of 'the forbidden fruit'. We all want what we cannot have… but usually only after we have been told that it is out of bounds. When it is freely available, we usually aren't stirred to seize it and we decide instead to think about it. When it is scarce, or worse, forbidden, we struggle to have it!!

This is so powerful! Please try using this! Create packages or options and then selling scenarios where you offer a client something they want (and get the desire high first), then create a reason why they cannot have it. Your prospect will then fight to have his or her own way!

So *please* go and create situations. Plan it and use it and as you become proficient at it, you will manage to have lots more sales. Have fun!!

Deliberately use the intelligence gathered in the fact find to present options that would appeal and then say, "But that's not for you." Talk freely about all of the extras you can provide and make sure they are excited or interested in them before telling them they actually cannot have what they are now wanting because they don't qualify (or similar). You will have sooo much fun as prospects become slightly indignant then start trying to make a deal with you, and all the time you know you are winning them towards you!

Again, when you master this and use it properly, you will have huge business upturn and much more fun! Like all things new, when you first try these ideas, you will probably feel uncomfortable and worry about getting it right... and indeed you may well get it 'wrong' and the client doesn't respond in the ideal way... but keep trying and one day you will get it right and from then onwards you will be winning and having masses more fun.

Please trust me, this works and is great fun!

Good luck.

The Final Word!

Phew! There you go, you made it through! We've covered a bit of ground, you and I really, haven't we?

I sincerely hope that all that we have talked about over these pages has been an enjoyable and entertaining read... but more than ever I pray that you didn't merely read through and that you have stopped and given some thought to how you might apply these techniques to grow your business.

I promised you when we started out, that inside these book covers are some powerful ideas that when applied can add thousands of pounds to your income and make the whole process more enjoyable and less stressful... and I meant it.

If you have understood everything, then try applying it. If it hasn't made sense immediately, then go back and reread because it usually makes a lot more sense second time around, but otherwise don't struggle on alone. Contact our team through our websites and invite us to help you with it (www.thebusinessboosteracademy.co.uk www.thebusinessbooster.co.uk). My passion is to make a difference... so contact us and we will share your load.

To recap though, let's quickly look at all that we have covered.

We started out with some basics. We started with the foundations of any business and the cornerstone of you as a business owner. Such vital ingredients as to where **you might be headed** in the form of goals, **why you want to go through all of this** and endure the stress and strain **and, of course, a plan as to how** you might bridge the gap from where you are now to where you want to be. We learned to **be specific**

and to ask **for help from our universal Butler!** (Are you talking to him yet?)

When you have these core elements, you will need to **look at a strategic approach** so that all of your time isn't consumed in reaction to your environment and **you will also need to major on the intelligence side of your business**. You can't fight a battle in small business land based upon strength... you are going to be outgunned by your corporate enemies so you need to be guerrilla-like and be smarter... get yourself and your business intelligent and take the time out to learn about your clients, your potential market, and **store and manage data in your CRM system**.

Put this with **a systemised thought process** and magic happens. Remember, your business has massive value and can easily be grown if it has a clear and identifiable system or process written down for each area of the workflow. You develop a system for everything and make it visible to all who join your company... and then a prospective purchaser might be more inclined to hand over millions and buy the company from you!

We understand the Millionaire Mindset and appreciate that it is all about us and the little things that add up in how we walk, talk, think and act.

Then we move on. Having set up your business on the correct foundations, we can look to how we grow it. You looked at **many new ways to market your business**... can you remember them?

How about **Networking**... especially targeting the areas where your prospects gather? We looked at the hugely powerful process of **strategic alliances**... where you make an ally of someone who serves your target group but who sells a complimentary offering and then essentially teaming up with them to share the data and advance your business in just a few months. (A well planned mutually beneficial joint venture can see you grow a client base that organically might have taken 10 years to grow... and you could do this in as many months!)

The natural alliance relationship you have now developed lends itself to **creating special events** and these in turn become newsworthy thus giving you a superb **PR process** to put you in front of every prospect's eyes. Not bad really, for saying you will not have spent hardly any money for all of this press exposure, unlike your less enlightened competition!

We looked at how to generate massive amounts of **referrals** and we talked about using **the Internet** to make you money while you are sleeping... and please do not ignore the critical role of **Social Media** as this area is going to play a huge role in the future. Please remember that every month and every year that passes sees this medium as a more and more the prominent player with the newer buyers coming through the ranks.

After considering the role of virtual exhibiting, we talked about traditional **exhibitions** and showed ways where you can do this without massive expense... simply apply principles of sharing and everybody wins. Throw away, please, the competitive scarcity mindset and embrace the sharing and abundance mindset... there really is no need to stress!

Next, we discussed **direct sales** outlets and also **agencies** where by you can get other businesses to do the work for you... affiliate schemes, for example, when using the Internet. Then a favourite for many companies, **telemarketing** which you can add without the strains of loads of staff and overhead, but with just a little more thought than others might bother to apply you can win the day. Finish this off with some **well planned and well executed mailing** and you steam ahead of all those around you. Enquiry overload, we decided, was yours for the taking!

Where do you go next? Simple. You have a strong foundation and you have created lots of enquiries... you must sell them to reap your cash rewards!

Selling scares a lot of people but by now, my friend, you can see that actually it **is more a question of learning to know people** than learning slick answers. Sales are a human interaction game. Selling is about watching and listening, but with a little more science thrown in to make you a sure fire success. You learned about how **lifestyle traits can indicate personality styles** and thus how certain personality types can react or act differently to varying stimulants. Your input can be varied to suit the individual, instead of just doing what you always did with every prospect, and hey presto! You suddenly become Lucky! You start winning more sales than ever and really enjoying it and connecting with people. You are now a business success and it feel absolutely fantastic!!

And what a journey it has been! Fun, difficult at times and not immediate... but like anything in life, if it's worth having, it's worth pushing for... and you have. You have pushed on and for that, I thank you and I am so proud. Please use these talents... **keep the lid off your box and jump higher**. Please do not let other people's short-sighted or low-level beliefs be yours. Keep strong and keep focussed because you can have it all... there is no such word as can't.

Think for a moment of giving gifts at Christmas time to your relatives. What does it feel like when you give someone a gift and they appear ungrateful and don't use the gift? Do you feel like giving more? On the other hand, when you give a gift to a relative and they are so evidently thankful that they use it all of the time, how do you feel then? Do you feel like giving more?

Well, I believe God gave you all of the gifts you need to make Him proud. He gave you all of the talents you need to succeed and I believe that if you use them fully, He will give you even more gifts. He will see to it that you receive more if you use what He has given you. Then with your wealth and success, you can make a difference to the lives of those you love. You deserve to be wealthy. Being poor is no good... in as much as your powers to influence and change lives are limited.

Go out there today and make it happen for you... make it happen for those you love, and make it happen to serve as an example of how you don't need massive resources or privileged backgrounds to be a winner. You can make it happen with a little more skill and a lot more application of effort. I am proud of you!

I thank you! Indeed you should be proud enough of your achievements to want to shout about it from a rooftop... but at least shout it back to us! Please share with me and my team your experiences. Join in and spread the word so that your message can inspire another... like a forest fire, you might ignite someone who hears your story and is in the same position as you until YOU spark him or her up. Start that fire spreading. Send me your story.

Keep in touch. Live the life you deserve.

With love
Yours in success
Ben.

The Business Booster

Want more Business Booster inspiration?

Why not experience our live event?

Two incredible, life changing days sharing and

learning. Check our websites for details.

Log on to our websites and join in the family

www.thebusinessbooster.co.uk

www.thebusinessboosteracademy.co.uk